The Melchizedek Thread

A SELECTION OF PUBLICATIONS BY MICHAEL J. ALTER

What Is the Purpose of Creation: A Jewish Anthology

Why the Torah Begins with the Letter Beit

The Resurrection: A Critical Inquiry

A Thematic Access-Oriented Bibliography of Jesus's Resurrection

The Name Israel

The Resurrection and Apologetics: Jesus' Death and Burial Vol 1

The Hypothesis of Undesigned Coincidences: A Critical Review

The Melchizedek Thread

Genesis 14, Psalm 110, and the Epistle to the Hebrews

MICHAEL J. ALTER

Foreword by David Instone-Brewer

RESOURCE *Publications* • Eugene, Oregon

THE MELCHIZEDEK THREAD
Genesis 14, Psalm 110, and the Epistle to the Hebrews

Resource Publications
An Imprint of Wipf and Stock Publishers
199 W. 8th Ave., Suite 3
Eugene, OR 97401

www.wipfandstock.com

PAPERBACK ISBN: 979-8-3852-7108-5
HARDCOVER ISBN: 979-8-3852-7109-2
EBOOK ISBN: 979-8-3852-7110-8

VERSION NUMBER 01/21/26

To Brandon

Contents

Foreword

Michael Alter traces the "thread" of Abraham's incident with Melchizedek from the world of ancient Near Eastern political expedients of honor and alliances through gifts. Meditations on this event are traced through the world of first temple worship songs (the Psalms) and intertestamental Judaism as preserved at Qumran. By the time of the New Testament, considerations of this ancient event had morphed into theological concepts that Abraham's contemporaries wouldn't have dreamed of.

This work also looks to the future, to see the various reactions to the ANE people group called Hebrews use of this material to establish Christological and soteriological conclusions. Later rabbinic Judaism tried to downplay the heightened significance given to Melchizedek in some earlier traditions. Alter regards this as an anti-Christian move that reacted against exegeses such as those found in the New Testament. In contrast, later Islamic meditations on the role of Melchizedek continue to explore this mystical and mysterious figure.

The question for us as readers depends on the tradition we come from. Jews may be surprised at yet another way in which Christianity reshaped teachings, albeit with the motive of preserving theology that was perceived to be under attack. Muslims may be interested in the long history of interpretation that lies behind the later meditations that may connect al-Khidr with Melchizedek. Secular biblical scholars may feel vindicated that the ANE context has been taken seriously, and that the so-called exegesis in Hebrews is shown to be theological typology that illustrates rather than derives Christian claims from the OT.

Christians will have the most to gain from this work, because it provides a wealth of background and history that helps to reveal what the author of Hebrews was trying to convey. He clearly was not trying to convince his readers that the OT proved Jesus was divine, or that

Judaism's sacrificial system had been created merely to be a retrospective illustration of Jesus' superior sacrifice.

His contemporaries knew about the previous meditations on Melchizedek, which had already transformed this interaction with an ancient city ruler into a mystical prophetic message. They knew that the reasoning in Hebrews was not exegeting the plain meaning of the text, but was continuing the centuries-long development of a theological theme to what it claimed was its ultimate conclusion.

His first readers also knew that the sacrificial system, which many of them were continuing to take part in, provided spiritual comfort, and that it encouraged them to grow close to God, who had requested this worship. Many Jews may have unthinkingly regarded ablutions and sacrifices as necessary for salvation, rather than being merely signs of obedience. However, after the temple was destroyed, most Jews were easily able to accommodate the concept that God still accepted their repentance and worship without these sacrifices. Some Jews continued to regard ablutions as spiritually efficacious and necessary for salvation, in the same way that many Christians regard baptism as necessary. However, many Jews and Christians regard them as symbolic of their commitment and consecration and signs of their obedience.

Alter has succeeded in revealing the message of Hebrews in the light of the author's context. It is seen to be an exploration of Christian theology in the light of contemplations about Melchizedek and other aspects of Jewish theology, and not a proof of that theology from the OT. It helped those first readers see the new revelations about Jesus as a development rather than a discontinuity of what they had known and practiced. For modern Christians, this insight should help us to have respect for those Jews who faithfully attempted to follow the instructions given by God, while they waited for a fuller revelation.

Rev. Dr David Instone-Brewer, 2025

Preface

This text examines the intricate and often disputed connection between Melchizedek in the Hebrew Bible and the Epistle to the Hebrews. The latter is a crucial foundation of high Christology. *The Melchizedek Thread: Genesis 14, Psalm 110, and the Epistle to the Hebrews* scrutinizes the theological assumptions and viewpoints of its unidentified author, as well as those of Bible commentators and theologians. The content in Hebrews and related to it by Bible commentators and theologians often lacks historical evidence and biblical support. Raymond Brown says, "Most Bible commentators' interpretations reveal more of the expositor's ingenuity than the message of Scripture."[1] This text aims to provide a robust review and critical analysis of various issues addressed by scholars who have commented on this letter and related texts. Notable topics include Genesis 14 and Psalm 110.

To achieve the objectives of this inquiry, we must openly engage with prominent Bible commentators on the Epistle to the Hebrews. Key figures in this field include Harold W. Attridge, F.F. Bruce, George Wesley Buchanan, Gareth Lee Cockerill, Paul Ellingworth, Gard Granerød, Sigurd Grindheim, George H. Guthrie, Donald Hagner, Fred Horton, Philip Hughes, Luke Timothy Johnson, Simon Kistemaker, Craig Koester, William Lane, Eric Mason, Alan Mitchell, David Moffitt, and others.

Each issue explored in a chapter opens usually with a quote from a leading commentator or source who argues for the high Christology in Hebrews, followed by an in-depth analysis of their reasoning. Afterward, this text presents alternatives to the interpretation put forward by these authors. The central points of focus are the *rebuttals*. In the interests of intellectual honesty, readers are encouraged to re-examine the material cited by the commentators in its entirety.

1. Brown, *The Message of Hebrews*, 127.

After quoting from these sources, additional defenders who share the same perspective are introduced. This format allows readers to explore the various arguments presented by a diverse group of supporters, ensuring fairness and academic integrity throughout the discussion.

This text incorporates diverse approaches that are crucial for a comprehensive understanding of its subject matter. Examples include archaeology, ancient history, Bible commentary, biblical criticism, biblical teaching, Genesis 14, Hebrews, lexicons, Melchizedek, Messiahship, Priesthood, Psalm 110, and worldview. However, we must acknowledge that no single text can encompass every perspective on such a complex and multifaceted topic. Readers are encouraged to consult the bibliography provided. It serves as a gateway to an expansive realm of knowledge, inviting readers to dive deeper into these critical subjects and broaden their understanding.

Chapter 1—The Melchizedek Personality. He is the golden thread linking Genesis 14, Psalm 110, and Hebrews. Melchizedek's description is an enigma, a mystery, and a riddle. In the Hebrew Bible, his name appears twice. It is noteworthy that the New Testament says more about Melchizedek than the Hebrew Bible. A mere three-verse segment is in Genesis 14:18–20 and one verse in Psalm 110:4. Together, they total four verses. His name also appears eight times in the Epistle to the Hebrews (Heb. 5:6, 10; 6:20; 7:1, 10, 11, 15, and 17).

Chapter 2- Commentary on Genesis 14 presents the first appearance of Melchizedek in the Hebrew Bible. There are many unresolved questions about him, including his real name, his hometown, his genealogy, his birth, and his death. Academics continue to debate whether Genesis 14:18–20 is an obtrusive insertion into the chapter. Chapter 2 concludes by investigating the topic of priests, kings, and king-priests.

Chapter 3- Psalm 110 continues its investigation of Melchizedek. This psalm provides a crucial foundation for the author of Hebrews. It is one of the most challenging psalms, both textually and exegetically. It is quoted in Matthew 22:44; Mark 12:36; Luke 20:42–3; Acts 2:34; Hebrews 1:13; 5:6; 11:21. The literature on Psalm 110 is extensive.

Chapter 4—The Epistle to the Hebrews is the primary focus of this text. Its anonymous author is uncompromising in his statements about Jesus, which reflect his high Christology. The literature relating to this epistle is extensive. Skeptics and detractors challenge the numerous claims made by its author.

Chapter 5—Jesus' Bodily Resurrection examines the claim that the author of Hebrews does not explicitly mention Jesus' bodily resurrection. Afterward, the chapter examines select insights from Judaism and Islam regarding the resurrection—in particular the observation that a resurrection cannot take place without a death.

Chapter 6—A Hypothetical Jewish View of the Epistle to the Hebrews examines the Epistle through a lens (worldview) of Judaism. Readers are requested to envision a hypothetical first-century Jewish opponent, Rabbi Troki, who engages in a spirited debate with the author of the Epistle to the Hebrews. He is not ashamed of the Torah. One of these arguments concerns Jesus' divinity.

Chapter 7—Worldview and Horizons: Christianity and Islam examines the subject of horizons and worldviews. It focuses on the worldviews of Christian theism and Islam. Their differing perspectives create an unnegotiable gulf between the two faiths. Presumably, the abyss cannot be closed.

Chapter 8: Skeptics and Detractors expands on the prior chapter. It incorporates three sets of questions for readers to contemplate: Questions Relating to Genesis 14, Questions Relating to Psalm 110, and Unresolvable Questions Relating to the Epistle to the Hebrews.

Chapter 9—Conclusion.

Appendix: Rabbinic Literature About Melchizedek by Topic. This section provides some rabbinic literature about this personality. Readers should examine it to understand Melchizedek's significance in a multifaceted and meaningful way.

This text will focus exclusively on English sources, engaging with Genesis 14, Psalm 110, and the Epistle to the Hebrews. It will briefly touch on the Dead Sea Scrolls, Apocrypha, Pseudepigrapha, Talmud, midrash (see the Appendix), haggadic, and rabbinic literature. These sources can provide invaluable insights and context that are crucial for a more comprehensive understanding of the concept of Melchizedek. A detailed examination of these resources will be conducted in a future project.[2]

The Melchizedek Thread: Genesis 14, Psalm 110, and the Epistle to the Hebrews offers a comprehensive review of key chapters in the Epistle to the Hebrews and related texts. It critically examines the extensive writings of prominent Bible commentators and theologians regarding

2. Interested readers should consult Kasper Dalgaard's dissertation, *A Priest for All Generations: An Investigation into the Use of the Melchizedek Figure from Genesis to the Cave of Treasure.*

high Christology, analyzing their claims, interpretations, and challenges. Readers are encouraged to consider material representing both perspectives within the religious spectrum thoughtfully.

Acknowledgments

Virtually all books are a team effort. This text would not be possible without a number of people to whom I am indebted. Several noteworthy people stand out.

First, I must acknowledge the Wipf and Stock staff. In particular, Matt Wimer, the acquisition editor, for accepting this text for publication. It was a pleasure working with the Wipf and Stock team.

Vincent J. Torley, who has a PhD and MA in philosophy, and who teaches in Japan, edited the text, helped identify key ideas that needed clarification and expansion. His insights were significant.

Christian Farren proofread, copyedited, and typeset the initial version of the text. Frequently, he identified errors. In addition, he also helped identify key ideas that required clarification and expansion.

Dr. Rev. David Instone-Brewer is a retired senior research fellow in Rabbinics and the New Testament at Tyndale House, Cambridge, England, and a member of the Divinity Faculty at the University of Cambridge and the British Association of Jewish Studies. He has authored several books, mainly on the Jewish background to the New Testament, and is a member of the Committee for Bible Translation (NIV). Previous publications include *Techniques and Assumptions in Jewish Exegesis Before 70 C.E.* (Mohr, 1992), *Divorce and Remarriage in the Bible* (Eerdmans, 2002), *Traditions of the Rabbis from the Era of the New Testament* (Eerdmans, 2011), and *Morale Questions of the Bible* (Lexham, 2019). He received his PhD from the University of Cambridge, where he specialized in early rabbinic literature. I am honored and grateful to have a distinguished scholar of his caliber to contribute the foreword to this text.

Lastly, I also wish to acknowledge Savanah N. Landerholm, PhD, for her cover design and typesetting.

Michael J. Alter, *Erev Rosh Hashanah*, 5786

Abbreviations

AD	*anno Domini (in year of our Lord)*
ANE	Ancient Near East
BCE	before the common era
CE	Common Era
cf.	[Lat.] *confer*, compare
e.g.	*exempli gratia*, for example
ff.	and the following one(s)
i.e.	*id est,* that is
LXX	Greek Septuagint
NT	New Testament
OT	Old Testament [Hebrew Bible]
PhD	Doctor of Philosophy
sic	'thus,' 'so,' 'in this manner'

BIBLICAL BOOKS OF THE HEBREW BIBLE

Gen	Genesis
Ex/Exod	Exodus
Lev	Leviticus
Num	Numbers
Deut	Deuteronomy
Josh	Joshua

Judg	Judges
Ruth	Ruth
1–2 Sam	1–2 Samuel
1–2 Kgs	1–2 Kings
1–2 Chr	1–2 Chronicles
Ezra	Ezra
Neh	Nehemiah
Esth	Esther
Job	Job
Ps	Psalms
Prov	Proverbs
Eccl	Ecclesiastes
Song	Song of Songs
Isa	Isaiah
Jer	Jeremiah
Lam	Lamentations
Ezek	Ezekiel
Dan	Daniel
Hos	Hosea
Joel	Joel
Amos	Amos
Obad	Obadiah
Jonah	Jonah
Mic	Micah
Nah	Nahum
Hab	Habakkuk
Zeph	Zephaniah
Hag	Haggai
Zech	Zechariah
Mal	Malachi

NEW TESTAMENT

Matt/Mt	Matthew
Mk	Mark
Lk	Luke
Jn	John
Acts	Acts
Rom	Romans
1–2 Cor	1–2 Corinthians
Gal	Galatians
Eph	Ephesians
Phil	Philippians
Col	Colossians
1–2 Thes	1–2 Thessalonians
1–2 Tim	1–2 Timothy
Tit	Titus
Phlm	Philemon
Heb	Hebrews
Jas	James
1–2 Pet	1–2 Peter
1–3 Jn	1–2–3 John
Jude	Jude
Rev	Revelation

DEUTEROCANONICAL

1 Macc	1 Maccabees

BIBLICAL TEXTS AND TRANSLATIONS

ASV	American Standard Version
CEB	Common English Bible
CEV	Contemporary English Version
ERV	English Revised Version
ESV	English Standard Version
FRCL	French Common Language Version
ISV	International Standard Version
JPS	Jewish Publication Society
KJV	King James Version
LXX	Septuagint
MT	Masoretic Texts
NAB	New American Bible
NABRE	New American Bible, revised
NASB	New American Standard Bible
NEB	New English Bible
NIV	New international Version
NJB	New Jerusalem Bible
NKJV	New King James Version
NRSV	New Revised Standard Version
RS	Revised Standard
RSV	Revised Standard Version
SPCL	Spanish Language Common Version
TEV	Today's English Version
UBS	United Bible Societies

APOSTOLIC FATHERS

1 Clem	*1 Clement*

Philo

De Agricult.	*On Agriculture*
De Leg. Alleg.	*Legum Allegoriare (Allegorical Interpretations of the Law)*
De Monarch	*De Monarchia ("On Monarchy")*
De Plant. Noe.	*De Plantatione Noe ("Concerning Noah's Work as a Planter")*
De Sacrificiis	*On the Sacrifices of Cain and Abel*

Josephus

Ag. Ap.	*Against Apion*
A.J.	*Antiquities*
Ant.	*Jewish Antiquities*

DEAD SEA SCROLLS (DSS)

11QMelch	11QMelchizedek (11Q13)

RABBINIC LITERATURE (MIDRASH/TALMUD)

Esth. Rab.	Esther Rabbah
Gen. Rab.	Genesis Rabbah
Lev. Rab.	Leviticus Rabbah
Ned.	Nedarim
Num. Rab.	Numbers Rabbah
Pirqe. Rab. El.	Pirqe Rabbi Eliezer
Sanh.	Sanhedrin
Tanh.	Tanchuma

Segue

THE CHRISTIAN MYSTIQUE

The Christian mystique spans the entire world, exerting a profound influence on believers and nonbelievers alike. The fundamental tenet of orthodox Christianity is that following Jesus' crucifixion, God raised him from the dead in his original physical body.[3] The Christians' faith in the resurrection rests on this bedrock belief. However, many of the assumptions that undergird this belief are left unsaid. The Epistle to the Hebrews delineates many of these assumptions.

- God exists and spoke to people through the prophets many times and in various ways [Heb. 1:2].
- Jesus [the Son] is the revealer (NB. The Son's revelation is superior to all other revelation.) [Heb. 1:2].
- Jesus [the Son] was appointed heir of all things [Heb. 1:2].
- Jesus [the Son] made the universe [Heb. 1:2].
- Jesus [the Son] is in the radiance of God's Glory [Heb. 1:3].
- Jesus [the Son] is the exact representation of God [Heb. 1:3].
- Jesus [the Son] sustains all things by his powerful word [Heb. 1:3].
- Jesus [the Son] is the redeemer [Heb. 1:3; elaborated later in chapters 5 to 10].
- Jesus [the Son] is superior to the angels [Heb. 1:4].

3. Yet it was transformed into a living, powerful, and glorious body (cf. 1 Cor. 15:43; Phil. 3:21). Tabor, *Paul and Jesus*, 64 elaborates, "Resurrection is rather the reclothing or 'reincorporation' of the essential self with a new immortal body that frees it from the Hadean state of death."

- Jesus [the Son] is God's first-born [Heb. 1:5–6].
- Jesus [the Son] is God's son [Heb. 1:5; 5:5].
- Jesus [the Son] will be worshipped by the angels [Heb. 1:6].
- Jesus sits at the right hand of God [Heb, 1:13; 8:1 and alluded in 1:3; 10:12; and 12:2].
- Jesus [the Son] is a high priest [Heb. 3:1].
- Jesus [the Son] is greater than Moses [Heb. 3:3–6].
- Jesus [the Son] is the great high priest [Heb. 4:14–16].
- Jesus [the Son] is a priest forever in the order of Melchizedek [Heb. 5: 6, 10; 7:17].
- Jesus [the Son] learned obedience through what he suffered. And being made perfect, he became the source of eternal salvation for all who obey him [Heb. 5:9].
- Jesus [the Son] is the guarantor of a better covenant [Heb. 7:22].
- Jesus [the Son] lives forever and has a permanent priesthood [Heb. 7:24].
- Jesus [the Son] is able to save to the uttermost those who draw near to God through him since he always lives to make intercession for them [Heb. 7: 25].
- Jesus [the Son] holy, innocent, unstained, separated from sinners, and exalted above the heavens [Heb. 7:26].
- Unlike the other high priests, Jesus [the Son] has no need to offer sacrifices daily, first for his own sins and then for those of the people [Heb. 7:27].
- Jesus [the Son] has been made perfect forever [Heb. 7:28].
- Jesus [the Son] is seated at the right hand of the throne of the Majesty in heaven [Heb. 8:1].
- Jesus [the Son] is a minister in the holy places, in the true tent [i.e., heaven] that the Lord set up, not man [Heb. 8:2].
- Jesus [the Son] obtained a ministry that is as much more excellent than the old as the covenant he mediates is better since it is enacted on better promises [Heb. 8:6].
- Jesus [the Son] is the mediator of a new covenant [Heb. 12:4].

- Jesus [the Son] is the same yesterday and today and forever [Heb. 13:8].
- Jesus [the Son, the great Shepherd of the sheep] was brought back from the dead by the God of peace [Heb. 13:20].

These theological statements require thorough analysis. Before we begin, a brief examination of mainline Christian orthodoxy is necessary. Its core beliefs can be summarized as follows:[4]

- There is a single God, and not a multiplicity of gods (Mark 12:29; 1 Tim. 2:5). Moreover, this single God, the Christian God, exists as a Trinity of three persons: the Father, the Son, and the Holy Spirit (Matt. 28:19; 2 Cor. 13:14; 1 Pet. 1:1–2). Other monotheistic religions, consequently, such as Islam and Judaism, are in error regarding the number of persons in the Godhead.
- God is omnipotent, omniscient, and omnipresent.
- Jesus, who is the only begotten Son of God (John 3:16), is God the Son made incarnate in human flesh (the Incarnation).
- Jesus is simultaneously one hundred percent (fully) God and one hundred percent (fully) human (two natures in one person; the Hypostatic Union).
- As God the Son, Jesus preexisted (John 1:1–18; 8:58; Col. 1:17; Rev. 22:13) as a member of a triune deity.
- Although Jesus pre-existed in the form of God before his incarnation, he laid aside his divine glory of his own free choice, took upon himself the form of a servant, and was made in the likeness of men.
- The reason why Jesus became incarnate was to rescue a fallen human race. When God created human beings, they were very good (Gen. 1:31), but the first man (Adam) disobeyed God and sinned. As a result, death came into the world (the Fall).
- God knew in advance that Adam would be disobedient and sin.
- As a consequence of the Fall, every human has a corrupted nature and is estranged from God. Thus, we are all born in a state of original sin. Original sin is the result of a personal act by Adam (Gen. 3).

4. An in-depth analysis is beyond the scope of this text. Readers are referred to standard reference sources (encyclopedia entries) and texts relating to Dogmatics and Systematic Theology.

- After revealing Himself to Moses and the Israelites, God established a system to remove sins and permit humankind to "return" and become "connected" to God. It incorporated (a) a temple, (b) a priesthood, (b) an operator's manual (the Hebrew Bible), (c) sacrifices (properly termed "offerings"), and (d) detailed rituals.
- However, God knew in advance the limitations associated with the priesthood and sacrificial system that He established and ordained for the Israelites.
- The reason why this system could not heal the breach between God and humanity was that only an infinite offering could atone for humankind's sins against an infinite God.
- The infinite offering to God had to be holy, innocent, pure, separated from sinners, sinless, unstained, and exalted above the heavens. Only Jesus, who is fully God, could fulfill God's requirement for an acceptable, infinite offering to Himself.
- Therefore, God the Father sent His only Son, Jesus (who is God the Son incarnate), to offer his life for us, in order to atone for *all humanity's* sins (the Redemption).
- Jesus was conceived by the power of the Holy Spirit and born of the virgin Mary (Matt. 1:20–23; Luke 1:27–35). For thirty years he lived a humble life with his family in Galilee, before being called at his baptism to proclaim the coming of the Kingdom of God.
- All the words that Jesus spoke during His earthly ministry were the words of God. They contain absolutely no error of any kind. That includes Jesus' explicit teaching that he came to offer his life as a ransom for many (Mark 10:45).
- Jesus' death by crucifixion, in which his blood was shed for us, was a one-time (eternal) offering (substitutionary work on the cross). Jesus, the high priest, did this once and for all when he offered up himself.
- Humanity's exclusive hope of redemption is through the shed blood of Jesus Christ, the Son of God.
- That is why God the Father permitted his Son to be assaulted, scourged, and crucified by pagan Roman soldiers under the rule of Pontius Pilate (Matt. 27:26–35; Mark 15:15–24; Luke 23:33; John

19:15–18), for the sake of accomplishing his plan of salvation for the human race.

- Jesus, who was fully God and fully man, died on the cross.[5]
- After his death, he was buried for three days and three nights (Matt. 12:40; cf. 1 Cor. 15:4).
- God the Father transformed Jesus' corpse into an immortal, powerful, and glorious body (cf. 1 Cor. 15).
- Over a period of forty days after his death, Jesus was seen by his disciples, who became convinced that he had appeared to them and that he had risen from the dead, despite their not recognizing him on multiple occasions (Matt. 28:17; Luke 24:15–31; John 20:15; 21:4; Acts 1:3).
- Jesus then ascended to heaven (the Ascension) and now acts as an intercessor and mediator for humankind (Acts 1:9).
- Each and every human being can only be saved through the death of Jesus on the cross (which expiated the effects of Adam's sin). In order to be saved, it is necessary to repent of one's sins, and believe in Jesus as humanity's one and only Savior. The believer is then made righteous, is born again by the Holy Spirit, and becomes a child of God. The believer who dies in a state of grace is assured of an ultimate destiny in heaven.

Biola University and Liberty University summarize these doctrines in their faith statement and doctrinal position, as illustrated by the excerpts below:

5. *Catechism of the Catholic Church*, "Part One: The Profession of Faith,"13–18; "I Believe In Jesus Christ," 106–114; "Paragraph 3. Jesus Christ was Buried," 162–163.

BIOLA UNIVERSITY ARTICLES OF FAITH

By His death on the cross, the Lord Jesus made a perfect atonement for sin, by which the wrath of God against sinners is appeased and a ground furnished upon which God can deal in mercy with sinners. He redeemed us from the curse of the law by becoming a curse in our place. He who Himself was absolutely without sin was made to be sin on our behalf that we might become the righteousness of God in Him. The Lord Jesus is coming again to his earth, personally, bodily, and visibly. The return of our Lord is the blessed hope of the believer, and in it God's purposes of grace toward mankind will find their consummation.[6]

LIBERTY UNIVERSITY DOCTRINAL POSITION

We affirm that Adam, the first man, willfully disobeyed God, bringing sin and death into the world. As a result, all persons are sinners from conception, which is evidenced in their willful acts of sin; and they are therefore subject to eternal punishment, under the just condemnation of a holy God.

We affirm that Jesus Christ offered Himself as a sacrifice by the appointment of the Father. He fulfilled the demands of God by His obedient life, died on the cross in full substitution and payment for the sins of all people, was buried, and on the third day He arose physically and bodily from the dead. He ascended into heaven where He now intercedes for all believers.

We affirm that each person can be saved only through the work of Jesus Christ, through repentance of sin and by faith alone in Him as Savior. The believer is declared righteous, born again by the Holy Spirit, turned from sin, and assured of heaven.[7]

ASSERTIONS ABOUT THE JESUS' SAVING DEATH

Returning to the Epistle of the Hebrews, the anonymous author makes the following assertions regarding Christ's saving death on the cross (the Atonement):

1. Jesus [the Son] *made purification for sins* (Heb. 1:3).
2. Jesus was crowned with glory and honor because of the suffering of death, *so that by the grace of God he might taste death for everyone* (Heb. 2:9).

6. "Theological Positions."
7. "Doctrinal Position."

3. [How?] Jesus [the Son] "*learned obedience through what he suffered*" *and "being made perfect*" (Heb. 5:9).
4. [Consequences] Jesus *became the source of eternal salvation to all who obey him* (Heb. 5:9).
5. [Requirement] Jesus [the Son] is able to save to the uttermost those who draw near to God through him since *he always lives to make intercession for them* (Heb. 7:25).
6. [Consequences] *Jesus always lives to make intercession for them* (Heb. 7:25).
7. [Moreover] Jesus [the Son] has no need, like those high priests, to offer sacrifices daily, first for his own sins and *then for those of the people* (Heb. 7:27).
8. Since he did this once and for all *when he offered up himself* (Heb. 7:27).
9. [How is this possible?] Now may the God of peace who brought again from the dead our Lord Jesus, the great shepherd of the sheep, by *the blood of the eternal covenant*, equip you with everything good that you may do his will, working in us that which is pleasing in his sight, through Jesus Christ, to whom be glory forever and ever (Heb. 13:20–21).

Most, if not all, of the author of Hebrews' assertions are matters of faith. They cannot be proven. These assertions are often referred to as *mysteries*. *The Catechism of the Catholic Church* is unequivocal in its affirmation that Jesus' death on the cross for humanity's sins is a mystery of faith.

> 624 "By the grace of God" Jesus tasted death "for every one." In his plan of salvation, God ordained that his Son should not only "die for our sins" but should also "taste death," experience the condition of death, the separation of his soul from his body, between the time he expired on the cross and the time he was raised from the dead. The state of the dead Christ is the mystery of the tomb and the descent into hell. It is the mystery of Holy Saturday, when Christ, lying in the tomb, reveals God's great sabbath rest after the fulfillment of man's salvation, which brings peace to the whole universe.[8]

8. *Catechism of the Catholic Church*, "Part One: The Profession of Faith," 13–18; "I Believe in Jesus Christ," 106–114; "Paragraph 3. Jesus Christ was Buried,"162–163.

In this passage, the *Catechism* openly admits that Christian theism and theology—supported by the Epistle to the Hebrews—are ultimately founded on faith in a mystery. In the minds of Christian and Jewish theists, God exists, and miracles can and do happen.

Skeptics and detractors object that there are alternative theistic rationales that challenge the Christian explanation for Jesus' alleged bodily resurrection. They point out that even if Jesus' body did rise from the dead by some supernatural agency (i.e., something not natural but able to affect nature), this event need not have been a miracle worked *by God* to vindicate the Christians' beliefs about Jesus. There are also conjoined (i.e., containing two or more assumptions) *naturalistic* explanations for the faith of Jesus' disciples in the resurrection. These explanations are (1) less *ad hoc* (i.e., less contrived as they contain fewer additional suppositions) than the Christian hypothesis that Jesus rose from the dead; (2) more plausible; (3) more probable; (4) greater in their explanatory scope and power; and (5) disconfirmed by fewer of our currently accepted beliefs. Furthermore, these skeptics and detractors assert that supernatural or conjoined naturalistic phenomena can better explain:

1. Why did Jesus' body go missing after the crucifixion?
2. Why did people repeatedly think they saw him alive despite his earlier public execution?
3. Why have numerous people come to believe in Jesus, even to the point of being willing to suffer persecution and martyrdom?
4. How did the early church manage to grow?

This text will unpackage three interconnected Hebrew and Christian Bible readings: Genesis 14:18–20, Psalm 110:1–4, and Hebrews. Some of the questions addressed therein are whether the Epistle to the Hebrews provides convincing evidence that Jesus is a high priest, became the source of eternal salvation to all who obey him, and rose from the dead.

1

The Melchizedek Personality

> There is probably no more enigmatic a figure in all of scripture than Melchizedek, and no more difficult a problem in biblical studies than tracing the Melchizedek tradition through its various developments in Jewish and Christian literature.[1]

Melchizedek is a mystery. He appears only twice in the Old Testament and in only one document in the New Testament. However, Melchizedek is interpreted in such an odd way he becomes quite important. The New Testament document in which he appears is Hebrews. Hebrews is, in itself, quite mysterious. Next to nothing is known about the author of the document. Next to nothing is known about to whom it was written. Next to nothing is known about the document in general. Scholarship makes a lot of guesses, but really no answers are to be found. The mysteriousness of Melchizedek in Hebrews should surprise no one; Hebrews is itself one of the most mysterious works of the New Testament.[2]

> This chapter still poses a vast number of riddles to which an even larger number of conjectures have been offered as solutions . . . Innumerable suggestions have been offered, but this proliferation implies the doubt that any one of them may be the finite and only one.[3]

1. Longenecker, "The Melchizedek Argument of Hebrews," 161.
2. Hambrick, "The Paradox of Melchizedek," 1.
3. Margalith, "The Riddle of Genesis 14 and Melchizedek," 501.

> However, a much more weighty consideration relates to the author's discussion of the high priesthood. Of Christ. When the writer is about to discuss the topic of Jesus as high priest in the order of Melchizedek, he says that this subject "is hard to explain because you are slow to learn" (5:11). The word *hard* had overtones that reverberated in the Hebrew community.[4]

WHO WAS MELCHIZEDEK, HOW IS HE DESCRIBED IN THE BIBLE, AND HOW DOES HEBREWS LIKEN JESUS TO HIM?

Nowadays, many Christians take it for granted that Jesus was a high priest. However, where did the idea come from? Neither the disciples, the gospel authors, nor Jesus himself said he was a priest.

"The first known literary source to attribute the title 'high priest' to Jesus is Hebrews"[5] (see Heb. 3:1; 4:14–16; 5:5; 9:11–12; and indirectly in 2:17). Therefore, the Messiah is also a priest. Ole Jakob Filvedt and Martin Wessbrandt explore several possibilities regarding the origin of this idea in Hebrews: (1) Jesus was recognized as high priest in some strands of the early Christian tradition, (2) the idea that Jesus was high priest originated from the general theological creativity of the author of Hebrews, or (3) there was an intimate link between worship/liturgy and the idea that Jesus was high priest.[6] They conclude, "There is strong intuition to suggest that the concept originated with the author of Hebrews."[7]

Christian apologists, Bible commentators, and theologians argue that Jesus is "likened" to Melchizedek in Psalm 110, which refers to him as a high priest.[8] For example, Michael Brown, a leading Messianic Jew, writes:

4. Kistemaker, *Exposition of the Epistle to the Hebrews*, 16, cf. 140, 147–48.

5. Filvedt and Wessbrandt, "Exploring the High Priesthood of Jesus in Early Christian Sources," 97.

6. Filvedt and Wessbrandt, "Exploring the High Priesthood of Jesus in Early Christian Sources," 96–114.

7. Filvedt and Wessbrandt, "Exploring the High Priesthood of Jesus in Early Christian Sources," 112.

8. Also spelled Malkiṣedeq, Melkiṣedeq and Melchisedec. See Staley, "The MELKISEDEQ Memoirs," 1n1.

> Why do I say that the Messiah will also function as a priest? Once again, David is the prototype, and while king, he sometimes did what only priests were supposed to do, offering sacrifices in 2 Sam 24, wearing the linen ephod in 2 Sam 6, and eating the consecrated bread in 1 Sam 21. It even says in 2 Sam 8:18 that David's sons were priests. Then, in Psalm 110, speaking either of David, the prototype of the Messiah, or of the Messiah himself, God says, "*You are a priest forever after the order of Melchizedek*." This is quite significant, since Melchizedek was himself a priestly king.[9]

The only other biblical reference to Melchizedek in the Hebrew Bible is a short passage in Genesis 14.

Ian Vaillancourt's literature review highlights that most scholars characterize Genesis 14 as distinct, describing it with terms such as "unique," "difficult," "enigmatic," and even "strange and perplexing."[10] Steven Pahl's literature review also notes, "Scholars describe Genesis 14 as 'difficult,' 'a puzzle,' and 'an erratic boulder in the Genesis landscape.'"[11] Fred Horton adds that "Melchizedek is mentioned only twice in the Old Testament in passages that present significant challenges in terms of text, language, and date. The difficulty in understanding the references to Melchizedek is compounded by the fact that, in both passages, the primary focus is not on Melchizedek but on other figures: Abram in the first instance and the king of Jerusalem in the second."[12]

These observations underscore an important warning. Relying on three verses—whose meanings are unverifiable and highly debated—should prompt serious consideration. Skeptics may question whether it is reasonable to accept Christian theism or convert to Christianity based on a few select Bible verses that are often taken out of context and misrepresented. Given these caveats, they wonder if any sensible person today would choose to follow Jesus and change their faith simply because Christian apologists, Bible commentators, and theologians claim that, like Melchizedek, Jesus serves as both priest and king and is also the Messiah. Ultimately, readers must judge these assertions for themselves.

However, interpreting these verses can be difficult. Scholars, Bible commentators, and theologians disagree on the personae, date, source,

9. Brown, "The Real Jewish Messiah."

10. Vaillancourt, "The Canonical Melchizedek," 6.

11. Pahl, "Thematic Connections in Psalm 110 and Genesis 14," 55.

12. Horton, *The Melchizedek Tradition*, 12.

unity, and meaning of portions of the chapter. "This lack of biblical information, and the presence of extra-biblical writings concerning the details of Melchizedek's life, has produced a plethora of opinions regarding his nature and person throughout history and even to this day."[13] First, readers must decide whether to work exclusively with the Hebrew or the Christian Bible or to include the Jewish oral traditions. The latter include the Midrash (Gen. Rab. 43:6; 46:5; 55:6; Lev. Rab. 25:6; Num. Rab. 4:8) and Talmud (b. Ned. 32b; see the Appendix). Further sources of interest include the Apocrypha (Enoch), the Dead Sea Scrolls (Qumran), Targums, and writings of Philo and Josephus. However, only two references to Melchizedek occur in the Hebrew Bible. In addition, the New Testament mentions Melchizedek more frequently than the Hebrew Bible. A mere three-verse segment is in Genesis 14:18–20 and one verse in Psalm 110:4. Together, they total four verses.

> Genesis 14: 18–20 And Melchizedek king of Salem brought out bread and wine. (He was priest of God Most High.) And he blessed him and said,
> "Blessed be Abram by God Most High,
> Possessor of heaven and earth;
> and blessed be God Most High,
> who has delivered your enemies into your hand!"
> And Abram gave him a tenth of everything (ESV).
> Psalm 110:4 The Lord has sworn
> and will not change his mind,
> "You are a priest forever
> after the order of Melchizedek." (ESV)

Fred Horton expounds on the importance of these four verses, "Providing Christ a priestly order and prefiguring its superiority to the Jewish priesthood."[14] The late American New Testament theologian and professor of biblical studies William Lane (1931–1999) concurs: "The writer's main concern in 7:1–28 is to delineate the nature of Jesus' priestly office and prove that it is superior to the Levitical priesthood . . . In the Genesis narrative and Ps 110:4, the writer finds the unmistakable implication that the Levitical priesthood will be replaced by the eternal priesthood foreshadowed and prefigured in the person of Melchizedek."[15]

13. Anderson, "An Examination of the Figure of Melchizedek," 1.
14. Horton, *The Melchizedek Tradition*, 29.
15. Lane, *Hebrews* 1–8, 163.

Melchizedek appears eight times in the Epistle to the Hebrews (Heb. 5:6, 10; 6:20; 7:1, 10, 11, 15, and 17). Steven Donnelly notes:

> The writer of the *Epistle to the Hebrews* draws a unique parallel between the priesthood of Melchizedek and that of Christ himself. While the royal component of Melchizedek's identity is noted, the text focuses upon his ongoing priesthood and shows no regard for genealogical records. Indifference toward familial background distinguishes Melchizedek's priestly status as transcendent over the sons of Levi and Aaron as well as any ordinances of the Mosaic legal code (7:11–13).[16]

Donnelly continues, "Melchizedek's undisclosed history (e.g., records regarding family background, date of birth) corresponds with qualities intrinsic to the pre-incarnate Christological Son whose priesthood, in reciprocal fashion, mirrors the figurative description of Melchizedek's own priesthood (cf. Heb. 7:3)."[17] Furthermore, he points out a crucial fact: the writer of Hebrews considers Melchizedek's priestly role as superior to that of Levi and the sons of Aaron. Donnelly argues that the writer of Hebrews frames his argument around three points:

1. Levi was not yet born at the time of the Melchizedek-Abraham meeting of Genesis 14.
2. Abraham paid tithes to Melchizedek (the priest).
3. Melchizedek blessed Abraham.[18]

James Moffatt elaborates: (a) Melchizedek "is never recorded to have lost his priesthood by death" and (b) "in his ancestor Abraham, Levi yet unborn did homage to Melchizedek."[19] Chronologically, these three texts (Genesis 14, Psalm 110, and Hebrews 5–7) will be the subject of further examination in this text.

16. Donnelly, "The Divine Rites," 27.
17. Donnelly, "The Divine Rites," 29.
18. Donnelly, "The Divine Rites," 29.
19. Moffatt, *The Moffatt New Testament Commentary*, 94.

2

Commentary on Genesis 14

> We have four things in the story of this chapter. I. A war with the king of Sodom and his allies, ver. 1–11. II. The captivity of Lot in that war, ver. 12. III. Abram's rescue of Lot from that captivity, with the victory he obtained over the conquerors, ver. 13–16. IV. Abram's return from the expedition, Genesis 14:17, with an account of what passed, 1. Between him and the king of Salem, ver. 18–20. 2. Between him and the king of Sodom, ver. 21–24. So that here we have that promise to Abram in part fulfilled, that God would make his name great.[1]

COMMENTARY AND ANALYSIS ON GENESIS 14

The figure of Melchizedek is one of the most enigmatic personalities in the Bible. The first mention of Melchizedek in the Hebrew Bible appears in Genesis 14. This passage will be analyzed in the following sections. The questions below will be explored in detail, incorporating the views of scholars in the field:

2.1.1 What Does the Name "Melchizedek" Mean?

2.1.2 Who was Melchizedek?

2.1.3 Where was Melchizedek's Home?

2.1.4 Melchizedek's Genealogy, Birth, and Death

1. Henry, *An Exposition of the Old and New Testament*, 93.

2.1.5 The Break in Genesis 14: Insertion or Original?

2.1.6 Abram Meets Melchizedek: Who Paid Whom a Tithe?

2.1.7 Kings in the Ancient Near East?

2.1.8 Priesthood in the Ancient Near East?

2.1.9 The Union of Kingship and Priesthood: Was Melchizedek the First King-Priest?

2.1.10 Would Jesus have Qualified as a Priest in the Ancient Near East?

Before proceeding with a historical analysis of Melchizedek, we must provide some background information concerning the events recorded in Genesis 14.

The chapter describes a coalition of four powerful kings and their armies fighting against five kings of weaker city-states who rebelled against them after twelve years of forced allegiance and servitude. The identities of the kings and their city-states are the subject of considerable academic debate.[2] The four kings emerge victorious and seize all the goods and food of Sodom and Gomorrah. In addition, they kidnap Lot—the nephew of Abram (later known as Abraham), who is living in Sodom—and seize his possessions.

When Abram learns about the kidnapping, he assembles 318 armed men to defeat the coalition. Ultimately, he liberates Lot and other people with him and recovers the stolen goods. Commentators have remarked that Abram's behavior in this chapter is strikingly different from what is shown in the book of Genesis. As Victor Hamilton pithily remarks: "Nowhere before or after this chapter do we find Abram taking part in military activity."[3] Cale Staley elaborates:

> Abram's character also exhibits qualities in this narrative that do not fit with his image throughout the rest of the Abram cycle. The Abram known in the rest of Genesis is a small pastoralist with a smaller group of people surrounding him. But, the Abram of Gen. 14 is more akin to a mercenary, surrounded by a group of 318 soldiers, who is in league with the Amorites Aner, Eschol, and Mamre.[4]

2. See the overview of Staley, "The MELKISEDEQ Memoirs," 22–29.

3. Hamilton, *The Book of Genesis*, 389–90.

4. Staley, "The MELKISEDEQ Memoirs," 31.

The king of Sodom, who survived the war, meets Abram in the Valley of Shaveh. Next, Melchizedek, king of Salem (who has not been mentioned until this point in the narrative), presents bread and wine to Abram. Melchizedek, who is also a priest of God Most High, blesses Abram and praises God for delivering Abram's enemies into his hands. According to David Elgavish, "Melchizedek's presenting himself before Abram corresponds to the well-known practice of kings from the vicinity coming to greet the victor."[5] For instance, the same action can be observed in 2 Samuel 8:9–10, "When Toi king of Hamath heard that David had defeated the whole army of Hadadezer, Toi sent his son Joram to King David, to ask about his health and to bless him because he had fought against Hadadezer and defeated him, for Hadadezer had often been at war with Toi. And Joram brought with him articles of silver, of gold, and of bronze" (ESV) in recognition of the victor. Elgavish also argues that offering bread and wine was a peace covenant.[6]

Thomas Alexander observes, "Abraham's encounter with the kings of Salem and Sodom can also be viewed in the light of the promise recorded in 12:2–3."[7] He points out that both kings acknowledge Abram's importance due to his victory. Alexander argues, "Here we find a fulfilment of the promise, 'I will make your name great.'"[8] Instead, Nahum Sarna argues that Melchizedek's words of blessing in Genesis 14:19 are significant because it is the first time another person blesses Abram/Abraham: "The incident is the first example of the fulfilment of God's initial promise back in Haran that Abraham's name would become great and be invoked in blessings."[9]

In verses 18–20 of Genesis 14, Melchizedek makes his first appearance in the Hebrew Bible. Several "firsts" are found in this narrative:

1. Melchizedek is described as the priest of God Most High, *'El 'Elyon*. This divine title is first mentioned in the Bible here.
2. This section of text contains the first biblical reference to tithing.
3. The passage features the first biblical use of the Hebrew word for "priest."

5. Elgavish, "The Encounter of Abram and Melchizedek King of Salem," 495–508.
6. Elgavish, "The Encounter of Abram and Melchizedek King of Salem," 495–508.
7. Alexander, "A Literary Analysis of the Abraham Narrative in Genesis," 42.
8. Alexander, "A Literary Analysis of the Abraham Narrative in Genesis," 42.
9. Sarna, *Understanding Genesis*, 117.

4. Genesis 14:18 is the first biblical verse to speak of "bread and wine."
5. Genesis 14:19 records a priest's first blessing of a human being in the Bible.
6. Genesis 14:19 is the first verse to describe God as the "possessor/ acquirer of heaven and earth."[10]

The biblical character of Melchizedek is shrouded in mystery. Various scholarly opinions exist regarding his name, identity, origins, and lineage. In addition, his interactions with Abram are the subject of lively debate, as are his dual roles as a king and a priest. This text examines those topics in greater detail in Part 2. There, we will see that scholars have yet to reach a consensus on Melchizedek. The lack of solid and reliable information about this enigmatic figure casts doubt on Jesus' portrayal as an eternal priest in the order of Melchizedek. His situation is akin to building a house on a foundation of sand.

2.1 What Does the Name "Melchizedek" Mean?

There is a lack of consensus regarding the meaning of the name Melchizedek. Common interpretations include phrases such as "King of Righteousness," "Righteous is my king," or "righteous king."[11] Kaspar Dalgaard's literature review offers additional options, such as *my king is righteous*, *Sedeq is my king*, or *Malak is righteous*.[12] Joseph Fitzmyer opines, "The name must have originally meant '[the god] Sedeq is my king,' or less likely, 'My king is righteous(ness).'"[13] A third option is "The phrase מלכי צדק could refer to an actual person named "Melchizedek."[14] Fourth, it could refer to an ancient title, "Right(ful) King."[15] In other words, it could be a royal title. Pharaoh would represent another example of a title serving as a name. Margaret Barker says, "Melchizedek is written as two words, suggesting that it was not a name but a title: Malki Zedek perhaps

10. Haywood, *Targums and the Transmission of Scripture into Judaism and Christianity*, 379.

11. Staley, "The MELKISEDEQ Memoirs," 35; Cockerill, "Melchizedek or 'King of Righteousness?'" 307–10; Koester, *The Anchor Yale Bible*, 346.

12. Dalgaard, *A Priest for All Generations*, 18.

13. Fitzmyer, "Melchizedek in the MT, LXX, and the NT," 65.

14. Pahl, "Thematic Connections in Psalm 110 and Gen 14," 104.

15. Pahl, "Thematic Connections in Psalm 110 and Gen 14," 104.

King of Righteousness or Righteous King."[16] Similarly, Emmanouela Grypeou and Helen Spurling explain, referring to Genesis Rabbah 43:6, that Melchizedek is "understood to be a title rather than a name, that is, 'King of Zedek' with Zedek referring to a place name."[17] Granerød discusses the thesis that in Psalm 110:4, "it does not represent a personal name but either a nominal phrase or a nominal clause" whereas the reference in "Gen. 14:18–20 indeed is to a *person*, that is 'Melchizedek.'"[18]

Gordon Wenham offers three options:

> My king is Sedeq, 'Milku is righteous' or 'my king is righteous [i.e., legitimate].' The first two interpretations presuppose that either Melek or Sedeq is the name of a god. The third does not: if it were correct, it would be the equivalent of Akkadian *Sarru Ken* (Sargon). Since theophoric names are frequent in the ancient orient, the first or second explanation is to be preferred.[19]

The discussion demonstrates that a compound name like Melchizedek raises unresolvable problems: (1) Is Melchizedek a proper name? (2) Does it combine the connotations of an epithet? or (3) Was it written as one word or two words? After posing these academic questions, Ann Madsen asks, "But who decides?"[20]

A weak argument against Melchizedek being a personal name is "an *ex nihilo* argument" based on "the fact that this person is not mentioned elsewhere in earlier sources."[21] It is noteworthy that Mitchell Dahood's translation of Psalm 110 does not use a proper name. Verse 4b, he translates as follows: "You are a priest of the Eternal according to his pact; His legitimate king, my lord."[22] Human error is another possibility: "Various scribal errors have also been suggested as the reason behind the name's sudden appearance in Gen 14:18: instead of a proper name, it may have resulted from misreading *Salem* as *Sodom*, with 17–20 then narrating the first part of the meeting between Abraham and the king of Sodom, named Melchizedek."[23]

16. Barker, "Who was Melchizedek and Who was God?" 2; cf. Gruenwald, "Melchizedek," 11.

17. Grypeou and Spurling, *The Book of Genesis in Late Antiquity*, 210.

18. Granerød, *Abraham and Melchizedek*, 195.

19. Wenham, *Genesis 1–15*, 316.

20. Madsen, "Melchizedek the Man and the Tradition," 32.

21. Granerød, *Abraham and Melchizedek*, 237.

22. Dahood, *Psalms III*, 112.

23. Dalgaard, *A Priest for All Generations*, 18.

An anonymous author writing under the pen name The Kingdom of Zion poses three rhetorical questions (listed below) about Melchizedek that readers should consider. He also points out that the name was written originally in two words: Malki Zedek. In the Septuagint and Vulgate, it appears as one word:

1. How probable is it for a person to take two words that describe their relationship to others and their spiritual nature or standing before God as their name?
2. How likely is it that a person's parents decide to call their child from birth, describing future deeds or events?
3. How probable is it that a person will eventually merge their name into a new single word?

The writer concludes, "So we can soundly say that this was probably never His birth name."[24]

There is another factor to consider when analyzing the name. Scholars note that Melchizedek's name is a Canaanite formulation, with parallels found in the Hebrew Bible. Two frequently cited examples are Adoni-Zedek, the king of Jerusalem (Joshua 10:1–3) and Abimelech, the king of Shechem (Judg. 9:1–57). The second, Abimelech, was a wicked king. Kings in the ancient Near East also bear similar names. One example is Ami-Saduqa ("Saduq is my kinsman"). This was an Amorite name of a Babylonian king, c. 1600 BCE. Madsen adds, "A significant parallel is to the name Sargon. The Akkadian spelling of the name is Sarru(m) Ken ("the king is just, legitimate"; cf. PS cx 4). E.A. Speiser calls Melchizedek the 'Canaanite counterpart of Sargon.'"[25]

Another variable that academics discuss is theophoric names. El and Yahweh frequently appear in the Hebrew Bible as component names, such as Ariel, Gabriel, Ishmael, Israel, Elijah, Hezekiah, and Joshua.[26] Madsen discusses the relevance of this fact:

> If Melchizedek is divided into its two Hebrew elements, *mlk, and sdq, there is an immediate and apparent problem in identifying the theophoric name. Which element is the divine name? Although mlk is commonly "King,"* it is known as a divine name

24. The Kingdom of Zion, *History of Melchizedek, the Great High Priest*, 2,
25. Madsen, "Melchizedek, the Man and the Tradition," 33; Speiser, *Genesis*, 104.
26. For multiple examples, see Alter, *The Name Israel*, 138–41 (*El* theophory).

> in Ugarit, Mari, and Assur. Melchizedek could mean "*Mlk* (a god) is righteous (upright)."[27]

According to Rosenberg, *Sdq* has also been identified as a deity in the area of Canaan.[28] Consequently, "two divine names make up the name Melchizedek."[29] Madsen concludes, "Various translations are possible but none is certain to be the primary denotation. Examining each word element opens a semantic cave, therefore, scholars are not agreed."[30]

Ultimately, convincing information is necessary to determine the meaning of Melchizedek. Scholars can only provide their opinions based on the best available information. However, readers must acknowledge that information is lacking and contradictory.

2.2 Who was Melchizedek?

Collectively, Melchizedek appears only ten times in the Hebrew Bible and the New Testament. Eight of these times occur in Hebrews (Heb. 5:6, 10; 6:20; 7:1, 10, 11, 15, 17). Martin Bodinger notes that "Melchizedek is unique, in that he is the only non-Jewish character of the Old Testament to appear in the Psalms and the only mortal, in eschatological literature, who becomes a divine figure with Messianic features."[31] Moshe Reiss adds, "Melchizedek appears in Genesis as one of two non-Israeli priests who appear in the Hebrew Scriptures; the second is Jethro, the father-in-law of Moses."[32] From the Genesis narrative, what is known about Melchizedek? His description is in three verses (Genesis 14:18–20). Christian commentators list the following characteristics:

1. He is the king of Salem (probably Jerusalem).
2. He is a Canaanite priest-king (i.e., king and priest).
3. He has no recorded family history (genealogy).
4. He brings out bread and wine.
5. He is the priest of God Most High/the Most High God.

27. Madsen, "Melchizedek, the Man and the Tradition," 33; Cf. Kistemaker, *Exposition of the Epistles to the Hebrews*, 184.

28. Rosenberg, "The God of Sedeq," 161–77.

29. Madsen, "Melchizedek, the Man and the Tradition," 34.

30. Madsen, "Melchizedek, the Man and the Tradition," 34.

31. Bodinger, "L'énigme de Melkisédeq," 298.

32. Reiss, "The Melchizedek Traditions," 259.

6. He is a contemporary of Abram.
7. He blesses Abram (gives blessings or at least one blessing).
8. He receives from Abram a tribute of a tenth (or tithe) of everything (Not stated explicitly; to be discussed below.)

In Genesis 14:18, the first description of Melchizedek is the third Hebrew word, *melek*, meaning king. Is this title accurate? Fred Horton cautions readers against taking the title too literally:

> It has not yet become obvious to scholars that there are many assumptions involved in making Melchizedek the king of pre-Israelite Jerusalem. One must assume, first of all, the literary unity of Gen. xiv and assign that chapter to an early date. Secondly, one must accept the equation Salem = Jerusalem which is not completely certain. Thirdly, one must give historical value to Gen. xiv. All three of these conditions must at least hold true before one may speak of Melchizedek's pre-Davidic priest-kingship in Jerusalem. Even if true, such assumptions deserve more study and attention than they are usually given.[33]

Horton's approximately thirty-page review and analysis of the biblical and extra-biblical evidence for a pre-Davidic Jerusalem is telling. Readers should carefully examine his material. In closing, he identifies three significant difficulties about the presumed priest-kingship of Melchizedek:

1. In neither of the extra-biblical sources is there evidence of any ruling dynasty in pre-Israelite Jerusalem, and the evidence of the El-Amarna tablets is against such views.
2. In the biblical records, there is no evidence of a ruling dynasty in Jerusalem of a sacral variety or otherwise.
3. Melchizedek, in the Old Testament, is never unequivocally identified as the king of Jerusalem.[34]

Genesis 14:18 also contains the word כֹּהֵן, *kohen*, "priest," and it is the very first mention of the term in the Hebrew Bible.[35] The other appearances of *kohen* in Genesis are: 41:45, 50, 46:20, 47:22, 26.[36] The

33. Horton, *The Melchizedek Tradition*, 39n3.
34. Horton, *The Melchizedek Tradition*, 45.
35. Gustavsson, "The Melchizedek Mystery," 23.
36. Chan, *Melchizedek Passages in the Bible*, 44.

word *kohen* has various uses in the Hebrew Bible. It can refer to (1) the Jewish nation or people as a whole, as when Exodus 19:6 declares, "And you shall be to me a kingdom of priests and a holy nation" (ESV), (2) a descendant of Aaron (Exod. 28:1), and (3) a descendant of Aaron serving in the Temple. The statement in 2 Samuel 8:18, that "Benaiah the son of Jehoiada was over the Cherethites and the Pelethites, and David's sons were priests" (ESV), is a matter of controversy and subject to academic debate. The controversy centers on how David's sons could be priests, given that they belonged to the tribe of Judah and were not descendants of Aaron. Children have only one biological father. One possible solution is that the word "priest" was flexible. It could also mean or refer to (4) priests serving as officials on the king's side, (5) royal advisors, (6) administrators or ministers or stewards, or (7) non-Levitical priests. Gerald Kennedy advocates the following reading: "and the sons of David were ministers."[37] Therefore, in secular contexts, the term *kohen* could refer to a high administrative office in the royal government. Mitchell Dahood comments, "The new king, like all early Israelite kings, enjoyed the privileges of a priest; 2 Sam 8:18, 1 Kings 3:4."[38]

Horton reports that Josephus declares, "Melchizedek is the first priest mentioned in the Torah."[39] Additionally, he points out that nowhere in the Old Testament apart from Psalm 90:4 is the king described as a *kohen*.[40] Jane Allison adds, "Therefore, he is non-Levitical without successor."[41] Moreover, Melchizedek was *not* a priest of Israel, as that nation did not yet exist at that time. Accordingly, he was Salem's king, and his priesthood pre-dated Abraham's covenant with God. Notably, Abram had no children yet. Thus, the Levites would not become a priestly tribe for another four centuries. Consequently, he appears well before the establishment of the Law and the Levitical succession.

The Hebrew Bible does not explain how a Canaanite city-king became a priest of God Most High. However, Josephus, writing in Book Six of the *Wars*, states that Melchizedek was called *the righteous King* because he really was one, "On which account he was the first priest of

37. Kennedy, "St. Paul's Conception of the Priesthood," 13

38. Dahood, *Psalms III*, 117.

39. Horton, *The Melchizedek Tradition*, 157, 160.

40. Horton, *The Melchizedek Tradition*, 45.

41. Allison, "A Study of the Priestly Christology of the Epistle to the Hebrews," 100.

God [there]; and first built a temple [there]; and called the city *Jerusalem*: which was formerly called *Salem*."[42]

"Then, "Melchizedek departs from the story with a suddenness matched only by his abrupt arrival (v.20b)."[43] In reverse, John Sailhamer says, "that Melchizedek appears in the narrative out of nowhere and just as quickly is gone."[44] Crucially, his description is both a priest *and* a king.

Christian commentators propose several options regarding his identity:

1. Melchizedek is a heavenly being (angelic).
2. Melchizedek as the pre-incarnate Christ.
3. Melchizedek is a type of Christ.
4. Melchizedek is a historical individual.
5. Melchizedek is a local deity in Canaan.[45]

Paulus Kim expands on the possible identity of Melchizedek. He says scholars' opinions on how the author of Hebrews depicts Melchizedek in his epistle can be summarized under three headings: "1) Celestial being: Fitzmyer—Elohim, De Jonge and Van der Woude—Angel, 2) Historical being: Horton, Parsons—the first priest in the Torah, 3) Celestial and Historical being: Kobelski—not as an angelic being but a celestial and historical being—as a type of Jesus Christ."[46]

Dale Leschert, in his doctoral dissertation, compares Melchizedek in 11Q Melch [Qumran] and Jesus in Hebrews. He writes:

> Both Melchizedek and Jesus appear to be called "God." 11Q Melch 2, 9, 10 seems to designated Melchizedek as [Elohim] . . . Melchizedek in 11Q Melch and Jesus in Hebrews are both are exalted heavenly figures (11Q Melch 2:10, 11; Heb. 1:3, 4; 7:26; 8:1); both make atonement for sin) 11Q Melch 2:6–8; Heb. 2:17); both defeat the enemies of God (11Q Melch 2:9–15; Heb. 2:14, 15); both free captives from bondage (11Q Melch 2:2–6; Heb. 2:14, 15) and both perform an eschatological role (11Q Melch 2:7; Heb. 1:2).[47]

42. Josephus, "The Jewish War," 438.
43. Mathews, *Melchizedek's Alternative Priestly Order*, 53.
44. Sailhamer, *Genesis*, 165.
45. Bodinger, "L'énigme de Melkisédeq," 297–332.
46. Kim, "Antitype of Jesus," 3.
47. Leschert, "Hermeneutical Foundations of the Epistle to the Hebrews," 280–81;

Reiss adds:

> P.J. Kobelski suggests that Melchizedek, as he appears in Genesis, is an angel who has helped Abraham defeat his enemies and released Lot. Thus, Abraham gives the tithe to Melchizedek. This is consistent with the DSS (11Q13) and the Nag Hammadi texts discussed below. The Talmud suggests (on Gen 14,15, several verses before Melchizedek is introduced) that angels helped Abraham fight his enemies that night (BT San. 96a also see Midrash Rabbah Gen 42,2.4 and 43,3).[48]

Ceslaus Spicq's comment about Melchizedek's identity bears diligent consideration: "But no matter how difficult the identification of its author may be—Oepke describes it as a search for a 'square hole' (Oepke, 1950, p. 17)—the critics have not grown tired of looking for a solution."[49]

The bottom line is that nobody knows Melchizedek's identity with certitude. Moreover, convincing information is needed to determine who Melchizedek was. Scholars can only present their conjectures based on the best available information at the time. However, readers must acknowledge that the information is contradictory here as well.

2.3 Where was Melchizedek's home?

The hometown of Melchizedek is subject to academic debate.[50] Rabbinic sources suggest that Salem is Jerusalem. One explanation is that Salem is an early synonym for Jerusalem because of the equation between Zion and Salem in Psalm 76:3 and later texts. Alternative suggestions are that "the name Salem instead refers to a geographic location near Shechem, that there was indeed a city named Salem distinct from Jerusalem, or that it was a result of a scribal error."[51] Some commentators postulate that it centers on the Samaritan Pentateuch's rendering of Genesis 33:18. It follows that Salem is not Jerusalem but a city in the region of Shechem.[52]

---

cf. Kobelski, *Melchizedek and Melchiresa*, 128; Horton, *The Melchizedek Tradition*, 167.

48. Reiss, "The Melchizedek Traditions," 262.

49. Spicq, "The Epistle to the Hebrews," 181. (See Oepke, Albrecht. *Das Neue Gottesvolk*. Gütersloh: Bertelsmann.)

50. Gammie, "Loci of the Melchizedek Tradition," 385–96; "Melchizedek: An Exegetical Study of Genesis 14 and the Psalter," 81–93.

51. Dalgaard, *A Priest for All Generations*, 19; cf. Horton, *The Melchizedek Tradition*, 49.

52. Mason, "Hebrews 7:3 and the Relationship Between Melchizedek and Jesus," 44–45.

Here, too, there is a lack of certitude—in this case, regarding the identity of Melchizedek's home.

2.4 Melchizedek's Genealogy, Birth, and Death

Genesis lacks any biblical record of his genealogy, birth, or death. Many Christian commentators interpret this lack of genealogy as suggesting he was *an eternal, heavenly figure.*[53] This claim is an argument from silence (*argumentum e silentio*). Readers must answer a fundamental question: does this interpretation make sense? What can be said is that "In the narrative discourse of Genesis 14, Melchizedek was the 'tenth' king to appear on the scene."[54] Although the author of Genesis does not explicitly say so, the appearance of Melchizedek as the tenth king may indicate a discourse-literary device commonly employed by Hebrew writers.[55]

1. The phrase "God said" in the creation narrative appears ten times (verses 3, 6, 9, 11, 14, 20, 24, 26, 28, and 29).
2. Before the Great Flood, there were ten generations of humans on the Earth.
3. Noah was in the tenth generation of mighty men chosen to give rise to a new generation on a new Earth.
4. Abraham was the tenth generation from Shem, son of Noah.
5. A tenth (ten percent) was paid in tithes (Gen. 14:20).

Readers must face the reality that the absence of biblical records is, in fact, an absence of biblical records. For example, Philo asserts that Cain did not die because his death is not recorded in Scripture.[56] Any hypothesis about the lack of records of his birth and death is an argument from silence. Nonetheless, the anonymous author of Hebrews and the Christian Bible commentators who follow in his steps argue as follows:

1. Scripture is silent regarding Melchizedek's genealogy.
2. Consequently, Melchizedek has neither beginning nor end and thus, he is beyond time.

53. Larsen, "After the Order of Melchizedek." (see also Psalm 110:4).

54. Chan, *Melchizedek Passages in the Bible*, 45.

55. Chan, *Melchizedek Passages in the Bible*, 45.

56. Philo, *The Works of Philo Judaeus*, 286. [see "On the Principle that the Worse is accustomed to be always plotting against the Better."]

3. This "reality" points to his eternity.

Hebrews 7:3 describes Melchizedek as "without father or mother or genealogy, having neither beginning of days nor end of life, but resembling the Son of God he continues a priest forever" (ESV). Charles Baylis, in a literature review, observes that this phrase "is normally taken to mean that the literary absence of Melchizedek's birth or death has prefigured Christ's eternal life," adding that "What is allegorically true of Melchizedek was literally true of Jesus, who had neither beginning of days nor end of life."[57]

Readers must decide whether this assumption is reasonable. For instance, in the Bible, there is the character of Jethro, the father-in-law and advisor of Moses. Scripture does not identify his parents or describe his death (Exod. 2:18; 3:1; 4:18; 18:1–12; Num. 10:29). Two other scriptural examples are Ephron (Gen. 23:1) and Potiphar (Gen. 39:1). M. J. Paul poses a thought-provoking question based on the premise that the author of Hebrews assumes Melchizedek to be eternal because he has neither beginning nor end, namely: could the author attribute "to Jethro the same qualifications as he now ascribes to Melchizedek?"[58] Similarly, Horton writes, "Many secondary characters in Genesis have no family or genealogy and have no account of their birth or death. Indeed, in Gen 14 alone, this might be said of all of the kings Abram defeated, as well as the king of Sodom. Why does the author single out Melchizedek?"[59] Moreover, assuming that Melchizedek lived forever and never died, as the author of Hebrews supposed, the order of Melchizedek would have been contemporaneous with the order of Levi for more than a thousand years. If so, did their living simultaneously with the Levites necessitate a change in the Torah?

2.5 The Break in Genesis 14: Insertion or Original?

Stephen Germany, in the *Encyclopedia of the Bible and Its Reception*, writes, "The Melchizedek episode in Gen 14:18–20 is regarded by most commentators as a later insertion into Gen 14, as it interrupts the dialogue between Abram and the king of Sodom in vv. 17, 21–24."[60] John

57. Baylis, "The Author of Hebrews' Use of Melchizedek," 31.

58. Paul, "The Order of Melchizedek," 209.

59. Horton, *The Melchizedek Tradition*, 29.

60. Germany, "Melchizedek I. Hebrew Bible/Old Testament," 525; cf. Gammie, "Melchizedek: An Exegetical Study of Genesis 14 and the Psalter," 59–73; Granerød,

Gammie begins his article in the *Journal of Biblical Literature* by stating, "There is virtually unanimous opinion among scholars that vss. 18–20 were not originally of a piece with the rest of Genesis 14."[61] Ronald Hendel bluntly states, "The current consensus is that there is little or no historical memory of pre-Israelite events or circumstances in Genesis."[62]

Herbert E. Ryle, an Anglican bishop and a dated source, explains why most scholars believe this passage to be an insertion:

> That the episode of Melchizedek has been introduced from a distinct source of tradition is very probable. (*a*) It interrupts the narrative in *v.* 17, which is continued in *v.* 21. (*b*) Its contents are not in harmony with the context. In *v.* 22, Abram refuses to take anything from the spoil: in *v.* 20, Abram is said to give Melchizedek "a tenth of all." If "a tenth of all" refers to the spoil, it contradicts *v.* 22: if it refers to "all" his own property, then it assumes for Abram quite different surroundings from those of the story in chap. xiv.[63]

Joseph Fitzmyer, S.J., adds the following observations:

> Moreover, even vv. 18–20 may not have been an original part of the story in that chapter, because they interrupt the account of the meeting of Abram with the king of Sodom. They are not, however, necessarily a 'later addition,' as some have tried to argue, but may be part of an independent ancient poetic saga, as old as the rest of Gen 14. Verses 18–20 seem, however, to have been incorporated secondarily into the account of the meeting of Abram with the king of Sodom, because they interrupt the continuity of vv. 17 and 21. This gives these verses an isolated and rootless character, which explains some of the details in them, but it also shows why Melchizedek appears for a brief moment here and has little connection with the rest of the story in Gen 14.[64]

In writing about this event, Matthew Hambrick adds, "Beyond any outside evidence, if one removes Genesis 14:18–20 from the text, it reads

Abraham and Melchizedek, 32, 46, 170–71, 217.

61. Gammie, "Loci of the Melchizedek Tradition," 385; cf. "Melchizedek: An Exegetical Study of Genesis 14 and the Psalter," 38, 59–73.

62. Hendel, "Historical Context," 64.

63. Ryle, *The Book of Genesis*, 184.

64. Fitzmyer, "Melchizedek in the MT, LXX, and the NT," 64.

as if the passage were never there, without any real problems or gaps.[65] Additionally, Janet Lamarche notes that readers can hardly fail to notice that "Before uttering a word, Melchizedek, the king of Salem, greets Abram and his troops with a meal (vv 18–20), thereby interrupting the flow of the account in vv 17, 21–24. The majority of scholars view this interruption as a literary seam; a visible and awkward insertion made by a redactor."[66] The reader is invited to carefully examine the narrative below, paying attention to the ellipses that represent the deleted insertion in Genesis 14.

> [17]After his return from the defeat of Ched-or-lao′mer and the kings who were with him, the king of Sodom went out to meet [Abram] at the valley of Shaveh (that is, the King's Valley). [. . .] [21]And the king of Sodom said to Abram, "Give me the persons, but take the goods for yourself." But Abram said to the king of Sodom, "I have sworn to the Lord, God Most High, maker of heaven and earth, that I would not take a thread or a sandal-thong or anything that is yours, least you should say, "I have made Abram rich" (Gen. 14:17, 21–23 ESV).

Horton concludes, "That vss. 18–20 are an insertion into Gen. xiv is shown quite easily by showing vss. 17 and 21 together."[67]

John Gammie, in his PhD dissertation, identifies four reasons for viewing verses 18 to 20 as an interpolation:

> (1) The flow of the narrative is altogether smooth if vs. 21 is read immediately after vs. 17. (2) Vss. 18–20 are more poetical in form and language than vs. 17, 21–24 from which they may be easily distinguished. (3) In vs. 17 the king of Sodom is portrayed as the one who has come forward to meet Abram. In vs. 18, however, no mention of the king of Sodom is found at all, rather a new figure is introduced who had not been previously mentioned and who is not mentioned again after vs. 20. (4) The mention of the tithe in vs. 20, but silence about it elsewhere, can best be explained on the supposition that vss. 18–20 were a late interpolation.[68]

65. Hambrick, "The Paradox of Melchizedek," 11–12.

66. Lamarche, "The Meaning of Genesis 14:11–24," 4.

67. Horton, *The Melchizedek Tradition*, 13.

68. Gammie, "Melchizedek: An Exegetical Study of Genesis 14 and the Psalter," 60.

In addition, parts of the Genesis 14 narrative are also subject to academic debate. J.A. Emerton, writing in *Vetus Testamentum*, offers the following analysis:

> First, it is generally agreed that the explanatory notes in verses 2, 3, 7, 8, and 17 are glosses. Secondly, it is likely that the references to Aner, Eshcol, and Mamre in verses 13 and 24 are not original, for they play no part in the rest of the story and are ignored in the account of the battle and the pursuit of the eastern kings.[69]

Academics suggest that this text in Genesis 14 was an insertion during David's reign to legitimize his role as king and priest of Jerusalem and justify Jerusalem as the political and religious center for the united nation of Israel. Lamarche's literature review identifies three reasons scholars date this text to David's time. These scholars argue that the text addresses three main issues.

1. It would have promoted religious syncretism between the cult of YHWH and the Jerusalemite cult during David's takeover of Jerusalem and spoke to both groups (Israelite and Jerusalemite) under David's authority.
2. It would have legitimized David's reign in Jerusalem for the Israelites and local residents.
3. This passage can be seen to justify David's role as a priest (after the order of Melchizedek—Ps. 110:4) and king.[70]

Emerton, one of the authors cited by Lamarche, performed an extensive analysis of Genesis 14. Based on his article's reconstruction of the history of Genesis 14, he concluded that verses 18–20 were an interpolation:

> The Melchizedek passage in verses 18–20 was added, probably in the reign of David. It was hoped to encourage Israelites to accept the fusion of the worship of Yahwe with the cult of El Elyon, to recognize the position of Jerusalem as the religious and political capital of Israel, and to acknowledge that the status of David as king had behind it the ancient royal and priestly status of Melchizedek. It was also hoped to encourage Canaanites

69. Emerton, "The Riddle of Genesis XIV," 404.

70. Lamarche, "The Meaning of Genesis 14:11–24," 5. She cites Emerton, "The Riddle of Genesis XIV," 437; Goldingay, "The Patriarchs in Scripture and History," 32. See also Andersen, "Genesis 14: An Enigma," 499.

> to accept the same combination of religious and political traditions, to acknowledge David as the heir of the old Canaanite royal traditions, and to regard the Israelites, under David's leadership, as their protectors against foreign attack.[71]

Kaspar Dalgaard provides a competing rationale for the insertion of Melchizedek into Genesis 14:

> The reason behind Melchizedek's insertion into the narrative was the redactor's intention of using a mythical character to lend importance to the patriarch. The aim of the text makes it plausible that a Melchizedek was known to both the redactor and the recipients of the text. The question of whether there ever was a historical person named Melchizedek will remain a mystery. What can we discern, however, is how the story and figure served the objectives of the redactor—objectives that may have included a validation of the king's priestly aspects and the prerogative of Jerusalem and its temple, but whose primary purpose was to emphasize the importance of the Abraham figure, as it appears in Gen 14, is an appearance of a king and priest, whose importance the redactor uses to emphasize the greater importance of Abraham.[72]

Gammie summarizes a German article by Walther Zimmerli that challenges the Genesis 14 text. The article aims to deepen the reader's understanding and perception of verses 1 through 17 and 21 through 24. Gammie writes:

> Whereas before the interpolation the chapter glorifies Abraham's victory, courage, and generosity, after the interpolation the profane and almost un-theological character is removed. The effect of the interpolation is to make not Abraham but El Elyon, i.e., Yahweh, appear as the ultimate source of Abraham's accomplishments.[73]

In contrast, Granerød discusses the possibility that the Genesis 14 narrative was an anti-Persian polemic.

Germany presents another set of facts to consider:

71. Emerton, "The Riddle of Genesis XIV," 437–38.

72. Dalgaard, *A Priest for All Generations*, 25

73. Gammie, "Loci of the Melchizedek Tradition," 385; Zimmerli, "Abraham Und Melchisedek," 255–64.

> Furthermore, the appearance of Melchizedek in Gen 14:18–20 constitutes a structural parallel with the appearance of Jethro in Exod 18. Both figures appear immediately after a military victory (cf. Gen 14:1–17 and Exod 17:8–16); both are "foreign" priests who are nevertheless associated with the worship of YHWH and who bless *'el elyôn*/YHWH; and both episodes occur immediately before YHWH's making of a covenant with Abram and Israel, respectively (cf. Gen 15 and Exod 19–24.)[74]

The anonymous author of Hebrews completely reverses the prior agendas by offering a high Christological text (to be discussed below). Interested readers should examine Emerton's literature review of seven attempts to interpret the evidence via the literary history of the chapter.[75]

2.6 Abraham Meets Melchizedek: Who Paid Whom a Tithe?

Many Christian commentators argue that the text says that Abram paid a tithe *to* Melchizedek. Traditionally, Christians accept that the "he" in verse 20 is Abram and that "he," Abram, gave his tithe to Melchizedek. Eric Mason says, "As for the tithe, the Hebrew of Gen 14:20 actually is ambiguous about who pays whom, though most readers no doubt assume that the priests are on the receiving end of the tithes."[76] Emerton says, "'And he gave him a tenth of all', but does not state explicitly whether it was Abram or Melchizedek who made the gift."[77] Similarly, Horton suggests that there is no reason, based on the Masoretic text (MT), that the language could not mean Melchizedek was giving a tithe *to* Abram.[78] To support this opinion, the text in the MT reads "he."[79] Matthew Hambrick elaborates:

> Is it not possible that the story could actually be referring to a payment from Melchizedek to Abraham in order to prevent Abraham from destroying Melchizedek in further warfare? There seems to be no reason, in the Genesis text alone, to keep this from being an arguable option.[80]

74. Germany, "Melchizedek: Hebrew Bible/Old Testament," 525–26.

75. Emerton, "The Riddle of Genesis XIV," 427–29.

76. Mason, "*You Are a Priest,*" 27.

77. Emerton, "The Riddle of Genesis XIV," 407.

78. Horton, *The Melchizedek Tradition*,14; Fitzmyer, "Melchizedek in the MT, LXX, and the NT," 66; Kennedy, "St. Paul's Conception of the Priesthood," 87.

79. Speiser, *Genesis*, 100.

80. Hambrick, "The Paradox of Melchizedek," 10.

Margaret Barker, a biblical scholar, offers a robust analysis:

> The Christians claimed that Abraham *gave* a tithe to Melchizedek (Heb. 7.2–4), implying that Melchizedek was the greater, whereas the pre-Christian tradition as recorded in the *Genesis Apocryphon* says that Abraham *received* a tithe of the captured flocks from Melchizedek, implying that Abraham was the greater. The Hebrew text is ambiguous here, saying simply that 'he received a tithe . . . but the most natural reading of the Hebrew is that Abraham received a tithe, that Abraham was the greater. This was disputed even as late as the time of Jerome, who died in 420 CE. He recognised that this was delicate matter, because both the Hebrew and the Greek texts of Genesis could be read either way (Jerome, *Letter* 73.6).[81]

Joseph Fitzmyer adds, "The lack of clarity in the text has been known at least since the time of Jerome (*Epist.* 73.6)."[82] He concludes with the following opinion:

> In the original saga Melchizedek, as an allied king, probably paid tithes to Abram, as a sign of tribute to him, but then, when the verses were incorporated into the story of Abram in Genesis, the statement about tithes came to be understood the other way round. As such, it is interpreted in the Epistle to the Hebrews, where the fact that Abram paid tithes to Melchizedek is made to show the superiority of Melchizedek's priesthood over that of Levi, for '[Levi] was still in the loins of his father [Abram], when Melchizedek met him' (Heb 7,10).[83]

Commentators acknowledge that the pronoun "he" is vague. Nonetheless, many Bible translations insert the name Abram as the subject of the sentence. For instance, the NRSV reads, "And Abram gave him one tenth of everything." Other Bibles that explicitly name Abram include the English Standard Version, New International Version, Holman Christian Standard, Common English Bible with Apocrypha, Jubilee Bible 2000, The Message Bible, New Revised Standard, New Century Version, New Living Translation, and Revised Standard Version.

Later, the author of Hebrews 7:4 adds, "See how great this man was to whom Abraham the patriarch gave a tenth of the spoils!" (ESV) The reader is not told how great Melchizedek was relative to Abram on a scale

81. Barker, "Who Was Melchizedek and Who Was His God?"

82. Fitzmyer, "Melchizedek in the MT, LXX, and the NT," 67.

83. Fitzmyer, "Melchizedek in the MT, LXX, and the NT," 67.

of 0 to 100. Here, the author claims and judges without evidence. Notably, according to Genesis 14:20, Abram gave Melchizedek one-tenth of the spoils. As previously discussed, there may be other reasons why Abram may have given the tithes if he did. Furthermore, even if Abram paid a tithe, it is not proof that Melchizedek was eternal or great. Lastly, Mitchell writes, "It is only here in the NT that Abraham is called a patriarch."[84]

Jeremy Punt clarifies that "the unborn Levites in his [i.e., Abraham's] loins actually participated in Abraham's gift, and on the principle of the greater blesses the lesser, ranked Levi together with Abraham as subordinate to Melchizedek."[85] Readers must judge if it makes sense that the unborn Levites in his [i.e., Abraham's] loins participated in Abraham's gift. This assertion is grounded in an argument from silence.

Various rabbinic interpretations make it clear that Abram gave the tithe to Melchizedek. The Midrash emphasizes Abram's virtue for his generous action after defeating the four kings rather than Melchizedek's status. For example, Grypeou and Spurling quote Genesis Rabbah 43:8.

> *And he gave him a tenth of everything* (Gen 14:20). R. Yehudah in the name of R. Nehorai said: By virtue of that blessing, the three great pegs in the world, Abraham, Isaac, and Jacob ate (i.e., had plenty). Concerning Abraham. It is written, *And the Lord blessed Abraham in everything* (Gen 24:1). On account of merit for *And he gave to him a tenth of everything* (Gen 14:20). (ed. J. Theodor—Ch. Albeck, *Midrash Bereshit Rabba*, vol. 1, 422).

Grypeou and Spurling elaborate on the Midrash:

> GenR 43:8 states that the comprehensive blessing given to Abraham by God, as recorded in Gen 24:1, came as a direct result of giving the tithe to Melchizedek. Furthermore, Abraham, Isaac, and Jacob received blessings on account of the merit of Abraham for giving a tithe to Melchizedek. In giving Melchizedek the tithe of the spoils of war, Abraham is the first patriarch to practice tithing and again foreshadows and keeps the covenantal laws before they are made known (Lev 27:30–33).[86]

There is another rationale for Abram paying a tithe to Melchizedek. Abram/Abraham's character is known for his hospitality, generosity, and humility, which are visible in the Bible. (1) *Abraham gladly served others,*

84. Mitchell, *Sacra Pagina: Hebrews*, 140.

85. Punt, "Politics of Genealogies in the New Testament," 392.

86. Grypeou and Spurling, *The Book of Genesis*, 208.

and when he caught sight of the three visitors, he immediately set out to accommodate their needs (Gen. 18:1–8). (2) *Abram/Abraham listened to* and acted on Sarah's suggestions (Gen. 16:2; 21:8–14). (3). Abraham said, "Behold now, I have taken on me to speak to the LORD, which am but dust and ashes" (Gen. 18:27). (4) Abram gave Lot the choice of land (Gen. 13:9–11). (5) Afterward, Abram helped redeem captives (Gen. 14:14–16); (5) Abram refused to take booty following his successful military campaign (Gen. 14:22–24). Therefore, (6) when encountering Melchizedek, Abram offers him a tithe of the spoils from the battle (debated in the literature) (Gen. 14:20). This act of generosity reflects Abram's character. Readers must be cognizant here and later about accepting or committing a *possibiliter fallacy* (treating something that is merely possible as if it is probable).

Many Christian commentators argue that Abram presented Melchizedek with a tithe (a tenth) of all the items he had gathered, demonstrating the latter's superiority. Their claim is based on their interpretation of Scripture and is subject to academic debate. Additionally, they argue that by this act, Abram acknowledged that he recognized Melchizedek as a priest who ranked spiritually higher than he did. This interpretation, too, is subject to academic debate. As suggested earlier in this reading, perhaps Abram's actions had nothing to do with demonstrating Melchizedek's alleged superiority.

Instead, the following possibilities suggest themselves: (1) Tithing exemplified Abram's character. (2) George Buchanan and Alan Mitchell offer another hypothesis. Perhaps Abram paid Melchizedek a tariff for crossing his land, or (3) it was a simple customary act.[87] (4) Gammie offers the proposal "That it was necessary for Abram to pay homage to 'El 'Elyon in order to establish his right to remain in Palestine and rule over the land."[88] (5) Conceivably, the interaction between Abram and Melchizedek was more of a voluntary offering or gesture of goodwill rather than a structured tithe. (6) Since Abram predates the giving of the law, the concept of tithing may not have been established as a law. (7) Melchizedek's blessing on Abram was possibly seen as a sufficient exchange, and a formal tithe might not have been required. (8) Abram's giving the tithe to Melchizedek may have symbolized acknowledgment of Melchizedek's unique status or a recognition of God's sovereignty. (9)

87. Buchanan, *To the Hebrews*, 118; and Mitchell, *Sacra Pagina: Hebrews*, 142.

88. Gammie, "Melchizedek: An Exegetical Study of Genesis 14 and the Psalter," 129.

Similarly, Abram's tithe to Melchizedek may have acknowledged God's role in the victory. Therefore, it could be a symbolic act of recognizing God's blessing rather than a declaration of Melchizedek's superiority. (10) Abram's action might have aligned with the norms of that time without indicating Melchizedek's superiority. (11) Then, tithing can be seen as a sign of respect and recognition of Melchizedek's priestly role rather than an indication of superiority. Therefore, Abram may have honored Melchizedek's priestly position without implying superiority. (12) Another possible explanation is that "Melchizedek appears in Genesis as an angel who has helped Abraham defeat his enemies and released Lot. Thus, Abraham gives the tithe to Melchizedek."[89]

In addition, it is worth noting that many scholars have questioned the historicity and reliability of Genesis 14:18–20. Many commentators take the position that these three verses are an interpolation. If they are correct, there was no offering of tithes. Furthermore, in verse 20, readers must determine to whom the pronoun "he" refers.

> 18 And Melchizedek king of Salem brought forth bread and wine: and he was the priest of the most high God.
> 19 And he blessed him, and said, Blessed be Abram of the most high God, possessor of heaven and earth:
> 20 And blessed be the most high God, which hath delivered thine enemies into thy hand. And *he* gave him tithes of all. (KJV)

> 18 And Melchizedek king of Salem brought out bread and wine; now he was a priest of God Most High.
> 19 He blessed him and said, "Blessed be Abram of God Most High, Possessor of heaven and earth.
> 20 And blessed be God Most High, Who has delivered your enemies into your hand." *He* gave him a tenth of all. (NAS)

> 18 And Melchizedek, the king of Salem, brought out bread and wine. (He was the priest of God Most High).
> 19 And he blessed him and said, "Blessed [be] Abram by God Most High, Maker of heaven and earth.
> 20 And blessed [be] God Most High who delivered your enemies into your hand." And *he* gave to him a tenth of everything. (Lexham English Bible)

89. Reiss, "The Melchizedek Traditions," 262.

> 18 But Melchisedech, the king of Salem, bringing forth bread and wine, for he was the priest of the most high God,
> 19 Blessed him, and said: Blessed be Abram by the most high God, who created heaven and earth.
> 20 And blessed be the most high God, by whose protection, the enemies are in thy hands. And *he* gave him the tithes of all. (Douay-Rheims Catholic Bible)

> 18 And Melchizedek king of Salem brought forth bread and wine; and he was the priest of the Most High God.
> 19 And he blessed him and said, "Blessed be Abram of the Most High God, possessor of heaven and earth;
> 20 and blessed be the Most High God, who hath delivered thine enemies into thy hand." And *he* gave him tithes of all. (Third Millennium Bible)

Emerton explains why verses 18–20 is an interpolation:

1. There is a contraction between verses 21–3 and the statement about the payment of a tenth in verse 20.
2. Verses 18–20 interrupt the flow of the narrative.
3. The Melchizedek passage interrupts strangely and breaks off very abruptly after recounting Melchizedek's blessing.
4. The framework makes sense without the Melchizedek passage, whereas the Melchizedek passage can scarcely stand on its own.
5. The Melchizedek passage begins without a proper introduction and does not explain what Abram is doing at Salem or who the foes he has just defeated are.[90]

As previously mentioned, many Christian apologists, Bible commentators, and theologians argue that the "he" refers to Abram. If true, this interpretation supplies the necessary proof that Melchizedek is superior to Abram. Consequently, the Levitical priest line is *inferior* to Jesus being a priest. However, the Genesis narrative does *not* say Melchizedek's order of the priesthood is superior to Levi's. In addition, Yitchok Cohen counters the argument that Abram giving tithes to Melchizedek proves the latter is superior. He argues that Abram "gave him [Melchizedek]

90. Emerton, "The Riddle of Genesis XIV," 408–9.

tithes as he was the reigning 'priest' of that era."[91] This essential topic is examined below in relation to Psalm 110:4 and the Epistle to the Hebrews.

In the *Journal of Biblical Literature*, Loren Fisher investigates why Abram pays a tithe to Melchizedek. Her inquiry probes ancient Near Eastern texts for a possible answer:

> We have known for a long time that the tithe was a common tax in the ancient Semitic world. Recently, I. Mendelsohn has shown that the tithe was an important form of taxation at Ugarit. He based his studies on the Akkadian texts. Could it be that Abraham the merchant was paying an expected obligation to his king? . . . .
>
> Malkiṣedeq was a Canaanite priest-king, and his encounter with Abraham is in accord with Canaanite tradition. It is what we would expect between a priest-king and a merchant of Ura.[92]

Meanwhile, readers must ask an essential question. For what purpose would this three-verse passage be inserted into the Genesis narrative? Horton offers the following opinion: "Specifically, it has been held that Gen. xiv.18–20 is an aetiological legend showing Abraham's submission to the Jerusalem (i.e., Salem) priesthood."[93]

Granerød presents a different understanding of the Genesis 14 narrative. He provides a multifaceted argument that Melchizedek who gave a tithe to Abram!

> However, contrary to this identification, which is based on a prior understanding of the events taking place, the most natural reading is to follow the Hebrew text, which merely says, 'And he gave . . .' In my opinion, it is likely that one should identify the donor with Melchizedek and the receiver with Abram. The reason for this is that Melchizedek is also the subject of the verbal actions, that is, the blessings, in the two proceding verses. Because no shift of grammatical subject is indicated between vv. 18–19 on the one hand and v. 20a on the other, the most natural reading is that Melchizedek, in the capacity of being the last-mentioned person, also is the subject of וַיִּתֶּן 'and he gave'.[94]

91. Cohen, "Can You Elaborate More on Melkizedec Giving."
92. Fisher, "Abraham and His Priest-King," 268–69.
93. Horton, *The Melchizedek Tradition*, 17.
94. Granerød, *Abraham and Melchizedek*, 229.

Another implication Granerød mentions is that the Melchizedek episode in Genesis 14 describes Abram as a priest because he receives tithes from Melchizedek.[95] Readers must peruse Granerød's argument in its entirety.

Lastly, readers need to understand Hebrews 7:7 because it explains why its author thinks Melchizedek is superior to Abram: "It is beyond dispute that the inferior is blessed by the superior" (ESV). Bibleref elaborates:

> Blessings are given from higher authority or power to the lower. As stated here, this is "beyond dispute," especially in the context of ancient culture. The author is making a point about how Abraham, who was blessed by Melchizedek, recognized that Melchizedek was a greater figure (Genesis 14:14–24). This is further emphasized by the fact that Abraham paid a tithe to Melchizedek (Heb. 7:6).[96]

Unfortunately, the author of Hebrews fails to engage or interact with biblical verses, demonstrating cases in which blessings are given from a lower authority or power to a higher one.

> Genesis 47:7 Then Joseph brought in Jacob his father and stood him before Pharaoh, and Jacob blessed Pharaoh. (ESV)
>
> Genesis 47:11 And Jacob blessed Pharaoh and went out from the presence of Pharaoh. (ESV)
>
> 2 Samuel 8:10 Toi sent his son Joram to King David, to ask about his health and to bless him because he had fought against Hadadezer and defeated him, for Hadadezer had often been at war with Toi. And Joram brought with him articles of silver, of gold, and of bronze. (ESV)
>
> 2 Samuel 14:22 And Joab fell on his face to the ground and paid homage and blessed the king. And Joab said, "Today your servant knows that I have found favor in your sight, my lord the king, in that the king has granted the request of his servant." (ESV)
>
> 1 Kings 1:47 Moreover, the king's servants came to congratulate our lord King David, saying, 'May your God make the name of Solomon more famous than yours, and make his throne greater than your throne.' And the king bowed himself on the bed.
>
> 1 Kings 8:66 On the eighth day he sent the people away, and they blessed the king and went to their homes joyful and glad of

95. Granerød, *Abraham and Melchizedek*, 229.

96. "Hebrews 7:7."

heart for all the goodness that the Lord had shown to David his servant and to Israel his people. (ESV)

Ruth 2:4 And behold, Boaz came from Bethlehem. And he said to the reapers, "The Lord be with you!" And they answered, "The Lord bless you." (ESV)

Ruth 2:19 And her mother-in-law said to her, "Where did you glean today? And where have you worked? Blessed be the man who took notice of you." So she told her mother-in-law with whom she had worked and said, "The man's name with whom I worked today is Boaz." (ESV)

The Gospels (presumably unavailable to the author) also provide examples. John 12:12–13 says, "The next day the large crowd that had come to the feast heard that Jesus was coming to Jerusalem. So they took branches of palm trees and went out to meet him, crying out, "Hosanna! Blessed is he who comes in the name of the Lord, even the King of Israel!" (ESV)

In his text, *To the Hebrews*, George Buchanan provides another example of a contradiction. "There are blessings which the inferior gives to the superior, such as the anonymous woman in a crowd who said to Jesus, 'Blessed is the womb that bore you, and the breasts that you sucked' (Luke 11:27).[97] Moreover, the argument that the "less is blessed of the better" [blessings are given from higher authority or power to the lower], which is often put forward as if it is some general rule or principle, is self-evidently false (Ps. 66:8; Luke 1:64; 2:28; 24:53). People bless God, and God blesses people. Blessings work both ways. It is noteworthy that Melchizedek blesses God: "and blessed be God Most High, who has delivered your enemies into your hand" (Gen. 14, 19, ESV)! In addition, there is controversy surrounding the text. The Hebrew text is ambiguous and lacks the clarity that the official Latin translation has enjoyed since Jerome's time: Melchizedek gave a tithe *to* Abram.

Gerald Kennedy says, "A point to be noted at the outset is that the sacred writer makes no mention of the origin or development of the tithal system. He took it for granted that his readers understood precisely what he was writing." The date of the text is unknown.[98]

The upshot of this discussion is that we have no way of knowing whether Abram paid a tithe to Melchizedek or vice versa. In addition,

97. Buchanan, *To the Hebrews*, 121.

98. Kennedy, "St. Paul's Conception of the Priesthood," 42.

the origin of tithing remains shrouded in mystery: numerous hypotheses have been put forward, but none commands general assent.

2.7 Kings in the Ancient Near East

Readers must ask at least two essential questions. (1) What do kings do? Furthermore, (2) what was a king's job description? These roles are embedded in a complex political, religious, military, and economic system. The potential answers to these questions depend upon the kingdom, religious practices, location, and time when a king rules people. A literature review identifies numerous descriptions. These descriptions include the following: rulers of their kingdoms and empires, religious leaders, priests or high priests, mediators between God and his people, warriors, hunters, defenders of the kingdom, scholars, lawmakers, dispensers of justice, builders, and producers of heirs. A crucial task relating to Melchizedek was that of being a priest.

Gammie's research focuses on another significant aspect of kingship. He cites Johs Pedersen, among others, as declaring that the word *melekh*, the common designation for 'king,' has had varying connotations. "It is employed indiscriminately about the mighty rulers of great empires and about the small chiefs of the Canaanite communities (Judg. 5:19; 9:6; cf. Gen. 20:2; Josh. 10:1; 11:1)."[99] Gammie explains the importance of this fact. "In view of the fact that the city of Melchizedek, Salem, is to be located somewhere in Canaan, the meaning of *melek* when applied to Melchizedek is clear. It must be understood to mean a small chief of a Canaanite community rather than a mighty ruler of a great empire."[100] Lastly, as a king, Melchizedek is never reported as a leader in war, an effector of victory and deliverance, a leader, or a judge. Nevertheless, these qualities are frequently associated with kings of the Ancient Near East (ANE).

2.8 Priesthood in the Ancient Near East

Numerous texts, including dissertations, books chapters, journal articles, and encyclopedia entries, engage with the topic of the priesthood. Here, too, readers must ask at least two essential questions. (1) What do priests do? Moreover, (2) what was a priest's job description? These roles, too,

99. Pedersen, *Israel—Its Life and Culture III–IV*, 46.

100. Gammie, "Melchizedek: An Exegetical Study of Genesis 14 and the Psalter," 71.

were embedded in a complex religious system. The potential answers to these questions depend upon the kingdom, religious practices, location, and time. Besides being religious leaders, priests were mediators between God and his people and performed cultic functions (sacrifice). Priests were present in all ancient religions and held a significant influence on society. The function of the high priest was similar to that of an ordinary priest but with stricter requirements and added responsibilities. Deborah Rooke inquired about the relationship between the monarch's role, that of the high priest, and that of the priesthood. Specifically, she asks, "Was there something distinctive about the royal priesthood which set it apart from the 'ordinary' priesthood, and if so, what?"[101]

In the patriarchal period (2000–1700 BCE), Israel had no official priesthood. In ancient times, certain individuals were made appointed to offer prayers of supplication, sacrifice, and expiation to on behalf of the entire community in the name of God. Ada Taggar-Cohen's insights about the Hittite priesthood duties and tasks are instructive. Several examples include: "They offered food and beverages to the gods; they took care of the divine statues and officiated in rituals on behalf of the royal family and the people" and were responsible for "washing, anointing and carrying the statues of the gods."[102] Bruce Power's literature review identifies numerous tasks, including cultic functions, meditation, performing religious rites, listening to confessions, healing, sacrifices, maintaining the calendar, providing for the gods, funeral cults, and administrative responsibilities for the temple.[103]

2.8.1 How People Became Priests

People became priests through various means, depending on the specific tradition(s) of each kingdom, city, village, or tribe. A literature review by Powers identifies various processes by which one could become a priest. Means of assuming the priesthood included exhibiting sacred attributes such as experiencing religious ecstasy, possessing unique attributes, exemplifying the figure of a King-Priest, being nominated by the elders of a family, hereditary assumption of the position, selection by lots, and purchasing the position. Another option was obtaining the position through violence (assassination). Powers remarks, "*When we examine the texts*

101. Rooke, "Kingship as Priesthood," 187.

102. Taggar-Cohen, "Hittite Priesthood," 162.

103. Powers, "The Development of the Priesthood in Ancient Israel," 7–20.

regarding cultic officials which come to us from the ancient near east it is remarkable that these writings do not take up the matter of origins."[104]

Importantly, the origin of Melchizedek's priesthood to El Elyon, the Most High, is unknown and a subject of unverifiable speculation.[105] In contrast, at Mount Sinai, God designated Aaron and his descendants to serve as priests (Exod. 28:1, 44; 30:30; 40:13–15; Num. 3:3). Thus, the books of Exodus, Leviticus, and Numbers maintain that Aaron received from God a monopoly over the priesthood for himself and his male descendants (Exod. 28:1). Given God's unequivocal injunction, "You shall not add to the word that I command you, nor take from it, that you may keep the commandments of the Lord your God that I command you" (Deut. 4:2, ESV), it follows that Aaron's descendants, the Levites, were the exclusive priests of the Children of Israel.

2.8.2 Qualification for Priestly Service in the Torah

In the Torah, general rules and qualifications outline the requirements that must be met by those called to the priesthood. The congregation and the priests strictly followed and observed these rules. They are as follows:

1. The priest must be a male (Exod. 28:1).
2. The priest must descend from Aaron with a documented lineage (Exod. 28:1).
3. The priest must be between thirty and fifty (Num. 4:3).
4. The priest must be unblemished (he must not be lame or a limb too long) (Lev. 21:18).
5. The priest must have a proper marriage (Lev. 21:9, 14).
6. The priest must not be married to a harlot or a divorced woman (Lev. 21:14).
7. The priest must not marry a widow other than a priest's widow (Ezek. 44:22).
8. The high priest must marry a virgin from among his own people (Lev. 21:13).
9. The priest must have no uncleanliness (e.g., leprosy) (Lev. 22:3–9).

104. Power, "The Development of the Priesthood in Ancient Israel," 12.
105. Power, "The Development of the Priesthood in Ancient Israel," 3–5.

10. The priest must have an untrimmed beard with well-trimmed (but unshaved) hair (Lev. 21:5).
11. The priest must be dressed appropriately (Exod. 28:1–4; Ezek. 44:17–19).

As Mitchell points out, "There were some Levites who were not priests (Num 3:5–10; Neh 10:35–39) . . . It is not clear whether the author of Hebrews knew the distinction between Levites and priests."[106] Moreover, John Scholer notes that the term "high priest" appears only about fifteen times in the Hebrew Bible, and points out an interesting oddity. "For on the one hand, the high priest alone is anointed, but on the other hand, all priests are anointed as well."[107]

In addition, the qualifications and the level of specialization among priests differed. Mark Christian elaborates:

> The term 'specialist' connotes individuals who through training acquire specific knowledge of—though not necessarily mastery in—a particular subject . . . . clerical elites often obtain elevated status through means other than expert knowledge and skillful performance! Thus caution is in order when positing intellectual or qualitative difference in the competency and skills of the elite priests on the one hand, middle-tier priests on the other.[108]

2.9 The Union of Kingship and Priesthood: Was Melchizedek the First King-Priest?

Christian apologists, commentators, and theologians (not all) repeat the claim that Melchizedek was the first person who was a king-priest because he was the first mentioned in the Hebrew Bible. Readers must contemplate whether this assertion makes sense in light of the following examples:

1. Genesis 9:14 is the first biblical text to mention a rainbow. Should it be thought that there never was a rainbow before this one?
2. Genesis 9:20 contains the Bible's first mention of planting a vineyard. Should it be thought that a person never planted a vineyard before this one?

106. Mitchell, *Sacra Pagina: Hebrews*, 140.
107. Scholer, *Proleptic Priests*, 21–22.
108. Christian, "Priestly Power That Empowers," 12–13.

3. Genesis 12:8 contains the first mention of building an altar. Should it be thought that there never was a person who built an altar before this one?
4. Genesis 12:10 contains the first mention of a famine. Should it be thought that there never was a famine before this one?
5. Genesis 12:17 contains the first mention of plagues. Should it be thought that there never was a plague before this one?
6. Genesis 13:7 marks the first mention of strife between herders in the Genesis narrative. Should it be thought that there never was an instance of strife between herders before this one?
7. Genesis 14:2 describes the first war in Genesis. Should it be thought that there never was a war before this one?
8. Genesis 14:8 is the first passage to mention a king-priest in Genesis. Should it be thought that there never was a king-priest before this one?
9. Genesis 14:20 is the first passage to mention the word "tithe" in Genesis. Should it be thought that there never was a tithe before this one?
10. Genesis 48:1 contains the first mention of illness in Genesis. Should it be thought that episodes of illness never occurred before this one?

> The *ancient Near East* was the home of early civilizations within a region roughly corresponding to the modern Middle East: Mesopotamia (modern Iraq, southeast Turkey, southwest Iran, and northeastern Syria), ancient Egypt, ancient Persia (Elam, Media, and Persia), Anatolia and the Armenian highlands (Turkey's Eastern Anatolia Region, Armenia, northwestern Iran, southern Georgia, and western Azerbaijan, the Levant (modern Syria, Lebanon, Israel, Palestine, Jordan and Cyprus) and the Arabian Peninsula . . .
>
> The history of the ancient Near East begins with the rise of Sumer in the 4th millennium BC, though the date it ends varies.[109]

During the approximately three-thousand-year history of the ancient Near East, numerous cities, city-states, tribes, villages, and kingdoms existed. In Deuteronomy 7:1–2, seven Canaanite nations or tribes are listed: the Hittites, the Girgashites, the Amorites, the Canaanites, the Perizzites, the Hivites, and the Jebusites. Genesis 14 mentions nine kings,

109. "Ancient Near East."

and their cities or kingdoms are enumerated. The tenth is Melchizedek. As previously mentioned, *he is the first recorded king-priest in the Hebrew Bible*. However, that fact does not preclude the possibility that the nine kings may have held joint titles as king-priests before Melchizedek, but for unknown reasons, the author of Genesis 14 omitted that detail.

Moreover, the same argument can be made for the leaders of the seven Canaanite nations or tribes. Perhaps their rulers were also king-priests and held that title before Melchizedek. An absence of evidence shows only that the evidence is absent. It does *not* mean that the title itself was absent before Melchizedek.

John Day, writing in *King and Messiah in Israel and the Ancient Near East* provides some significant information for the general reader to ponder:

> In Genesis 14 Melchizedek is said to have been both king and priest. That Canaanite kings could be priests is supported by various pieces of evidence. Menander of Ephesus, as reported by Josephus (*Apion* 1.18) says that Ithobalus, king of Tyre (= Ittobaal, father of Jezebel) was also a priest of Astarte. Similarly, Phoenician inscriptions speak of Tabnit, king of Sidon, as 'priest of Astarte', and his father King Eshmun'azar I is also 'priest of Astarte'. In inheriting the role of Melchizedek, David and the Israelite kings in Jerusalem therefore took over the role of priest; Ps 110.4 is conclusive evidence that the Israelite kings did indeed function as priests. This is consistent with the fact that David wore a linen ephod, a priestly garment, when taking the Ark up into Jerusalem (2 Sam. 6:14), and with various references to the kings offering sacrifice—Saul at Gilgal (1 Sam. 13.9–10), David at Jerusalem (2 Sam. 6.1, 17–18; 24.25), Solomon at Gibeon (1 Kgs 3.4, 15), at Jerusalem for the dedication of the Temple (1 Kgs 8.5, 62–64), and then the three great feasts of the year (1 Kgs 9.25). Although in some instances it might be argued that this means that the king 'had sacrifice offered', this will not fit 2 Kgs 16.12–25, where Ahaz goes up to the new altar he has made and offers the first sacrifice, and then commands the priest to continue the liturgy there; further, in 1 Kgs 12.33 it is said that Jeroboam 'went up to offer sacrifice' (cf. 13.12), which is interesting in shedding light on the sacral nature of kingship in the Northern Kingdom, a subject on which we understandably have less information. Again, David and Solomon bless the people in the sanctuary (2 Sam. 6.18; 1 Kgs 8.14), a rite which is reserved to the priests by Num. 6.22–27 and 1 Chron. 23.13).

> Clearly, the king's priesthood was not a full-time occupation, but a special priesthood since the general upkeep of the cult would have been the job of the professional priests.[110]

A.A. Anderson agrees with Day's assessment:

> When David captured Jerusalem, it is thought that he took over the Jebusite kingship, and thus the Psalm [i.e., Ps. 110] may allude to this conferment of the twin offices (i.e., kingship and priesthood] upon David. The Judean kings played an important role in the cult (cf. 2 Sam. 6:13–18; 1 Kg. 8:14, 55f) but on the other hand, Rowley (p. 471) points out that what 'is required is not evident that the King played a priestly part in certain festival rites, but that he ordinarily exercised the functions of the priest, and was truly the priest de facto as he was the King'.[111]

Presumably, there were hundreds of king-priests at that time. Notably, the functions of the king and priest are not mutually exclusive. Alan Kam-Yau Chan comments, "It is not uncommon in the ANE for the union of king and priest to be bound in one person."[112] In a similar vein, Raymond Brown writes, "The idea of a priest-king may seem rather unfamiliar to us, but it was not at all unknown in the ancient world."[113] However, many Christian commentators focus on Melchizedek because he is the first king-priest identified in the Bible, serving their theological agenda. Readers must understand that many researchers and academic scholars believe Israel and its neighbors' culture, including their cultic institutions, literature, and sacred texts, *drew on sources common to their environment*. Researchers have limited information about many cities/kingdoms, leaders, and their priesthoods. Well-known exceptions include Egypt, Assyria, Babylonia, and the Hittite Empire. Readers must ask themselves if Melchizedek was unique in being a king-priest. Archaeologists have uncovered the names of other king-priests in neighboring cultures.

Wikipedia identifies numerous cities and kingdoms. Select names from their handy chart, from oldest to youngest, include Egypt, the Akkadian Empire, Assyria, Elamite, Sumero-Akkadian, Minoa, Babylonia, Hittites, Hayasa-Azzi, Mitanni, Kizzuwatna, Ugarit, Phoenicians, and

110. Day, "The Canaanite Inheritance of the Israelite Monarchy," 74–75.

111. Anderson, *The Book of Psalms: Psalms 73–150*, 771.

112. Chan, *Melchizedek Passages in the Bible*, 43n173; cf. Gammie, "Melchizedek: An Exegetical Study of Genesis 14 and the Psalter," 71–72.

113. Brown, *The Message of Hebrews*, 128.

Phrygia. Wikipedia, the Department of Ancient Near Eastern Art from The Metropolitan Museum of Art, and other sources provide lists of dynasties and rulers.[114] This reality raises another question for readers to consider. Why do many apologists, Bible commentators, and theologians fail to engage with texts and peer-reviewed journals in the fields of anthropology, comparative religions, and sociology, and in-field experts that provide indisputable primary sources that king-priests were common in the milieu of the ancient Near East?

The Sumerians are known for building the first big cities. Sumer existed from around 4000 BCE to 2000 BCE. Uruk was the world's first major city and capital of the Sumerian empire. They were governed by a king-priest who served as a political and religious leader. Another ancient civilization was the Hittites.[115] Ada Taggar-Cohen's insights about the Hittite priesthood duties and tasks are instructive. Among their many duties, she lists the following: "They offered food and beverages to the gods; they took care of the divine statues and officiated in rituals on behalf of the royal family and the people" and "washing, anointing and carrying the statues of the gods."[116]

Moreover, "the Hittite priesthood was an institution headed by the royal family, with king and queen as high priests, and that descended hierarchically down to the different temples throughout the kingdom."[117] Similarly, Richard Purcell discusses and provides visual illustrations of Egyptian and Neo-Assyrian kings depicted in a priestly and ritualistic role. He remarks, "In light of the artistic evidence presented here, I suggest that the ideology of the king as priest was shared and widely held across the ancient Near East."[118] Marcella Frangipane displays a photo of a seal depicting a King-Priest from Uruk-Warka of the late Uruk period.[119] Ivan Engnell describes the Babylonian rulers: "In the cult, the king functions as high priest *par excellence*."[120] More precisely, the king as high priest has two basic religious duties: the maintenance of the worship rite

114. "Template: Rulers of the Ancient Near East"; "List of Rulers of Mesopotamia,"; Van de Mieroop, *A History of the Ancient Near East*, 324–29.

115. Taggar-Cohen, "Hittite Priesthood," 160, 162.

116. Taggar-Cohen, "Hittite Priesthood," 162.

117. Taggar-Cohen, "Covenant Priesthood," 13.

118. Purcell, "The King as Priest?," 299; cf. Dick, "The Neo-Assyrian Royal Lion Hunt," 250.

119. Frangipane, "Archaeological Evidence," 99, Figure 3c.

120. Engnell, *Studies in Divine Kingship*, 5.

and the appointment of priests.[121] Loren Fisher goes on to say that that Melchizedek, as the priest-king of Salem, "performed a dual function not uncommon in Canaan."[122]

Shania Zaia, writing in the *Journal of Ancient Near Eastern Religions*, describes the role of the head of the Assyrian state: "Furthermore, most previous studies have focused on the Assyrian king as the *šangû*, the high priest, of the god Aššur . . . In his priestly role, the Assyrian king served as the god's political and religious representative on earth. Moreover, the king had a duty to support and patronize the temples in his empire, and temple rebuilding, sacrifices, and royal rituals are highly visible in the official texts."[123] Stefan Maul elaborates:

> The office of High Priest remained a central one for Assyrian rulers from the Old Assyrian period onwards. The rulers cared for the well-being of their god, by means of which they also guaranteed the well-being of their subjects, whom the god had entrusted to them . . . The Assyrian kings' functions as High Priest and "vice-regent" of the highest god had a significant impact, at least since the time of Samsi-Adad [ca. 1808–1776 BCE), on the topography of the city Ashur, which remained fundamentally unchanged until the late period.[124]

In conclusion, skeptics and detractors would argue that it is fallacious to claim that Melchizedek was the first king-priest. Moreover, given the abundant evidence of the existence of king-priests within the Ancient Near East, it is most *unlikely* that Melchizedek was the first. In any case, there is no evidence of a priestly line of Melchizedek continuing in ancient Israel. On the contrary, the evidence from the Torah strongly indicates that only descendants of Aaron could be priests.

2.10 Would Jesus have Qualified as a Priest in the Ancient Near East?

Karen H. Jobes provides a list of qualities of Jesus as a *high priest*, adopted from Hagner. Readers must assiduously analyze these qualities. Are they exceptional, or are they exemplified in ordinary people? Are they verifiable? Is the catalog of high priestly qualities from Hebrews, which was

121. Engnell, *Studies in Divine Kingship*, 62.

122. Fisher, "Abraham and His Priest-King," 265.

123. Zaia, "Kings, Priests, and Power in the Neo-Assyrian Period," 153–54.

124. Maul, "Assyrian Religion," 341, 346.

composed by an anonymous author, written years after Jesus' death, and based on unknown sources (possibly hearsay and evolving oral traditions), sufficient to validate his priestly status?

It is crucial to note that during his life, Jesus was never called a high priest, never claimed to be a priest, and never fulfilled the functions of a high priest (in the Second Temple). If being a high priest is defined on a *functional basis*, then those doing the job are the high priests. Jesus' occasional performance of minor actions (offering blessings, teaching) resembling those of a high priest is no objective basis for calling him a high priest. Jobes writes, "The author of Hebrews explains that Jesus did not enter the temple in Jerusalem with the blood of an animal but entered into the Most Holy Place of heaven itself by his own blood (9:11–14)."[125] These words amount to an argument from silence, based on circular logic, as they employ Hebrews to confirm Hebrews.

A meticulous examination of the qualities of Jesus as a high priest finds little meaningful support for the claim that he was one. The author of Hebrews tries to confirm his argument by appealing to his assertions, which leaves his argument without external support. In the Epistle, Jesus is declared to be:

1. "merciful and faithful" (2:17)—an unconvincing and unverifiable claim that he never acted in a contrary fashion, even once.
2. "able to help those who are being tempted" (2:18)—an unverifiable claim with no convincing evidence.
3. one who "has ascended to heaven" or "has gone through the heavens" (4:14)—an unverifiable claim for which there is no evidence.
4. "not unable to sympathize with our weaknesses" (4:15)—an unverifiable claim.
5. "one who . . . has been tempted as we are—yet he did not sin (4:15)—an unverifiable claim made without presenting any convincing evidence that Jesus never sinned, and one which is refuted by both the Hebrew Bible and the Christian Bible (Eccles. 7:3; Rom. 3:10; 1 John 1:18).
6. "appointed by God" (5:5)—a claim without convincing evidence.
7. "a forerunner . . . on our behalf" (6:20)—a claim without convincing evidence.

125. Jobes, *Letters to the Church*.

8. "holy, blameless, set apart from sinners"—a vague and ambiguous claim that is unconvincing and lacks evidence.
9. "exalted above the heavens" (7:26)—an unconvincing claim without supporting evidence.
10. "a Son who has been made perfect forever" (7:28)—an unconvincing claim for which there is no evidence.
11. "seated at the right hand of the throne of the Majesty in heaven" (8:1)—an unconvincing claim without supporting evidence.
12. "a minister in the sanctuary, the true tabernacle" (8:2)—an unconvincing claim without supporting evidence.
13. "a high priest of the good things that are now already here" (9:11)—an unverifiable claim without supporting evidence.
14. a high priest who "entered the Most Holy Place once for all by his own blood" (9:12)—a claim that contradicts the Hebrew Bible and is neither verifiable nor convincing.[126]
15. a high priest who "obtained eternal redemption" for us (9:12)—an unverifiable and unconvincing claim that contradicts the Hebrew Bible.[127]

Bible commentators, theologians, and apologists associate these fifteen qualities with Jesus because the anonymous author of Hebrews does so. Moreover, these qualities are all mentioned in the book of the Hebrews. The reader must determine whether these fifteen qualities support the belief that Jesus was a high priest.

126. The author claims (9:11) that Jesus entered "through the greater and more perfect tent (not made with hands, that is, not of this creation" (ESV). Skeptics and detractors demand convincing evidence that Jesus entered this non-physical sanctuary, the Tabernacle in heaven, where he is in the presence of God as high priest. This claim is unverifiable.

127. Hagner, *Encountering the Book of Hebrews*, 104 (cf. Jobes, *Letters to the Church*.)

3

Psalm 110

INTRODUCTION

> 4The Lord has sworn
> and will not change his mind,
> "You are a priest forever
> after the order of Melchizedek" (ESV).

> Ps. cx is one of the most difficult of the psalms textually and exegetically. The interpretation of the psalm is complicated by its great importance for the New Testament where it is quoted at Matt. xxii. 44; Mk xii. 36; Lk. xx. 42–3; Acts ii. 34; Heb. i. 13; v. 6; xi. 21. Because of its importance for the New Testament, literature on Ps. cx is massive.[1]

3.1 When Do Scholars Believe Psalm 110 was Composed?

3.2 Who is the Psalmist Referring to When He Speaks of "my lord" as Sitting at the Lord's Right Hand?

3.3 Is Psalm 110 About a Priest Being Made King, or is it About a King Being Made Priest?

3.4 How Do Scholars Interpret the Phrase, "a Priest Forever After the Order of Melchizedek" in Psalm 110:4?

1. Horton, *The Melchizedek Tradition*, 23–24.

3.1 When Do Scholars Believe Psalm 110 was Composed?

A literature review by Barry Dick concludes that most commentators hold one of three views about the date of writing of the Psalm: pre-Israelite Canaanite origins, postexilic Israelite origins, or pre-exilic Israelite origins.[2] Robert Bratcher and William Reyburn, writing for the United Bible Societies (UBS), declare, "There is much disagreement concerning the time of its composition, with opinions ranging from the tenth century B.C. to the Maccabean age, in the second century B.C."[3] S.E. Gillingham adds, "But most commentators, on account of the archaic language and the disputed textual corruptions, assume the psalm to refer obliquely to some ancient sacral rites in the royal cult, although the exact setting of such rites is unclear."[4]

Psalm 110 is one of the most controversial and analyzed psalms. Academic versus traditional interpretations of Psalm 110 abound, as well as the questions they engender: (1) Who wrote the Psalm? (2) When was the Psalm composed? (3) What was the agenda of its author? The interpretation of verse 4 is particularly controversial.

Mitchell Dahood bluntly declares, "The traditional rendering, 'You are a priest for ever after the order of Melchizedek,' creates problems of interpretation that have proven insoluble."[5] Luke Timothy Johnson writes, "In the psalm, the Davidic 'Lord' who sits at the 'Lord's' right hand

2. Davis, "Is Psalm 110 A Messianic Psalm?," 160–61; cf. Granerød, *Abraham and Melchizedek*, 178–79, 181–88.

3. Bratcher and Reyburn, *A Translator's Handbook on The Book of Psalms*, 951; Rooke, "Kingship and Priesthood," 947.

4. Gillingham, "The Messiah in the Psalms," 222.

5. Dahood, *Psalms III*, 117.

in enthronement is declared a priest forever 'according to the order' of Melchizedek—with no explanation of who Melchizedek is or what the 'order' of his priesthood might mean."[6]

3.2 Who is the Psalmist Referring to When He Speaks of "my lord" as Sitting at the Lord's Right Hand?

The first question we must ask is: who is *adoni*, "my Lord" in Psalm 110:1?" "The first verse of Psalm 110 is quoted or alluded to in the NT more frequently than any other passage."[7] Most Christian commentaries and translations advocate employing an uppercase "L": "The LORD said to my Lord." In contrast, Jewish and some translators argue for a lowercase "l": "The LORD said to my lord." The former translation makes it appear that God (LORD) speaks to someone Divine and is referred to as (Lord with an upper case "L"). Therefore, the former translation implies divinity, and the latter a human being.

In verse 1, the first word (LORD) in Hebrew is the four-letter (*yud-he-waw-he*) sacred name of God (the tetragrammaton). However, the second "lord" in verse 1 is an entirely different word spelled (*aleph-dalet-nun-yud*). This "lord" is not capitalized and is the Hebrew word "*adoni*" (pronounced adonee), with a "*chirik*" vowel under the letter *yud*. It means "*to my master*" or "*to my lord*" with a lowercase "*L*" like the "*lord of the manor*." Crucially, in English, the words "*Lord*" and "*lord*" may be pronounced the same, but one is divine, and the other is not. Bentzion Kravitz writes, "In Biblical Hebrew, the Tanach uses the word '*adoni*' more than 130 times. In every instance it means a "*master*" or "*lord*," and refers to a human being. In addition to Psalm 110:1, the word "*To my master*" (*L'adoni*) appears 20 times and always refers to a human being."[8]

Herbert W. Bateman, PhD from Dallas Theological Seminary (DTS), is an American New Testament scholar who has taught at DTS, Liberty University, Moody Bible Institute, Southwestern Baptist Theological Seminary, and other institutions. In *Bibliotheca Sacra*, he weighs in on the controversy over the translation of the first verse of the psalm:

> David wrote in verse 1, 'The Lord [יְהוָה] says to my lord (לַאדֹנִי).' The form of 'to my lord' (לַאדֹנִי) is never used elsewhere in the

6. Johnson, *Hebrews: A Commentary*, 175.

7. Leschert, "Hermeneutical Foundations of the Epistle to the Hebrews," 289.

8. Kravitz, "Psalm 110—A Jewish Perspective"; e.g., Gen. 23:6; 24:36; 32:5; 44:16; Exod. 21:5; 32:22; 1 Sam. 24:7. Readers must examine his online essay.

> Old Testament as a divine reference.[9] He elaborates in his footnote, "Excluding Psalm 110:1, לַאדֹנִי occurs 21 times in the Old Testament." Then he cites the examples: "men or women to men (Gen. 24:36, 54, 56; 32:5–6, 19; 44:9, 16, 33: 1 Sam. 25:27–28, 30–31), men to a king (2 Sam. 19:29; 1 Kings 1:2; 18:13; 20:9; 1 Chron. 21:3), and David to the king (1 Sam. 24:7).[10]

Next, he points out: "Also none of the 138 forms of 'my lord' (אדֹנִי) and none of the 9 other prefixed forms of 'my lord' [וַאדֹנִי בַּאדֹנִי] is a divine reference."[11] Here, too, he cites all the verses in his footnotes. Herbert Bateman makes a concluding remark, with citations:

> These observations lend further credence to the generally accepted fact that the masoretic pointing distinguishes divine references (אֲדֹנָי) from human references (אדֹנִי). Furthermore, when 'my lord (אדֹנִי) and 'Lord' (יְהוָה) are used in the same sentence, as in Psalm 110:1, 'my lord' (אדֹנִי) always refers to an earthly lord. Thus the phrase 'to my lord' (לַאדֹנִי) apparently indicates that David was directing this oracle from Yahweh to a human lord, not to the divine messianic Lord nor to himself.[12]

Readers are encouraged to read entries of the names of God and lord or master: *Adonai*, *adoni*, and YHWH.[13]

In a literature review, Oliver Rankin presents a Jewish response to Psalm 110:1.

> It was appropriate that the Levite recited in the sanctuary should say "the Lord said to my lord—namely to David—Sit thou at my right hand." The meaning of the expression sitting (at the right hand of God) is that the Holy One, Blessed be He, would protect David all his days and deliver him and make him prevail over his foes. As happened when one (of David's mighty men, cf. 1 Chron. 11.11; 2 Sam. 23:8) lifting up his spear against eight hundred men slew them at one time.[14]

9. Bateman, "Psalm 110," 448.

10. Bateman, "Psalm 110," 448.

11. Bateman, "Psalm 110," 448.

12. Bateman, "Psalm 110," 448.

13. Names of God Study Group, "How to Translate the Name," 403–6; Loewen, "The Names of God in the Old Testament," 201–7; Moulton, "The Names and Attributes of God," 71–80; Mundhenk, "Jesus is Lord," 55–63;

14. Rankin, *Jewish Religious Polemic*, 203.

Bratcher and Reyburn are precise in their observation: "The psalm begins with Yahweh's command to the psalmist's *lord*."[15] However, the focus of this section is verse 4. Notably, the author of Hebrews refers four times to Jesus as "a priest forever after the order of Melchizedek.[16] This crucial verse is analyzed below.

3.3 Is Psalm 110 About a Priest being Made King, or is it About a King Being Made Priest?

Should Psalm 110 be categorized as a coronation ritual? Is it messianic/eschatological, royal, or both? What is the correct heading? Deborah Rooke's assessment is crisp and concise:

> From the point of view of modern scholarship, it is clear that Ps 110,4 does have royal significance. Although some have argued that Ps 110 dates from the Maccabaean period and was written to legitimate the kingship of the high priest Simon Maccabee, the more compelling conclusion is that it is an early royal psalm which legitimizes the priestly prerogative of the monarch. In other words, it is not about a priest who is being made king but about a king who is also being declared a priest. It addresses a king in the first verse (110,1), and then goes on to swear in this royal figure as a priest for ever, citing Melchizedek the king who is also a priest as the model for the priesthood of the monarch (110,4).[17]

In addition, Rooke argues that Psalm 110 "is not about a priest who is being made king but about a king who is also being declared a priest."[18] Rooke elaborates, "In support of the royal interpretation, it may be noted that that the psalm clearly addresses a royal figure to whom priestly prerogatives are subsequently granted by divine oath. And not a priestly figure who is being granted some kind of kingly rule."[19]

Rooke adds a critical question. Assuming that the psalm addresses a king and confirms or bestows upon him priestly prerogatives, "the question is whether his priesthood differs essentially from that of the

15. Bratcher and Reyburn, *A Translator's Handbook on the Book of Psalms*, 947 (bold and underline in the original).

16. Hebrews 5:6, 10; 6:20; and 7:17.

17. Rooke, "Jesus as Royal Priest," 86.

18. Rooke, "Jesus as Royal Priest," 86.

19. Rooke, "Kingship as Priesthood," 188.

non-royal priests who surround him."[20] Therefore, several categories of potential priests exist: the king, the high priest, the senior priests, and the ordinary priests.

Verse three will not be the subject of analysis here. Bratcher and Reyburn observe, "There is no way adequately to summarize the many reasons for the varied interpretations of this verse." The focus of this chapter is verse 4. It opens with the verb "*sworn*," meaning "took a solemn vow" or "*made a solemn promise*."[21] (Italics in the original.)

3.4 How Do Scholars Interpret the Phrase, "a Priest Forever After the Order of Melchizedek" in Psalm 110:4?

The crucial question is: what does "a priest forever after the order of Melchizedek" mean? Kennedy's insight is essential:

> The most controversial element of verse four is the determination of significance of the words "according to the order of Melchisedek." Let it be remarked at the outset that the final word has not been said, nor does it appear that it will ever be said, for the words border on the enigmatic.[22]

Matthew Emadi acknowledges, "The exact nuance of 'after the order of' (על־דברתי) is difficult to determine."[23] That question has been the subject of multiple studies and interpretations. Paul Ellingworth, a United Bible Societies (UBS) Translations Consultant, writes in the *Bible Translator* that there are three main ways in which readers can understand this problematic phrase:

1. There are two *orders or successions* of priests (rather like the succession of bishops in the Roman Catholic Church and some other churches). One series consists of Aaron and his descendants (Heb 7.11); the other, as far as we know, consists of Melchizedek and his only successor, Christ.
2. There are priests of two *ranks*: Melchizedek, who is "like the Son of God" (Heb 7.3, TEV), is of one rank; Aaron and his descendants are of a different and lower rank (compare Heb 7.23–24, 28).

20. Rooke, "Kingship as Priesthood," 188
21. Bratcher and Reyburn, *A Translator's Handbook on The Book of Psalms*, 951.
22. Kennedy, "St. Paul's Conception of the Priesthood," 65–66.
23. Emadi, "You Are Priest Forever," 61.

3. Christ is simply *like* Melchizedek, and Melchizedek is *like* Christ, as Hebrews says, using different Greek words, in 7.15 and 7.3.[24]

Gard Granerød declares:

> In Christian scholarship and its more or less secular aftermath, the MT Ps. 110:4b has, almost without exception, been rendered in accordance with the LXX Ps. 109:4: . . . ., 'Thou art a priest for ever, after the order of Melchisedec—a reading which in turn has been reflected in the New Testament (see Heb. 5:6; 6:20; 7:17). An exception among modern translations is the JPS TANAKH translation, which renders the Hebrew by 'You are a priest forever, a rightful king by My decree'.
>
> In this chapter I will discuss the phrase עַל־דִּבְרָתִי מַלְכִּי־צֶדֶק ['*al dibrati malki-sedeq*]. I will argue that the traditional (Christian) rendering of the Hebrew (e.g., the one found in the NRSV, 'You are a priest forever according to the order of Melchizedek') probably is wrong and only possible when the Hebrew text is translated via the interpretation offered in LXX Ps. 109:4 and the subsequent New Testament quotations of the same verse.[25]

Horton notes, "'You are a priest forever according to the order of Melchizedek.' By the word 'priest,' we should understand priest-king, and 'forever' refers to the perpetual holding of this priest-kingship by the Davidic dynasty."[26] James Barr remarks, "The question of the extent of time involved by relating an object to *'olam* is therefore relative to what the object is."[27]

Dae-I. Kang writes:

> It is crucial to interpret the meaning of *kata tēn taxin* in verse 4. Most English versions translate *taxin* as "order" (ASV, ESV, KJV, NASB, NIV, RSV). The translation as "order" conveys a sense of "succession." The translation is not reasonable, because there is no reference to any king succeeding to the order of the priesthood of Melchizedek in the Old Testament. Thus, Deborah Rooke [p. 91] suggests the translation "because of" or "for the sake of,"40 John Goldingay, "after the manner of,"41 and L. D. Hurst, "according to the character of."42 In my opinion [Kang], Hurst's translation is appropriate. He points out that

24. Ellingworth, "Just Like Melchizedek," 237.
25. Granerød, *Abraham and Melchizedek*, 195.
26. Horton, *The Melchizedek Tradition*, 38.
27. Barr, *Biblical Words for Time*, 74.

> the author of Hebrews paraphrases *kata tēn taxin Melchisedek* in Psalms 109:4 (LXX) into *kata tēn homoiotēta Melchisedek* in Hebrews 7:15. If Christ succeeds to the order of the priesthood of Melchizedek, it is unacceptable, because Melchizedek is just an earthly king. Therefore *kata tēn taxin Melchisedek* in Psalms 109:4 (LXX) should be understood as "according to the character of' in light of Hebrews 7:15," as Hurst's translation shows. What, then, is the character of Melchizedek? From the context of Psalm 110, it is the character of the priestly king.[28]

Theologian Jannes Reiling, writing an entry in the *Dictionary of Deities and Demons in the Bible*, observes:

> His priesthood is defined as 'in' or 'after' the manner of Melchizedek' (*'al* dibrātî malkî-sedeq). The exact meaning of this phrase is hard to establish. It may mean 'in the line of Melchizedek', i.e., inheriting the priesthood of Melchizedek, 'like Melchizedek', or 'on account of Melchizedek'. The common translation 'order' is due to the LXX where *'al* dibrātî is rendered *kata tēn taxin.* Probably the formula shows that the kings of Israel, beginning with David, inherited the tradition of the priest-king of pre-Israelite Jerusalem.[29]

Deborah Rooke notes in *Biblica*:

> Although Heb 7,11 refers to the priesthood of Jesus in the words of Ps 110,4 (LXX 109,4) with the phrase κατὰ τὴν τάξιν Μελχισέδεκ [*kata tēn taxin Melchisedek*], which is often rendered in English 'after the order of Melchizedek', in Heb 7,15 the phrase is glossed with κατὰ τὴν τάξιν Μελχισέδεκ, 'after the likeness of Melchizedek', implying that this is how the writer interpreted the quotation from Ps 110,4. Such an understanding certainly seems to be nearer the meaning of the Hebrew original than does the traditional English rendering. The relevant Hebrew phrase from Ps 110,4, עַל־דִּבְרָתִי מַלְכִּי־צֶדֶק, is a rather obscure construction, but on balance it most probably means 'because of Melchizedek' or 'for the sake of Melchizedek' rather than strictly 'after the order of Melchizedek.'[30]

28. Kang, "The Royal Components of Melchizedek in Hebrews 7," 104.
29. Reiling, "Melchizedek," 560.
30. Rooke, "Jesus as a Royal Priest," 90–91.

In another work, Rooke provides an extended evaluation of the critical phrase at the end of verse 4. Her assessment warrants meticulous examination:

> The important part of the verse for illuminating the royal priesthood is not, however, the reference to Melchizedek, which would make defining the nature of the king's priesthood dependent upon defining priesthood 'after the order of Melchizedek'. Indeed, the translation 'after the order of Melchizedek' is based on the LXX's *kata tēn taxin Melchisedek*, whereas the Hebrew *'al dibratî malkî-sedeq* signifies 'because of' or 'for the sake of Melchizedek' rather than 'after the order of Melchizedek'. . . If the Hebrew is followed and the rendition 'because of' or 'for the sake of Melchizedek' is preferred, Melchizedek does not in fact appear as the founder or the defining element of a succession of priests into which the present Hebrew monarch is incorporated—it is not a question of the king becoming a 'priest after the order of Melchizedek'. Rather, the two distinctive features of the royal priesthood are its bestowal by divine oath (The Lord has sworn and will not change his mind) and its eternity (You are a priest for ever). Melchizedek is then cited as a paradigm or precedent for such priesthood (because of Melchizedek), but he is an adjunct to the main message rather than a part of its substance. The point of such an interpretation is this: if priesthood is usually defined on a functional basis so that it is those who are actually doing the job who are the priests, and not simply those who are eligible to do the job, then the king's occasional participation in cultic ceremonial is no real basis on which to call him a priest, because he is not doing the kind of job which a priest would normally be expected to do in order to earn the designation 'priest'. However, the oath has been sworn to him that he *is* a priest, and a priest *for ever*, so that even though he is not a priest in the sense of one who carries out the regular functions of a sanctuary attendant, because of his vocation and relationship to Yahweh he is nonetheless an *ex officio* priest, a mediator between his God and his people, he will remain such as long as he lives; no-one can deprive him of his mediating, priestly status. Indeed, it could also be taken as a kind of warning, that for the king there is no evading the responsibility of mediation, no choice not to be a priest or carry out priestly duties, unlike others who were permitted by their lineage but who were perhaps unable or unwilling to serve as priests.[31]

31. Rooke, "Kingship as Priesthood," 197–98.

It is noteworthy that "Psalm 110 does not say that Melchizedek's order of the priesthood is superior to Levi's . . . Psalm 110 does not explicitly say that Melchizedek is eternal."[32] Instead, as Dale Leschert points out, "Our writer turns to the Genesis account to discover the superiority of the Melchizedekian order in the seemingly trivial detail that Levi, through Abraham, paid tithes to Melchizedek (Gen.14:20; Heb. 7:4–10).[33]

After a lengthy, detailed, must-read analysis (195–214), Granerød concludes that (1) verse 4 was composed during the monarchic period; and (2) that that the enigmatic verse 4 should be translated as follows:

> Yahweh has sworn and will not repent:
> 'You are a priest forever.
> For my sake my king is loyal.'[34]

3.5 How Do Christian Bibles Translate Psalm 110:4 and How Do They Interpret the Verse?

There exist numerous translations of Psalm 110:4. Some examples are listed below (italics added for emphasis):

> King James Version (KJV): The Lord hath sworn, and will not repent, Thou art a priest for ever *after the order of Melchizedek.*
>
> New King James Version (NKJV): The Lord has sworn And will not relent, "You are a priest forever *According to the order of Melchizedek.*"
>
> New International Version (NIV): The Lord has sworn and will not change his mind: "You are a priest forever, *in the order of Melchizedek.*"
>
> English Standard Version (ESV): The Lord has sworn and will not change his mind, "You are a priest forever *after the order of Melchizedek.*"
>
> International Standard Version (ISV): The Lord took an oath and will never recant: "You are a priest forever, *after the manner of Melchizedek.*"
>
> American Standard Version (ASV): Jehovah hath sworn, and will not repent: Thou art a priest for ever *After the order of Melchizedek.*

32. Leschert, "Hermeneutical Foundations of the Epistle to the Hebrews," 293.
33. Leschert, "Hermeneutical Foundations of the Epistle to the Hebrews," 293.
34. Granerød, *Abraham and Melchizedek*, 213.

New American Bible (Revised Edition) (NABRE): The Lord has sworn and will not waver: "You are a priest forever *in the manner of Melchizedek*."

New English Translation (NET): The Lord makes this promise on oath and will not revoke it: "You are an eternal priest *after the pattern of Melchizedek*."

The New English Translation (NET) comments in its footnote section:

> The phrase עַל־דִּבְרָתִי (*'al divrati*) is a variant of עַל־דִּבְרַת (*'al divrat*; the final י [*yod*] being an archaic genitive ending), which in turn is a variant of עַל דָּבָר (*'al davar*). Both phrases can mean "concerning" or "because of," but neither of these nuances fits the use of עַל־דִּבְרָתִי in Ps 110:4. Here the phrase probably carries the sense "according to the manner of." See L. C. Allen, Psalms 101- (WBC), 81. . .
>
> The Davidic king exercised a non-Levitical priestly role. The king superintended Judah's cultic ritual, had authority over the Levites, and sometimes led in formal worship. David himself instructed the Levites to bring the ark of the covenant to Jerusalem (1 Chr 15:11–15), joined the procession, offered sacrifices, wore a priestly ephod, and blessed the people (2 Sam 6:12–19). At the dedication of the temple Solomon led the ceremony, offering sacrifices and praying on behalf of the people (1 Kgs 8).[35]

In its translation, the TEV (*Today's English Version*) adds a footnote at the end of verse 4, "*in the priestly order of Melchizedek; or like Melchizedek; or in the line of succession of Melchizedek*." In 2001, the TEV was renamed the *Good News Bible*, also called the Good News Translation in the United States. It is an English translation of the Bible published by the American Bible Society.

Bryan C. Babcock presents one translation of verse 4, showing the possible individuals to whom the pronouns could refer. "YHWH (God) has sworn and will not change His (God's) mind, 'You (David, Solomon, a future Davidic king) are a priest forever after the order of Melchizedek.'"[36]

Gammie advocates a different translation:

> Yahwe has sworn and will not repent:
> "Thou art a priest forever
> Because I have spoken righteously, my king."[37]

35. *NET (New English Translation)*, Psalm 110.
36. Babcock, "Who is 'My Lord' in Psalm 110?," 2.
37. Gammie, "Melchizedek: An Exegetical Study of Genesis 14 and the Psalter," 155.

Gammie offers five reasons in support of his translation: (1) It better suits the psalm's parallelism and repetitive character. (2) The use of עַל alone as a conjunction, meaning "because, because of," is known from Gen. 31:20 and Ps. 119:136. (3) The use of צֶדֶק [*zedek*] adverbially, meaning "righteously," though not frequent, is not unknown (Deut. 1:16; Jer. 11:20; Prov. 31: 9). (4) It is in keeping with how Ps. 89 records similar promises were made to the king. (5) Finally, we have a precisely parallel use of the direct address in the closely related Ps. 2, "I have set my king/on Zion, my holy hill" (vs. 6).[38] Afterward, he adds, "The above reasons seem not only to justify our rendering of the text, but to demand it, especially in view of the fact that no alteration of the consonantal text is required."[39]

3.6 How Do Jewish Bibles Translate Psalm 110:4 and How Do Jewish Scholars Interpret the Verse?

In contrast, Jewish translations of Psalm 110:4 differ from Christian sources:

> NJPS: The LORD has sworn and will not relent. "You are a priest forever, a rightful king by My decree."
>
> Rabbi A.J. Rosenberg, Judaica Press: The Lord swore and will not repent; you are a priest forever *because of the speech of Malchizedek.*
>
> *Tanach: Stone Edition* (Artscroll): HASHEM has sworn and will not relent. "You shall be a priest forever, because you are a king of righteousness."[40]
>
> Robert Alter: *The Book of Psalms* 2007: The Lord has sworn, He will not change heart. "You are priest forever. *By my solemn word, my righteous king.*"
>
> Benjamin Segal—*A New Psalm: The Psalms as Literature* (2013): The LORD has sworn never to take back: "You are a priest forever, *like the noted 'Righteous King.'*" (p. 531)
>
> Yitzchok Cohen (Chabad Lubavitch, May 28, 2021): My translation with translator's additions in brackets . . . G-d has sworn (regarding David) and He will not change His mind. (G-d said to David,) "You are a king (and your dynasty will rule) forever, *because (you are) a righteous king.*"

38. Gammie, "Melchizedek: An Exegetical Study of Genesis 14 and the Psalter," 156.
39. Gammie, "Melchizedek: An Exegetical Study of Genesis 14 and the Psalter," 156.
40 From Scherman, *Tanach: The Stone Edition.*

The following are quotes from select Jewish commentaries:

> Robert Alter:
> You are priest forever. At least in the David story, there is some indication of combining the functions of king and priest, though later they would be clearly separated. Some interpreters imagine that this psalm actually refers to David.[41]
>
> Benjamin Segal:
> "Priest": Although the reference is possibly to an honorific description of a servant (the Israelite people are called a "kingdom of priests," Exod. 19:6), kings in Israel on occasion were called, or functioned as, priests (cf. 2 Sam. 6:18; 8:18; 2 Kings 16:12–13.[42]
>
> Adele Berlin and Marc Zvi Brettler:
> A second divine quotation, mirroring v. 1; this, however, is likely a citation of an old oracle; note 1 Sam. 15:11, where God repents that he made Saul king. David and Solomon often perform priestly roles (e.g., 2 Sam. 6:14; 1 Kings ch 8), and 2 Sam. 8:18 concludes: "David's sons were priests . . ." Melchizedek, having the double role of priest and king at Jerusalem, is seen as offering precedent for the similar roles of Davidic kings.[43]

3.7 What are Some Reasons for Doubting the Traditional Interpretations of Psalm 110?

Does Psalm 110:4b lend credence to Jesus being forever a priest in the order of Melchizedek? Notably, this verse is cited frequently in commentaries and discussions about the priesthood of Jesus. It is important to note that the Bible is a complex and deeply interpreted text. Moreover, different individuals, especially skeptics, detractors or those from other faiths, may hold varying views that contradict mainline Christian theology. Gary Habermas aptly notes in his recent text on the resurrection, "That is, we all have perspectives and even biases that affect the way we write, read, and speak. In short, we are all prejudiced.[44] He goes on to

41. Alter, *The Book of Psalms*, 397.
42. Segal, *A New Psalm: The Psalms as Literature*, 532.
43. Berlin and Brettler, *The Jewish Study Bible*, 1395.
44. Habermas, *On the Resurrection*, 21.

add, "There is little question for virtually all scholars that personal biases can and do distort data and affect one's research, all the way from mild to twists to what we have termed more egregious manipulation."[45]

Some individuals might raise the following arguments or points in discussions related to Psalm 110:4b. Through a literature review by this author and ChatGPT, Gemini, and Grammarly, numerous rationales have been identified that explain why skeptics, detractors, or people from different religions may hold varying views that contradict mainline Christian theism. What follows is an extensive list:

1. *Contextual interpretation*: Some argue that Psalm 110's context is specific to Davidic kingship and not necessarily about Jesus as a priest.
2. *Melchizedek's historical ambiguity*: Melchizedek is a mysterious figure with limited information in the Bible. Building a theological doctrine on a figure with limited details could be problematic.
3. *Christ's eternal priesthood*: Critics may question the idea of an eternal priesthood, arguing that it contradicts the traditional understanding of priesthood as a temporal institution.
4. *Historical development of Christian theology*: Critics might point to the historical development of Christian theology and suggest that interpretations of Psalm 110:4b evolved to support specific doctrinal beliefs.
5. *Hebrew Bible vs. New Testament priesthood*: Some argue that the concept of priesthood in the Hebrew Bible is distinct from the New Testament understanding, making it challenging to apply Psalm 110:4b directly to Jesus.
6. *Different priesthood orders*: Some view the claim that Jesus belongs to the order of Melchizedek as an attempt to reconcile conflicting details in the biblical narrative rather than a straightforward assertion.
7. *Symbolic interpretation*: Critics may suggest that the language used in Psalm 110:4b is symbolic or metaphorical and not intended to convey a literal priesthood after the order of Melchizedek.

45. Habermas, *On the Resurrection*, 65.

8. *Theological diversity*: Different Christian denominations hold diverse views on interpreting this verse, reflecting the broader theological diversity within Christianity.
9. *Translation issues*: Some may argue that the translation of the original Hebrew text could impact the interpretation of Psalm 110:4b.
10. *Christ's fulfillment of the Law*: Critics may question the necessity of Jesus having a priesthood after the order of Melchizedek, especially considering the Christian belief that Jesus fulfilled the Law.
11. *Historical-critical approach*: Some scholars employ historical-critical methods to analyze biblical texts, which may result in interpretations that diverge from traditional theological perspectives.
12. *Allegorical interpretation*: Critics may argue that interpreting Psalm 110:4b allegorically or metaphorically diminishes the need for a literal priesthood after the order of Melchizedek.
13. *Human authorship and intent*: Critics may question the human authorship of the Psalms and the original intent behind Psalm 110:4b, arguing that theological interpretations could be projections of later beliefs onto the text.

3.8 How Verses 5 to 7 of Psalm 110 Undermine the Traditional Christian Interpretation of Psalm 110:4

Many Christian apologists, Bible commentators, and theologians often omit discussing the three verses that immediately follow verse 4. Attentive readers must ask why. Skeptics and detractors contend that these verses prove that Jesus is not the person being spoken to by God:

> 5 The Lord is at your right hand;
> he will shatter kings on the day of his wrath.
> 6 He will execute judgment among the nations,
> filling them with corpses;
> 7 he will shatter chiefs
> over the wide earth. (ESV)

Bratcher and Reyburn remark:

> The king is promised God's protection: the Lord will win victory for him over his enemies. The Lord stands by him, at his right

> side to protect him. The *day of his wrath* in verse 5b further defines *He will execute judgment* in verse 6a; these refer to the day of the Lord, when he will judge all peoples on earth. The verb translated "defeat" in verse 5b (literally "break in pieces") is in the perfect sense (see TOB, NEB "has broken"); some translate it as a timeless present (NJV, BJ, NJB, TOB, FRCL); it seems better to take it to speak of future action, as the tense is sometimes used (RSV, TEV, SPCL, NIV).[46]

There are three questions to ponder:

1. Did God shatter kings on the day of His wrath during Jesus' lifetime?
2. Did God execute judgment among the nations, filling them with corpses during the lifetime of Jesus?
3. Did God shatter chiefs (i.e., kings) over the earth during Jesus' lifetime?

While commenting on Hebrews 1:13, Craig Koester refers to a similar phrase from Psalm 110:1, "until I make your enemies a footstool for your feet." He writes, "David battled his enemies 'until the Lord put them under the soles of his feet' (1 Kgs 5:3)."[47]

Gerd Steyn elaborates in his dissertation:

> Being "a blessing on the national leader in war," the enemies of David's messiah-king are subjected under his feet. Imagery of Near Eastern monarchy' is utilised and the image corresponds with Sumerian-Akkadian imagery where the conqueror took an honorary position at the right hand side of the god. The Psalm also resembles Egyptian imagery in this regard. The footstool of Tutankhamen of Egypt is carved with pictures of his enemies, and with other Egyptian kings being shown resting their feet on their enemies' heads. The practice symbolises the victorious and conquering position of the ruler when he placed his feet on the neck of his enemy's defeated king in order to demonstrate his triumph. Examples of the practice is found in Josh 10:24, with allusions to it in Deut 33:29, Isa 51:23 and Ps 89:11.[48]

Did God ever put the enemies of Jesus under his feet? Jesus famously instructed in The Parable of the Ten Minas, "26 'I tell you that to everyone who has, more will be given, but from the one who has not, even what

46. Bratcher and Reyburn, *A Translator's Handbook*, 952.
47. Koester, *The Anchor Yale Bible*, 196.
48. Steyn, "A Quest for the Assumed LXX," 112.

he has will be taken away. 27 But as for these enemies of mine, who did not want me to reign over them, *bring them here and slaughter them before me*" (Luke 19:26–27, ESV, italics for emphasis). Yes, this is a parable. However, these words are instructive. Skeptics and detractors ask why that day never transpired. They argue that Christians have waited almost two thousand years to fulfill verses five through seven. To the contrary, the Romans continued to rule and subjugate Israel, which climaxed in the year 70 with the destruction of the Second Temple.[49] Consequently, they might suggest that it is no wonder the author of Hebrews and many Bible commentators omit to quote those verses.

3.9 Conclusion

Psalm 110 is an enigma. Traditional and mainline Jewish sources diametrically oppose the "standard" Christian translation and interpretations of verse 1 (*adoni*). The last part of verse 4 ("after the order of Melchizedek") is vague, ambiguous, and subject to extensive academic debate. How can non-Christians, skeptics, or detractors support the standard Christian proposal if the sentence's meaning is unknown? In addition, how can they attempt to verify or refute the traditional Christian usage of verse as proof that Jesus is a high priest (discussed later in Hebrews 7) if what the author of Psalm 110 says is unknowable?

49. If Hebrews was composed before year 70, the author would only be cognizant the Romans continued to rule and subjugate Israel.

4

The Epistle to the Hebrews

INTRODUCTION

> First-century Jewish believers faced some perplexing questions concerning Christ's high priestly ministry. Why wasn't He called a priest while here on Earth? How could He be a legitimate high priest and how could His atoning work be efficacious if He was not from the tribe of Levi?[1]

Understanding the significance of the Book of Hebrews and the author's intentions hinges on several key questions. When analyzing Melchizedek in Hebrews 7:1–28, the author employs a technique known in Greek as *synkrisis*. This figure of speech often compares opposing things or individuals to support the writer's argument. In Hebrews, there are at least eight notable comparisons: parentage, genealogy, birth, death, office, actions, status, and achievements.

4.1 Authorship, Date, and Audience

The Epistle to the Hebrews is a text composed by an anonymous author. It is unclear who the audience of this letter/sermon was or where they lived. Scholars generally believed that the author of Hebrews was a Hellenized Jewish Christian. Moreover, he was intellectually sophisticated. D.A. Carson and Douglas J. Moo elaborate:

1. Levy, "Who is Melchizedek?"

> In the earliest form of the text that has come down to us, P46, this book had the title (*Pros Hebraious*, "To[the]Hebrews"). Apparently, Clement of Alexandria, writing c. AD 180, knew the book under this title . . . (*Hebraios*, "for Hebrews": *H.E.* 6.14.3–4). Most scholars assume that this is a later editorial label attached to the work for convenient reference and therefore should not influence our efforts to establish the identity of the addressees.[2]

Notably, it was not written as a general epistle to all Jews.

Mason writes that "most propose a date between 60–100 CE."[3] Sigurd Grindheim says, "There is no clear indication that allows us to conclude in favor of a more precise dating than 60–100 CE. A date toward the end of this spectrum appears more likely, however."[4] If the epistle had been composed before the year 70, the Second Temple would still be standing. Consequently, *korban* (offerings or sacrifices) would still be a daily occurrence. Besides, the Second Temple and the *korban* were competing with the eucharistic assemblies of the early Christian community. A literary review identifies several of the most highly rated commentaries about Hebrews. These authors' opinions about its authorship require studious examination.

> F.F. Bruce:
> "But as to who actually wrote the epistle, God knows the truth of the matter." Even today, we have not got far beyond Origen's confession of ignorance . . .
> When was it written? In the absence of any clear evidence for the identity of the recipients or the author, the date of the epistle is also unknown.[5]

> Gareth Lee Cockerill
> When people discovered that I was writing a commentary on Hebrews they would almost invariably ask, "Well, who wrote it?" One certainly can and must study Hebrews within its first-century environment. In my judgment, however, the evidence available is insufficient to determine with certainty the name of

2. Carson and Moo. *An Introduction to the New Testament*, 609; cf. Dryer, "The Epistle to the Hebrews in Recent Research," 104–31.

3. Mason, *You Are a Priest Forever*, 5.

4. Grindheim, *The Letter to the Hebrews*.

5. Bruce, *The Epistle to the Hebrews*, 20.

the author or to be overly precise about the location, specific identity, and situation of the recipients.[6]

Sigurd Grindheim

"But who wrote the epistle, in truth, God knows." That was the verdict of the church father Origen regarding the authorship of Hebrews. Eighteen hundred years of subsequent New Testament scholarship has not brought us closer to the truth.[7]

Philip Edgcumbe Hughes:

The absence both of solid testimony, internal or external, and of any firm traditions mean that, as things are, the riddle of authorship of Hebrews is incapable of solution.[8]

Paul Ellingworth:

Ellingworth identifies and discusses *thirteen persons* as possible authors of Hebrews, devoting ten pages to Paul. In the first sentence discussing Paul, Ellingworth writes, "The idea of Pauline authorship of Hebrews is now almost universally abandoned."[9]

William L. Lane:

"Undefined are the identity of the writer, his conceptual background, the character and location of the community addressed, the circumstances and date of composition, the setting in life, the nature of the crisis to which the document is a response, the literary genre, and the purpose and plan of the work. Although these undefined issues continue to be addressed and debated vigorously, no real consensus has been reached . . ."

"The tradition concerning its authorship, purpose, and intended audience is conflicting and unreliable. The evidence provided by the text itself is open to divergent interpretations. These facts constitute a continual reminder that every statement about Hebrews is a personal synthesis, an interpretive statement."[10]

6. Cockerill, *The Epistle to the Hebrews*, xiv.
7. Grindheim, *The Letter to the Hebrews.*
8. Hughes, *A Commentary on the Epistle to the Hebrews*, 19.
9. Ellingworth, *Epistle to the Hebrews*, 3.
10. Lane, *Hebrews* 1–8, xlvii.

4.2 Hebrews and the Septuagint

As mentioned, prior, the Epistle to the Hebrews is an anonymous composition from about 2,000 years ago. Eric Mason writes, "Virtually all scholars assert that Scripture for the author was the Septuagint."[11] Martin Karrer elaborates:

> The origin and distribution of the quotations is worthy of attention . . .
>
> Regarding language, our author consistently chooses Greek traditions, as noted. We do not find a single Hebrew or Aramaic relic in the quotations or elsewhere in Hebrews. Moreover, no quotation presents us with undisputable evidence of a correction by our author toward the Hebrew (Proto-MT) text. The author abstains from checking Hebrew traditions, even in the Pentateuch (Torah), as 11:21 shows . . . So, there is no proof of a knowledge of Hebrew. In any case, the Qumranic or proto-rabbinic tendency to return to the Hebrew text of Scriptures is not found in this book. There is a clear conviction that the Greek language was appropriate to the speaking of God.[12]

Notably, the term "the Septuagint" is inexact and misleading. The Greek version of the Hebrew Bible is known as the Septuagint or LXX. According to tradition, the Hebrew Bible was translated into Greek by seventy translators between 246 and 283 BCE, hence the name LXX. Moreover, the Letter of Aristeas, a Jewish work from the 2nd century BCE claims that *only* the first five books of the Bible (i.e., the Torah) were translated by elders or rabbis. No original exists. The Scripture in Greek exists in many different forms and revisions. Several well-known early versions include Aquila, Symmachus, and Theodotion. Entire books and journal articles have been written on this topic.[13] It is crucial that we recognize that the author of Hebrews frequently did not use the Hebrew Bible and his sources are unknown.

Cockerill identifies twenty-eight passages in the Hebrew Bible where he quotes from the Hebrew Bible.[14] In addition, the author of Hebrews alludes to, summarizes, and recounts events involving persons and

11. Mason, *You Are a Priest Forever*, 2; cf. Attridge, *Hebrews: A Commentary*, 23; Combrink, "Some Thoughts on the Old Testament," 23–25; Ellingworth, *Epistle to the Hebrews*, 111; Steyn, "A Quest for the Assumed LXX," 6–7.

12. Karrer, "The Epistle to the Hebrews and the Septuagint," 338–39.

13. See Peters, "Septuagint," 1093–1105 for an excellent overview.

14. Cockerill, *The Epistle to the Hebrews*, 42.

often echoes the idioms of the Greek Old Testament. Cockerill goes on to add, "The rhetorical style of Hebrews and the quality of the pastor's Greek suggest that the recipients as well as the author were most at home in the Greek language. Thus it was only natural for the pastor to use the Greek text of the OT accepted by his hearers."[15]

4.3 Purpose

The Epistle to the Hebrews was composed for multiple purposes. Christian apologists, Bible commentators, and theologians frequently point out two goals that recur throughout Hebrews: (1) encouraging Christians to endure (perseverance) and (2) warning them not to abandon their faith in Christ (apostasy) (see Heb. 2:1–4; 3:7–4:13; 5:11–6:12; 10:19–39; 12:1–29). Additionally, the author's multifaceted theological agenda is readily apparent:

1. Showing the absolute supremacy and sufficiency of Jesus Christ as the revealer and mediator of God's grace. The prologue (1:1–4) presents Christ as God's complete and final revelation, far surpassing the revelation given in the Hebrew Bible.
2. Showing the supremacy and sufficiency of Christ as the high priest who intercedes for us, the Supremacy of Christ as God Himself, and as the Perfect, once-and-for-all sacrifice that takes away the world's sins.
3. Revealing Christ as greater than the prophets (1:1–3a), angels (1:3b–2:18), Moses (3:1–6), Joshua (4:1–10), the high priest (4:14–15), and the Aaronites or Levitical priests (5:1–12:29).
4. Supplanting the Hebrew Bible with a new Covenant (Chapter 8, especially Heb. 8:13).
5. Exhorting his audience to reject local Jewish teachings and to remain faithful to Jesus.

4.4 The Author's Theological Agenda and the Links He Draws Between Jesus and Melchizedek

Many of the statements in Hebrews are theological claims that have been made by its author without evidence and have their foundation in

15. Cockerill, *The Epistle to the Hebrews*, 41n181.

eisegesis. Therefore, the book repeats its author's opinions and reflects his worldview. Readers must differentiate between claims made by the author and the presence of tangible evidence. Ellingworth shows that the Christological development of the letter is clear:

> Jesus is Son (chapter 1)
> He is high priest (2:17)
> The same Christ is both Son and high priest (5:5–10)
> His priesthood is like that of Melchizedek (6:20–7:1)[16]

Interestingly, J. Cornelis de Vos notes that the last verse in Hebrews 6 (v. 20) serves as a transitional. Moreover, "It quotes Ps 109:4 LXX (= 110:4 MT) and thus introduces Melchizedek, 'the high priest for eternity.' Compared to Ps 109:4 LXX . . . Melchizedek is referred to as priest in Psalm 109 LXX whereas he is high priest in Hebrews."[17]

Daniel Harrington, S.J., is forthright about the author's goals:

> The basic theological thesis of Hebrews is that Christ's suffering and death constituted the one perfect sacrifice for sins, and that because Christ went willingly to his death he can be regarded as the great high priest. Thus, Christ is both the one perfect sacrifice for sins and the priest who offers that sacrifice.[18]

Notably, the author of Hebrews writes:

> So also Christ did not exalt himself to be made a high priest, but was appointed by him who said to him,
> "You are my Son,
> today I have begotten you";
> as he says also in another place,
> "You are a priest forever,
> after the order of Melchizedek" (Heb. 5:5–6, ESV).

Cockerill elaborates on the author's worldview, which is dependent upon common Christian tradition. He identifies several examples:

> The pastor is committed to the Son's eternal preexistence (1:1–3); incarnation (2:5–18; 8:1–10:18); crucifixion (5:7–10; 9:11–14; 10:5–10; 12:1–3); and exaltation (1:13; 8:1–2; 1011[*sic*]14), including belief in his resurrection (13:20–21). He joins the other

16. Ellingworth, *Epistle to the Hebrews*, 348.
17. Vos, "Abraham's Family in the Epistle to the Hebrews," 309.
18. Harrington, *What Are They Saying about the Letter to the Hebrews?*, 64.

> NT writers in his conviction that Christ has sufficiently dealt with sin and is, therefore, God's definitive provision of salvation (4:14–16; 10:19–25).[19]

The ramifications of these verses are crucial: (1) Jesus did *not* exalt himself as a high priest, (2) the author proclaims that God *appointed* Jesus a high priest forever, and (3) for supporting proof, he cites Psalm 110:4.[20] Panagiotis L. Kampouris elaborates, "In other words, Melchizedek's priesthood is divine –since he was not anointed with oil like Aaron– and therefore this capacity is considered eternal, superior to that of the Levitical institution."[21] Readers must ask themselves: does it make sense that Jesus is a priest forever, simply because the author of Hebrews believes he is a priest forever, "after or like" the order of Melchizedek? The anonymous author is expressing an unverifiable opinion.

4.5 Possible Historical Sources for the Author's Claims About Melchizedek

In an article on Melchizedek from the *International Standard Bible Encyclopedia*, David Francis Roberts asks:

> Where did the author [of Hebrews] get the material for this description of Melchizedek? . . . The answer is perhaps to be had among the Tell el-Amarna Letters, among which are at least 6, probably 8, letters from a king of Urusalim to Amenophis IV, king of Egypt, whose "slave" the former calls himself. Urusalim is to be identified with Jerusalem, and the letters belong to circa 1400 BC. The name of this king is given as Abd-Khiba (or Abd-ḫiba), though Hommel, quoted by G.A. Smith, Jerusalem, II, 14, note 7, reads Chiba. Zimmer, in ZA, 1891, 246, says that it can be read Abditaba, and so Sayce (HDB, III, 335b) calls him ʿEbhedh ṭōbh. The king tells his Egyptian overlord, "Neither my father nor my mother set me in this place: the mighty arm of the king (or, according to Sayce, "the arm of the mighty king") established me in my father's house.".. The conclusions we come to are . . . The Epistle to the Hebrews makes use of . . . oral tradition which was not found in the Old Testament. It is

19. Cockerill, *The Epistle to the Hebrews*, 24.

20. The author repeatedly states that Christ was appointed to the high priesthood by God (Heb. 5:5–10; 7:17, 21). However, skeptics and detractors demand convincing evidence to sustain the claim. In addition, they mandate knowing the source of the author's information.

21. Kampouris, "The Priesthood of Melchizedek," 129.

> this unwritten tradition that is possibly explained by the Tell el-Amarna Letters.[22]

In the *Westminster Theological Journal*, M.J. Paul offers an alternative explanation for the potential significance of the Tell el-Amarna Letters. He comments, "But he [Melchizedek] did not have the right of kingship or priesthood on account of his descent. If this is right, there must have been two possibilities: one could become priest or king either because of hereditary rights or in another way." Paul goes on to provide two letters that King Abdu-Heba of Jerusalem sent to the Pharaoh pleading for assistance: "Behold this land of Jerusalem: (It was) not my father (and) not my mother (who) gave (it) to me, (but) the arm of the mighty king (which) gave (it) to me." And in another letter:

> They blame me before the king, my lord, (saying): 'Abdu-Heba has rebelled against the king, his lord." Behold, as for me, (it was) not my father and not my mother (who) set me in this place; the arm of the mighty king brought me into the house of my father!

Paul elaborates, "These quotations demonstrate that there was a difference between hereditary succession and installation by one superior in rank . . . The only element in the letters of 'Abdu-Heba I want to stress is the difference which exists between the ways in which one could become a king."[23]

Bible commentators must engage with these texts and other crucial subjects in the book of Hebrews. To repeat the question: why do many Christian apologists, Bible commentators, and theologians fail to engage with texts and peer-reviewed journals in anthropology, comparative religions, and sociology, and in-field experts in their analysis of Hebrews?

4.6 Jesus' Lineage

A fundamental issue is the lineage of Melchizedek. John MacArthur highlights a significant contrast between the two kinds of priesthood discussed in Hebrews. He suggests that "The point in Hebrews is that Melchizedek's parentage and origin are irrelevant to his priesthood. Whereas to the Aaronic priesthood genealogy was everything, to the

22. Roberts, "Melchizedek."
23. Paul, "The Order of Melchizedek," 208.

Melchizedek priesthood it was nothing."[24] Jeremy Punt, writing in *Neotestamentica*, adds, "Hebrews disavows genealogy explicitly or, at least, praises its absence as a sign of superiority: Melchizedek's position and Abraham's subordination to him depended on Melchizedek not having any genealogy."[25] In contrast, Mitchell says, "Hebrews presents Melchizedek as the type of a priesthood that is superior to the Levitical priesthood in order to establish a basis for the high priesthood of Christ."[26]

4.7 The Lack of Evidence for the Claims Made About Jesus in Hebrews

How does the author know that God appointed Jesus "the heir of all things, through whom also he created the world" (Heb. 1:2, ESV)? Raymond Brown comments, "But surely by describing Christ as 'heir of all things,' he intends to convey to us the idea that the Lord Jesus will inherit not only this earth but the entire universe."[27] Moreover, Brown adds, the author is surely envisaging "a Christ whose hands had shaped the universe and summoned the galaxy of stars into being."[28]

Craig Koester elaborates that the term "universe" used in Hebrews 1:2 is plural. Therefore, that word can be used temporally for 'ages' and spatially for 'worlds.'[29] How does the author know that the hands of Jesus shaped the universe and summoned the galaxy of stars into being? How does the author know that he [Jesus] is the radiance of the glory of God and the exact imprint of his nature, and he upholds the universe by the word of his power" (Heb. 1:3; ESV)? Koester argues that "the radiance" is a metaphor for the fact that the Son actively radiates divine glory out from God or that "he passively reflects 'back' divine glory, like a mirror."[30] Therefore, the term may show either radiance or reflection.[31] Again, it requires asking, what is the author's evidence? How does the author know that "after making purification for sins, he [Jesus] sat down at the right hand of the Majesty on high" (Heb. 1:3, ESV)? Where is the sustaining

24. MacArthur, *Hebrews*, 177.
25. Punt, "Politics of Genealogies in the New Testament," 390.
26. Mitchell, *Sacra Pagina: Hebrews*, 139.
27. Brown, *The Message of Hebrews*, 29.
28. Brown, *The Message of Hebrews*, 30.
29. Koester, *The Anchor Yale Bible*, 176.
30. Koester, *The Anchor Yale Bible*, 179–80.
31. Koester, *The Anchor Yale Bible*, 180.

evidence for these claims? Skeptics and detractors are unconvinced by unsubstantiated claims by an anonymous author.

How does the author know that Jesus is greater than the angels? Does the author believe Jesus is greater than *all* the angels (e.g., the *Chayot haKodesh*, *Ophanim*, *Erelim*, *Seraphim*, *Hashmallim*, *Cherubim*, or *Malakim*)? Where is his evidence (not the Bible commentator's eisegesis of what the author was thinking)? The author's claim that angels worshipped Jesus is unverifiable (Heb. 1:6). It is no more than Hebrews confirming itself or material in Luke 2 (probably a composition after Hebrews) or an evolving oral tradition. The latter requires that Hebrews was composed after Luke and that the author read Luke. Similarly, Paul's claim in Colossians 1:16 that all things were created through him and for him is unverifiable. The author's exhortatory claim is found in Hebrews 1:5, which quotes Psalm 2:7 and 2 Samuel 7:14. The author, a passionate believer in Jesus, quotes Psalm 2, expressing his opinion without providing supporting evidence.

Karen H. Jobes expands the discussion by presenting five reasons the Son (Jesus) is superior to the angels:[32]

(1) God is his Father, whereas God is the creator of the angels. Jobes fails to provide convincing evidence that God is "the" Father of Jesus. Skeptics and detractors would respond that if Jesus is one-third of the Godhead (the Trinity) and always existed, how could Jesus have a father? Would not the Father, the Son, and the Holy Spirit coexist throughout eternity? Falling back to the argument that the Trinity is a mystery is unconvincing to skeptics and detractors.[33]

Matthew reports that an angel of the Lord appeared to Joseph in a dream. The angel said, "But as he considered these things, behold, an angel of the Lord appeared to him in a dream, saying, "Joseph, son of David, do not fear to take Mary as your wife, for that which is conceived in her is from the Holy Spirit" (Matt. 1:20, ESV). Skeptics point out that the narrative is unconvincing by itself, as it lacks sustaining evidence. Moreover, claiming this episode is a mystery is unconvincing.

(2) Jobes argues that the Son was the object of angel worship. In contrast, the angels are to worship God. Here, too, no evidence is provided to support this view. The support is within the Christian Bible (e.g., Luke

32. Jobes, *Letters to the Church*.

33. Trinitarian Christians would respond that the term "son" does not require a coming into existence; all it requires is a dependence on the Father or generator, much as an eternal magnetic field would still depend on the eternal magnet generating it.

2). Consequently, commentators use the Christian Bible to corroborate and substantiate itself.

(3) Next, there is the assertion that the Son is God's eternal king while angels are servants of God. Jobes provides no sustaining evidence to support her claim. For multiple reasons, this assertion is unsustainable. Assuming that the virgin birth occurred, Jesus could not be from the line of David. God's instruction manual, the Hebrew Bible, requires the king to be in the direct bloodline of David. Adoption does not render a person viable for kingship. Koester points out that Julius Caesar adopted Augustus as his son and heir. Afterward, Augustus adopted Tiberius to inherit the throne (*RomCiv*, 1:633–38; 2:2–7).[34] However, Roman practice is not Torah or Jewish law.

Moreover, never does the Christian Bible detail that Jesus was adopted by Joseph or anointed by a priest to be king or that he was accepted or acknowledged as king while alive.[35]

(4) None of the angels will rule over the universe (1:7 –8; 13:2:5), whereas this is the role the Son took on when he ascended to the throne of God after his death and resurrection. However, Jobes provides no support for Jesus assuming that role or ascending to the throne of God. The author of Hebrews makes an unverifiable assumption. Moreover, Jobes cites Hebrews to corroborate and substantiate Hebrews.

(5) Jobes alleges the Son co-occupies God's throne, whereas angels serve those who will inherit salvation. No convincing evidence exists that the Son, Jesus, co-occupies God's throne.

4.8 Virginal Birth vs. Davidic Kingship: Problems with the Notion of Jesus as the Adopted Son of Joseph

Another explanation put forward by commentators is that adoption in the Greco-Roman world became legally official when the father gave their child his or her name. By Joseph calling his name Jesus, Jesus' adoption was made complete, and Scripture fulfilled. This argument is unverified and not supported by traditional Christian teachings. Notably, a diversity of adoption practices existed. However, no supporting example of this procedure is known. Additionally, this argument relies on accepting the historicity of the angel instructing Joseph in a dream to name the future child "Jesus" (Matt. 1:21; Luke 1:31). If the original narrative is a literary

34. Koester, *The Anchor Yale Bible*, 185.

35. The words on the cross were to humiliate Jesus.

invention (modified Luke), the explanation fails. The inconvenient truth is that nowhere in the Hebrew Bible is there a verse stating that the Son, a human Messiah, co-occupies God's throne.

In addition, claims that support the idea that Jesus was adopted by Joseph amount to an argument from silence. Nonetheless, in the interests of fairness, supporting arguments adduced by commentators should be listed. Examples include the following:

1. *Silence in the Gospels*: Some commentators argue that the Gospels are silent about Jesus' childhood and adolescence, leaving room for the possibility that Joseph adopted him during that time.
2. *Lack of Genealogy in Luke*: Critics point to the absence of a *biological* genealogy for Jesus in the Gospel of Luke, suggesting that this omission might be intentional and related to an adopted status. (Luke's genealogy goes from Adam to Joseph, referring to Jesus as "the son (as was supposed) of Joseph.")
3. *Use of "son of Joseph" in John 6:42*: The Gospel of John refers to Jesus as the "son of Joseph." Some proponents of the adoption theory argue that this term supports the idea of a legal, rather than biological, relationship.
4. *Jesus' Designation as "son of David"*: Some argue that Jesus' designation as the "son of David" may imply a legal, adoptive connection to the Davidic line through Joseph rather than a biological one.
5. *Ambiguities in Biblical Language*: Critics of traditional views may point to ambiguities in biblical language or translations that support the notion of Jesus' adoption by Joseph.

However, there is another problem. Two verses later (Matt. 1:23), Matthew cites a fulfillment prophecy: "Behold, the virgin shall conceive and bear a son, and they shall call his name Immanuel (which means God with us)" (citing Isa. 7:14, ESV). Immanuel does not appear to be the name by which Jesus was known throughout his life. Christian commentators suggest the name highlights an essential aspect of his identity. However, this explanation is merely an opinion and is tantamount to an argument from silence. In addition, the alleged prophecy in Isaiah 7:14 has no connection to Jesus. The prophecy was for King Ahaz, not a future event that occurred approximately 700 years later.

4.9 The Speculative Connection with Philo

Several dated works suggest that the author of Hebrews drew upon numerous concepts from the Hellenistic Jewish philosopher Philo of Alexandria (c. 20 BCE—c. 50 CE).[36] Samuel Sandmel wrote an influential article in the *Journal of Biblical Literature*. His cautionary warning about *parallelomania* bears diligent consideration. Parallelomania is defined as:

> That extravagance among scholars which first overdoses the supposed similarity in passages and the proceeds to describe source and derivation as if implying literary connection flowing in an inevitable or predetermined direction.
>
> The key word in my essay is extravagance. I am not denying that literary parallels and literary influence, in the form of source and derivation, exist . . . However, I am speaking words of caution about exaggerations about parallels and about source and derivation.[37]

Therefore, Sandmel is stating that the simple observations of similarlity between historical events are often less than valid.[38]

So, what is the most appropriate way to assess the significance of the parallels between Philo and Hebrews? Dennis MacDonald has suggested multi-step criteria to test similarities between texts, which this text encourages its readership to employ.

- Accessibility or availability: Did the author of Hebrews have access to Philo's writings?
- Density: This topic refers to the volume of contacts between the two texts. Parallels between two texts may be numerous but trivial. In contrast, two or three weighty similarities may suffice.
- Distinctiveness: Occasionally, two texts contain distinguishing characteristics such as an unusual word or phrase. MacDonald points out: "Some interpreters consider this the best test of dependence."[39] A remarkably similar context hardly seems accidental (p. 41).

36. Besant, *Free-Thinker's Text Book Part 2 Christianity*, 367–75; Bryant, *The Sentiments of Philo Judeus*, 107–201 or 203–7 for a list of 52 terms and doctrines; and Lake, *Plato, Philo, and Paul*, 40–47.

37. Sandmel, "Parallelomania," 1.

38. Sandmel, "Parallelomania," 1.

39. MacDonald, *The Homeric Epics and the Gospel of Mark*, 8–9.

- Interpretability or intelligibility: The capacity of the presumed original text to make sense of the later text." This reality may include the solution to a peculiar problem that has eluded other explanations."[40]

In his 1797 text, *The Sentiments of Philo Judeus*, Jacob Bryant (1715–1804), an English scholar and mythographer, assumed that Philo had borrowed information from Christianity (Preface, vi). On pages 203–206 of his book, he lists fifty-two striking parallels between the two. For example, in the works of Philo, the Logos is referred to as the Son of God, the first-begotten of God, the Image of God, who is superior to the angels and all things. He is said to be the one by whom the world was created, the Light of the world, the one who can see God and who resides in God. He is the most ancient of God's works and is regarded as being the same as God. The Logos is eternal, beholding all things and supporting the world. He is said to be nearest to God, without any separation, free from all taint of sin, who presides over the imperfect and weak. The Logos is described as the Fountain of Wisdom, a Messenger sent from God, an Advocate for man, who ordered and deposed all things. He is spoken of as the Shepherd of God's flock, the Physician who heals all evil, the seal of God, and the sure refuge of those who seek him. Heavenly food is distributed by the Logos equally to all who seek it. Men are said to be freed by the Logos from all corruption. The Logos is described by Philo not only as the Son of God but also as his beloved Son. The just man is said to be advanced by the Logos to the presence of his Creator. The Logos is called the true High Priest and a mediator. Bryant elaborates on these parallels in the section of his book titled "*A Recapitulation of the Character and Attributes of the Logos*."[41]

John Lake corrected Bryant's assertion about seventy-five years later, arguing that Christianity had borrowed from Plato.[42] Annie Besant quotes Lake in her work, *The Freethinker's Text-Book*. She notes:

> Such are the most important passages of Keim's resume of Philo's philosophy, and its resemblance to Christian doctrine is unmistakeable, and adds one more proof to the fact that Christianity is Alexandrian rather than Judaean. It will be well to add to this sketch the passages carefully gathered out of Philo's works by

40. MacDonald, *The Homeric Epics and the Gospel of Mark*, 8–9; Litwa, *How the Gospels Became History*, 48 criticizes MacDonald's list. See also Mitchell, "Homer in the New Testament?" 244–58; Sandnes, "*Imitatio Homeri?*," 715–32.

41. Bryant, *The Sentiments of Philo Judeus*, 107–200.

42. Lake, *Plato, Philo, and Paul.* cf. 11; Remsburg, *The Christ*, 493–95.

> Jacob Bryant, who endeavored to prove, from their resemblance to passages in the New Testament, that Philo was a Christian, forgetting that Philo's works were mostly written when Jesus was a child and a youth, and that he never once mentions Jesus or Christianity. It must not be forgotten that Philo lived in Alexandria, not in Judaea, and that between the Canaanitish and the Hellenic Jews there existed the most bitter hostility, so that—even were the story of Jesus true—it could not have reached Philo before A.D. 40, at which time he was old and grayheaded. We again quote from Mr. Lake's treatise, who prints the parallel passages, and we would draw special attention to the similarity of phraseology as well as of idea.[43]

Table 1, which is modified from Bryant and Lake, exclusively displays points of contact between Philo and the Epistle to the Hebrews. Excerpts from Hebrews are visible in the order of their appearance.

Table 1. *Identity of the Christ of the New Testament with the Logos of Philo*[44]

Philo, describing the Logos, says	Hebrews speaking of Jesus says
'The divine word by whom all things were ordered and disposed.'—De Mundi Opificio.	'By whom also he made the worlds.'—Heb. i. 2.
'The Logos is the image and likeness of God.'—De Monarch.	'The brightness of his (God's) glory, and the express image of his person.'—Heb. i- 3
'The soul of man is an impression of a seal, of which the prototype and original characteristic is the everlasting Logos.'—De Plantatione Noë.	'Christ, the brightness of his (God's) glory, and the express image of his person. —Heb. i. 3.
'The Logos supports the world, is the connecting power by which all things are united.'—De Profugis.	Upholding all things by the word of his power.'— Heb. i. 3.
'The Logos is superior to the angels.'—De Profugis.	'Being made so much better than the angels. Let all the angels of God worship him.'—Heb. i. 4, 6.
'The Logos was eternal' —De Plant. Noë.	But to the Son he saith, Thy throne, O God, is for ever and ever.'—Heb. i. 8.
'The Logos is superior to all beings in the world.'—De Leg. Allegor.	'Thou hast put all things in subjection under his feet.' —Heb. ii. 8.

43. Besant, *Free-Thinker's Text Book Part II Christianity*, 366–67.

44. Besant, *Free-Thinker's Text Book Part II Christianity*, 367–72.

Philo says that the Logos is the true High Priest, who is without sin and anointed by God :—	The New Testament speaks of Jesus as the High Priest:
'It is the world, in which the Logos, God's First-born, that great High Priest, resides. And I assert that this High Priest is no man, but the Holy Word of God; who is not capable of either voluntary or involuntary sin, and hence his head is anointed -with oil.'—De Profugis.	'Seeing then that we have a great High Priest that is passed into the heavens, Jesus, the Son of God, let us hold fast our profession.'— Heb. iv. 14. 'For such an High Priest became us, who is holy, harmless, undefined, separate from sinners.'—Heb. vii. 26.
Philo mentions the Logos as the great High Priest and Mediator for the sins of the world. Speaking of the rebellion of Korah, he introduces the Logos as saying :—	The New Testament speaks of Jesus as the High Priest:
'It was I who stood in the middle between the Lord and you.	'We have such an High Priest, who is set on the right hand of the throne of the majesty in the heavens, a mediator of a better covenant.'—Heb. viii. 1—6.
'The sacred Logos pressed with zeal and without remission that he might stand between the dead and the living. —Quis Rerum Div. Haeres.	'But Christ being come an High Priest. . . . . entered at once into the holy place, having obtained eternal redemption for us.—Heb. ix. 11, 12.
'The Logos is free from all taint of sin, either voluntary or involuntary.'—De Profugis.	'The blood of Christ, who offered himself without spot to God.'—Heb. ix. 14.
'Those who relinquish human doctrines, and become the well-disposed disciples of God, will be one day translated to an incorruptible and perfect order of beings."—De Sacrificiis.	'But ye are come unto mount Zion, and to the city of the living God, and to an innumerable company of angels, and to the spirits of just men made perfect.'— Heb. xii. 22, 23.
'The Logos is the shepherd of God's flock. De Agricult.	'The great shepherd of the flock our Lord Jesus.'— Heb. xiii. 20.

The parallels between the Epistle to the Hebrews and Philo cry out for explanation. Several modern authors also discuss numerous parallels between Hebrews and Philo's writings.

In an article titled "Philo and the Epistle to the Hebrews," Robert W. Thurston, a Professor Emeritus of History at Miami University, Ohio, describes how the scholarly pendulum has swung back and forth on the question of whether the author of Hebrews borrowed from Philo, citing the work of Ceslaus Spicq, author of *L'Epitre aux Hebreux* (Paris, 1952), who mounted a cumulative argument for direct borrowing.[45] In contrast, Ronald Williamson, whose study, *Philo and the Epistle to the Hebrews*, reached an opposing conclusion:

> The relationship between Philo and the Christology of Hebrews would be impossible to treat in a short article if it were not for the monumental studies of C. Spicq and R. Williamson. Spicq has carefully cataloged an impressive list of parallels between Philo and Hebrews. So numerous are the parallels that many writers would agree with Spicq's conclusion that the author of Hebrews was well acquainted with Philo's writings, and was perhaps even a convert from Philonism. In Spicq's view, Philo's Logos doctrine underlies the Christology of Hebrews.[46]

But Williamson disagrees. In a thorough and painstaking analysis, he comes to the following conclusions:

1. There is no evidence that a single doctrine in Hebrews is borrowed from, or influenced by Philo. On the contrary, the teaching of Hebrews is in several respects in direct conflict with the teachings of Philo.
2. There is no clear evidence that Hebrews quotes any passage or phrase from Philo.
3. There is no clear evidence that any of the vocabulary of Hebrews is borrowed from Philo.[47]

The conclusion drawn by Thurston is that while the numerous parallels between Philo's terminology and that of Hebrews clearly demonstrate "a relationship between the Logos doctrine of Philo and the Christology of Hebrews . . . there is no evidence that Hebrews borrows doctrines, phrases or vocabulary from Philo."[48]

Why, then, are there so many terminological similarities between these two authors? Thurston suggests that Hebrews was composed to *refute* the heretical views of Christians who based their doctrines on those of Philo and envisioned the Logos as some kind of archangel who had appeared in human form at various times throughout history, including the advent of Jesus. For the author of Hebrews, the problem with Philo's

45. Spicq, "The Epistle to Hebrews," 182. He cites his text *L'Epitre aux Hébreux*, 39–91.

46. Thurston, "Philo and the Epistle to the Hebrews," 133.

47. Williamson, *Philo and the Epistle to the Hebrews*, 133–34.

48. Thurston, "Philo and the Epistle to the Hebrews," 135.

Logos doctrine is that it does not go far enough: "Philo speaks of the Logos as the 'image (eikōn) of God,' but Heb. 1:3 says that the Son is the 'express image (charaktēr) of God.'"[49]

In addition, the author of Hebrews contended that Christian disciples of Philo overlooked the once-and-for-all significance of Christ's death on the Cross: "If the Philonists' Logos Christology had been correct Christ would have needed to suffer many times since the foundation of the world. But this is impossible because 'it is appointed unto man once to die.'"[50] Thurston concludes that there is substantial "evidence suggesting that many statements concerning Jesus in Heb. 1–4 refute a Christology which was based on Philo's Logos doctrine," and that if correct, "the same is true of Hebrews' statements about the Great High Priest . . . But unlike Hebrews, Philo never directly links Melchizedek's name to the term 'Great High Priest.'"[51]

Cockerill devotes six pages to exploring the influence of Neoplatonism on the anonymous author.[52] He comments, "Because of their common heritage in the Hellenistic world Philo can be helpful in understanding Hebrews at the level of semantics and imagery."[53] Readers should consult Cockerill's analysis.

More recently, Kenneth Schenck, who is Professor of Religion at Indiana Wesleyan University, revisited the question of the relation between Philo and Hebrews in his paper, "Echoes of Philo in the Sermon of Hebrews," which was presented to the joint session of the Hebrews/Intertextuality Sections at the 2019 Society of Biblical Literature annual meeting in San Diego. Citing the work of Richard Hays, he distinguishes between an *allusion*, where there are "obvious intertextual references" between a later text and an earlier one, and an *echo*, or a subtler connection in which the writer need not consciously intend to refer to an earlier source but is nonetheless influenced by that source. Schenck states his thesis as follows:

> I am not trying to argue that the author of Hebrews had read the texts of Philo, although it is certainly possible. I am not even arguing that Hebrews is echoing the texts of Philo directly.

49. Thurston, "Philo and the Epistle to the Hebrews," 137.
50. Thurston, "Philo and the Epistle to the Hebrews," 142.
51. Thurston, "Philo and the Epistle to the Hebrews," 140.
52. Cockerill, *The Epistle to the Hebrews*, 28–34.
53. Cockerill, *The Epistle to the Hebrews*, 31.

An echo can be indirect. The texts of Philo may very well have left artifacts in the oral culture of Alexandria. In an oral culture, surely we should consider echoes of orality to be genuine echoes just as much as echoes of literary texts. Do we find in Hebrews echoes, perhaps unintentional, perhaps unconscious, to the language of Philo? . . .

> The cumulative effect of the linguistic parallels between Hebrews and Philo seems too great not to conclude that there are echoes of Philo's Alexandria in this sermon. The meanings that Philo gave those words differed significantly from the author of Hebrews, but the preponderance of parallel is there.[54]

Grindheim's conclusion bears consideration:

> There are also many other points of comparison between the author of Hebrews and Philo of Alexandria. In the history of New Testament interpretation, the predominant view has been that the author knew and had been influenced by Philo's thought even though he did not share all his views . . .
>
> While there are no clear examples of borrowing from Philo, there are a number of similarities between the two, similarities that require an explanation . . .
>
> If the author of Hebrews did not know Philo or his works personally, he had likely been influenced by a tradition that had much in common with Philo. It is plausible, therefore that the author's background was in Alexandria.[55]

Readers must ultimately judge the similarities for themselves and decide whether they are the result of a coincidence or Philo's direct or indirect influence.

Finally, readers must read Deuteronomy 13 and judge whether the author of Hebrews' theological goals conflict with God's operator manual:

> 6 If your brother, the son of your mother, or your son or your daughter or the wife you embrace or your friend who is as your own soul entices you secretly, saying, 'Let us go and serve other gods,' which neither you nor your fathers have known, 7 some of the gods of the peoples who are around you, whether near you or far off from you, from the one end of the earth to the other, 8 *you shall not yield to him or listen to him*, nor shall your eye pity him, nor shall you spare him, nor shall you conceal him. (Deut. 13: 6–8, ESV)

54. Schenck, "Echoes of Philo in the Sermon of Hebrews?," 2.

55. Grindheim, *The Letter to the Hebrews*.

4.10 The Author's Lack of Qualifications and the Need for Skepticism

What are the author's qualifications to write Hebrews, which Christians accept as Scripture? The author's exegesis of Genesis 14 and Psalm 110 reflects his high Christology. However, this raises many questions. Did the author know the Hebrew language? What was the author's knowledge of the Torah? Was he a rabbi? Was he a convert? Where did its author obtain his information? Was he a prophet? Was his information a revelation? If so, was it from God, Jesus, or an angel? Or is the author's composition the product of his own imagination, interpretation, and understanding of the Hebrew Bible (not the Septuagint)? If the latter, what was his hermeneutical methodology, and what makes his interpretation correct? If not, moreover (and again, it requires asking), when and where did the information come from? Under what conditions was the information received? Do the teachings in Hebrews conflict with God's operator manual, the Hebrew Bible? Suppose the answer to this question is affirmative. Why should people ignore God's operator manual (see Deut. 4:2)? Presumably, skeptics and detractors will respond that Hebrews is unconvincing, whereas Christians will believe. The following is a verse-by-verse analysis of select verses from Hebrews, primarily chapter 7.

HEBREWS 5:6, 10, AND 6:20

On three occasions prior to chapter 7, the author refers to Jesus as "a priest forever after the order of Melchizedek":

> Heb. 5:6 as he says also in another place, "You are a priest forever, after the order of Melchizedek" (ESV).
>
> Heb. 5:10 being designated by God a high priest after the order of Melchizedek (ESV).
>
> Heb. 6:20 where Jesus has gone as a forerunner on our behalf, having become a high priest forever after the order of Melchizedek (ESV).

The phrase "a high priest forever after the order of Melchizedek" carries profound significance in our exploration. Since we have already explored its translation and meaning in previous discussions, we will not rehash those details here. Instead, we will engage with and interact with Hebrews chapters 7, 8, and 13.

HEBREWS 7:1

> 1 For this Melchizedek, king of Salem, priest of the Most High God, met Abraham returning from the slaughter of the kings and blessed him. (ESV)

F.F. Bruce comments:

> In order to draw out the significance of Christ's being acclaimed as perpetual high priest "after the order of Melchizedek," our author goes back from his text, Ps. 110:4, to the only other place in the Bible where Melchizedek appears, the story of Abraham's rout of the four invading kings from the east (Gen. 14). From the part played by Melchizedek in that narrative, it will be shown how aptly he prefigures the high priesthood of Christ.[56]

The author of Hebrews opens chapter 7 with several vague references, which warrant careful examination:

1. *For this Melchizedek*: Is this a person's name or a title? Academics argue that Melchizedek is not a personal name but rather a title (a king of righteousness, a member of a royal priestly family). Like *Avimelech* (Judges 8:31), *Melchizedek* is a title, not a personal name. According to the Jewish oral tradition (Genesis Rabbah 46:7; Nedarim 32b), he is Shem, the youngest son of Noah.
2. *King of Salem*: (a) Was Salem Jerusalem, (b) a city distinct from Jerusalem, (c) a geographic location near Shechem, or (d) a city in the region of Shechem?
3. *Priest of the Most High God*: Who or what was this God?
4. *Met Abram from the slaughter of the kings and blessed him*: Is Genesis 14:18–20 a historical event or a literary insertion?

Notably, the name and titles of Melchizedek in Hebrews 7:1 are taken directly from Genesis 14:18. Harold Attridge points out that "Hebrews ignores the next portion of the verse, which describes Melchizedek's offering the bread and wine."[57] Ronald Williamson opines, "But no doubt the Writer of Hebrews, in a section in which he is showing Melchizedek's superiority to Abraham, did not wish to mention an incident—Melchizedek ministering to Abraham's needs—which could have been construed

56. Bruce, *The Epistle to the Hebrews*, 156–57.
57. Attridge, *Hebrews: A Commentary*, 188.

otherwise."[58] Specifically, Genesis 14:18 mentions that Melchizedek brought bread and wine and ministered to Abram's needs. Gerald Kennedy offers three explanations for the actions taken:

1. Melchisedech "brought forth bread and wine" to feed Abram and his weary warriors.
2. Melchisedech "brought forth bread and wine" to sacrifice them in thanksgiving for Abram's God-given victory over the four kings.
3. Melchisedech "brought forth bread and wine" not only for the refreshment of Abram and his weary warriors but also to thank God for the victory over the four kings.[59]

Kennedy devotes pages 19 through 41 to providing a detailed analysis of these options. Incidentally, from a rabbinic vantage, the wine in Genesis 14:18 is given a variety of symbolic interpretations in the Midrash. Grypeou and Spurling identify and discuss three: (1) it reflects aspects of Temple worship, (2) it symbolizes the Torah (knowledge), and (3) it prefigures the Israelites' oppression in Egypt, predicted in Genesis 15:13.[60]

HEBREWS 7:2

> 2 and to him Abraham apportioned a tenth part of everything. He is first, by translation of his name, king of righteousness, and then he is also king of Salem, that is, king of peace. (ESV)

William L. Lane comments on this verse (with a response):

1. and to him, Abraham apportioned a tenth part of everything: A topic of academic dispute. The word "he" is unidentifiable.
2. by translating of his name, king of righteousness: A topic of academic dispute. Are these words a name or title? What does the name/title mean?
3. and then he is also king of Salem: Was Salem (a) Jerusalem, (b) a city distinct from Jerusalem, (c) a geographic location near Shechem, or (d) a city in the region of Shechem?

58. Williamson, *Philo and the Epistles to the Hebrews*, 445; cf. Koester, *The Anchor Yale Bible*, 339.

59. Kennedy, "St. Paul's Conception of the Priesthood," 23.

60. Grypeou and Spurling, *The Book of Genesis in Late Antiquity*, 213.

4. that is, king of peace: A topic of academic discussion. This name is presumably a prefiguration of the promised Messiah.[61]

For reasons unknown, the author of Hebrews incorrectly refers to Abram as Abraham, a name he receives many years after meeting Melchizedek. This practice continues in Hebrews 7 (vv. 1, 2, 4, 5, 6, 9). Mason comments that the author "refers to the patriarch anachronistically as . . . Abraham, matching the Septuagint's spelling in the subsequent chapters of this changed name."[62] Mason elucidates, "Though the patriarch is still named Abram in Gen 14 he does not become Abraham until Gen 17:5, the author of Hebrews always refers to him as Abraham, as do most Second Temple Jewish writers who retell this encounter."[63] However, here, too, the author omits material from Genesis 14:19, in which Melchizedek blesses Abram. In verse 2, the author presents the etymology of Melchizedek's name. Although the name probably means "my king is Zedek," the author interprets it as "king of righteousness."[64] Attridge points out, "Zedek is the name of a Canaanite deity."[65]

HEBREWS 7:3

> 3 He is without father or mother or genealogy, having neither beginning of days nor end of life, but resembling the Son of God he continues a priest forever. (ESV)

Fred Horton comments:

> The reason for this strange interpretation of Melchizedek in Gen. xiv. 18–20 is almost universally said to be because of Melchizedek's sudden appearance in Gen. xiv and his almost sudden disappearance. He is tied to no family tree nor are his parents mentioned. No account is given of his birth or of his death. Strack-Billerbeck note that for the Rabbis what is not said in the Torah is just as important for Rabbinic exegesis as what is

61. Lane, *Hebrews 1–8*, 164.

62. Mason, *You Are a Priest Forever*, 26.

63. Mason, *You Are a Priest Forever*, 139n1.

64. Attridge, *Hebrews: A Commentary*, 189; cf. Kennedy, "St Paul's Conception of the Priesthood," 6.

65. Attridge, *Hebrews: A Commentary*, 189.

> said, and the principle is given a Latin formulation: *quod non in thora non in mundo.*[66]

Horton then elaborates, "The author of Hebrews has not selected just any figure without genealogy from the Old Testament; rather, the first priest on earth is not given any genealogy in the Torah . . . but for the first priest such omissions take on significance."[67] This essential verse requires extensive analysis.

The following discussion of Hebrews 7:3 is a lengthy one divided into seven sections:

a. Strack and Billerbeck's exegetical principle: what the scholars say.
b. Strack and Billerbeck defend their thesis.
c. Problems with Strack and Billerbeck's analysis.
d. "Without father, mother, or genealogy": is this a literal or figurative description, and what does it mean?
e. "Like unto the Son of God": what does this phrase mean?
f. Invoking Melchizedek to explain how Jesus, a member of the tribe of Judah, could be a priest.
g. The priesthood of Jesus: a superior priesthood?

These issues warrant careful analysis and a close engagement with the scholarly literature.

(a) Strack and Billerbeck's exegetical principle: what do the scholars say?

Hermann Strack and Paul Billerbeck (S-B), in their text, *Kommentar zum Neuen Testament aus Talmud und Midrasch*, make the following observation:

> 7:3B: Having Neither a Beginning of Days Nor End of Life.
> This is said because in Scripture neither the birth nor the death of Melchizedek is mentioned. Here the principle applies: quod non in thora, non in mundo. Some examples are given here for elucidation.[68]

66. Horton, *The Melchizedek Tradition*, 153. He cites Strack and Billerbeck, *Kommentar zum Neuen Testament*, 694.

67. Horton, *The Melchizedek Tradition*, 160.

68. Strack and Billerbeck, *Kommentar zum Neuen Testament*, 694; Instone-Brewer,

It is important to highlight that Strack and Billerbeck, who are both Lutheran ministers and scholars, are frequently referenced by commentators who engage with a specific principle of Rabbinic exegesis: "*quod non in thora, non in mundo*." This Latin phrase, which was coined by Strack and Billerbeck, translates to "that which is not in the Torah is not in the world."[69] Mikeal Parsons, a professor and the current Macon Chair in Religion at Baylor University, elaborates on this principle:

> Applying the rabbinical principle of exegesis, *quod non in thora non in mundo* (Literally. 'that which is not in the Torah, is not in the world'), the reader may logically deduce from the silence of the scripture that this first priest has neither father, nor mother, nor genealogy, but 'continues, as a priest forever.'[70]

Luke Timothy Johnson, a professor of New Testament and Christian origins at Candler School of Theology, comments:

> Whereas a present-day reader might take the narrative silence as an indication of a discrete source inserted into the ancient text, our author follows the interpretive principle that has been called *non in tora* [sic] *non in mundo* . . . Thus if Scripture does not report on his ancestors, Melchizedek had none. The reader may conclude that he is without human antecedent. But Hebrews goes further. Neither does Scripture report him as having a 'beginning of days or an end of life' . . . The reader can therefore conclude further that Melchizedek had no natural birth (beginning of days) and did not die (end of life). Melchizedek is somehow, by Scripture's own implicit testimony, eternal.[71]

Karen H. Jobes, Professor Emerita of New Testament Greek and Exegesis at Wheaton College and Graduate School in Wheaton, Illinois, clarifies the meaning of this term:

> In the ancient world, there was a Jewish exegetical technique referred to as *non in thora non in mundo* ("not in the Torah, not in the world"). This Latin phrase refers to the interpretive technique—which may seem very odd to our modern sensibilities—that was based on the idea that if the Torah (in this case, Genesis) was silent about something (in this case, the birth and death of Melchizedek), then that "thing" could be understood

"Introduction to the English Translation," xxi–xli.

69. Or, in other words: "What the Torah doesn't mention, doesn't exist."

70. Parsons, "Son and High Priest," 213.

71. Johnson, *Hebrews: A Commentary*, 177.

> not to exist (in this case, that Melchizedek hadn't been born or died) for interpretative purposes.[72]

Jannes Reiling, a theologian and leader of the Union of Baptist Churches in the Netherlands, writes:

> Since nothing of this is transparent in Gen 14 these qualifications may have been deducted *e silentio*, according to the rule *quod non in thora non in mundo*.[73]

Brian C. Small, in *The Characterization of Jesus in the Book of Hebrews* declares:

> Scholars are divided over whether the author of Hebrews was influenced by contemporary speculation about Melchizedek, regarding him as a type of supra-human or heavenly being or whether he was simply basing his argument on the scriptural passage by employing the rabbinic technique of the argument from silence, *quod non in thora est non in mundo*, "what is not in the Torah is not in the world."[74]

Paulus Jinu Kim observes:

> The Levitic priests are not eternal, but Melchizedek is eternal (vv. 3, 8). "There is no day to begin, no end of life" this developes [sic] another the fact in the principle of 'quod non in thora, non in mundo'. The fact that there is no mention of the birth or death of Melchizedek in the Torah means that Melchizedek did not die or had not been born. Based on this interpretation, the Hebrew author allows readers to form a consensus on the eternity of Melchizedek.[75]

Deborah Rooke adds in a footnote:

> "This is usually interpreted as an example of the exegetical principle that even silence is significant in the prophetic word of God — *quod non in thora non in mundo*."[76]

72. Jobes, *Letters to the Church*.
73. Reiling, "Melchizedek," 562.
74. Small, *The Characterization of Jesus in the Book of Hebrews*, 169n48.
75. Kim, "Antitype of Jesus Christ," 6.
76. Rooke, "Jesus as Royal Priest: Reflections on the Interpretation," 85.

In his work, *The Melchizedek Tradition: A Critical Examination of the Sources to the Fifth Century A.D. and in the Epistle to the Hebrews*, Fred Horton explains the exegetical significance of the principle:

> Strack-Billerbeck note that for the Rabbis what is not said in the Torah is just as important for Rabbinic exegesis as what is said, and the principle is given a Latin formulation: *quod non in thora non in mundo*.[77]
>
> For the Jewish exegete of the first century B.C., however, the fact that Melchizedek is the first priest mentioned in the Torah would be of great moment. Applying now the principle *quod non in thora non in mundo* to this dictum produces the exegetical result that there was no priest at all before Melchizedek or he would have been mentioned.[78]

Samuel Sandmel, in a dated but oft-cited article in the *Journal of Biblical Literature*, observes the limitations of Strack-Billerbeck's five-volume commentary, which merits consideration:

> What shall we make of the five immense books which constitute the Strack and Billerbeck *Kommentar zum Neuen Testament aus Talmud und Midrasch*? Let us grant that it is a useful tool. So is a hammer if one needs to drive nails. But if one needs to bisect a board, a hammer is scarcely useful. I would state here that NT scholars devoid of Rabbinic learning have been misled by Strack-Billerbeck into arrogating to themselves a competency they do not possess."[79]

To his credit, David Instone-Brewer, a former Baptist minister, Cambridge scholar, and Honorary Research Fellow in Rabbinics and the New Testament at Tyndale House, engages with the S-B controversy. In his introduction, he discusses multiple crucial topics: Historical Background, Potential Misuse, Scholarly Warnings, Lutheran Bias, the Importance of Dating, and the Usefulness of Strack-Billerbeck.[80]The reader must recognize these important arguments.

Other writers caution their readership about this text and the interpretive principle coined in Latin by Strack and Billerbeck. James W. Thompson warns:

77. Horton, *The Melchizedek Tradition*, 153.

78. Horton, *The Melchizedek Tradition*, 153, 157.

79. Sandmel, "Parallelomania," 8–9.

80. Instone-Brewer, "Introduction to the English Translation," xxi–xli.

> Interpreters have frequently observed that the claim that Melchizedek was 'without father, without mother, without genealogy' is an example of the author's use of a rabbinic interpretative principle that later interpreters called *quod non in Thora, non in mundo* (What is not in the Torah is not in the world), a common argument from the silence of scripture. *However, the author's use of these terms reflects more than an appeal to the silence of scripture, for he employs this interpretation to develop a theme that is important to him.*[81] (Italics for emphasis)

Sung Jin Park is Dean of Asian Studies and associate professor of Biblical Studies at Midwestern Baptist Theological Seminary. He cautions:

> "Due to Strack-Billerbeck's book, *Kommentar zum Neuen Testament aus Talmud und Midrasch*, this rabbic [sic] maxim has been quite widespread in the hermeneutics of this day. *However, there is still much debate about its application.*"[82] (Italics for emphasis)

Jack Kilcrease notes:

> Many commentators have connected this statement to the rabbinical interpretative principle: '*Quod non in thora, non in mundo*' ("what is not in Torah, is not in the world"). [Then, in a footnote, Kilcrease quotes Scott Hahn. "Scott Hahn argues that *it is not a genuine rabbinical interpretative technique.*"][83] (Italics for emphasis)

Scott Hahn, an American Catholic theologian, Christian apologist and a former Presbyterian minister, addresses the topic in a must-read, three-paragraph discussion that has been praised for its diligent analysis:

> Most Scholars believe the author is arguing here from the supposed rabbinical dictum that "Quod non in thora, non in mundo," literally, "what is not in the Torah, is not in the world." What the Torah doesn't mention, doesn't exist. Therefore, since the Torah does not record Melchizedek's birth, death, or lineage, he must be without ancestors and eternal, and therefore like Jesus.
>
> However, there are two major difficulties with this common view. First, "Quod non in thora, non in mundo," is not a genuine rabbinic interpretative principle—as one might gather from the fact that it is given in Latin, hardly the original language of

81. Thompson, *Hebrews*, 147.

82. Park, "Melchizedek as a Covenantal Figure."

83. Kilcrease, *Self-Donation of God*, 89n62.

> the Rabbis. It is an unfortunate phrase, invented by Strack and Billerbeck, which actually misdescribes the hermeneutical principles at work in the rabbinic texts to which it is applied, Neither the rabbis nor the Jewish tradition in general ever argued from the absence of a thing in Scripture to its absence in reality.
>
> Second, "being without father or mother or genealogy "would not suffice to make Melchizedek similar to Jesus. Jesus had "father and mother and genealogy" (cf. Matt 1:1–17; Luke 3:23–28); in fact, a few verses later the author will mention Jesus' Judahite lineage (7:14). Moreover, we have already seen how the author's application of the royal Davidic psalms to Jesus presumes Jesus' Davidic descent. Were the author here to suggest that Jesus' human descent from David was somehow unreal, it would undermine his assumption that Jesus fulfills the promises to the Davidic heir.[84]

In contrast, George Guthrie, Professor of New Testament at Regent College in Vancouver, Canada, subtly refrains from directly engaging with the well-known principle, *Quod non in thora, non in mundo*. Nonetheless, his words warrant careful consideration:

> The writer finds what the Old Testament narrative does *not* say especially relevant for his argument. Following a common exegetical practice known as 'argument from silence,' the author capitalizes on Genesis 14's lack of any reference to Melchizedek's ancestry, birth, or death. He has obviously drawn out from the narrative an interpretation which does not appear on the surface in the Genesis account."[85]

Is Strack and Billerbeck's principle, *Quod non in thora, non in mundo* ("What the Torah doesn't mention, doesn't exist") a valid one, or is it nothing more than an illicit argument from silence? Let us examine the arguments Strack and Billerbeck make in defense of this principle.

(b) Strack and Billerbeck defend their thesis

After introducing Hebrews 7:3B, Strack and Billerbeck devote two pages to their principle (in the original German), quoting an excerpt from the Talmud which employs hermeneutics to argue that until Abraham's time, the biblical patriarchs did not show any visible signs of aging.

84. Hahn, *Kinship By Covenant*, 301.

85. Guthrie, *The Tyndale New Testament Commentaries*, 253–54.

> Bava Metzia 87a
>
> § The Gemara continues discussing Abraham: *Until Abraham, there was no aging,* i.e., old age was not physically recognizable. Consequently, *one who wanted to speak to Abraham* would mistakenly *speak to Isaac,* and vice versa: An individual who wanted to speak *to Isaac* would *speak to Abraham,* as they were indistinguishable. *Abraham came and prayed for mercy, and aging was* at last noticeable, *as it is stated: "And Abraham was old, well stricken in age"* (Genesis 24:1), which is the first time that aging is mentioned in the Bible.
>
> *Until Jacob, there was no illness* leading up to death; rather, one would die suddenly. *Jacob came and prayed for mercy, and illness was* brought to the world, allowing one to prepare for his death, *as it is stated: "And one said to Joseph: Behold, your father is sick"* (Gen. 48:1), which is the first time that sickness preceding death is mentioned in the Bible. *Until Elisha, one did not fall ill and then heal, as everyone who fell ill would die. Elisha came and prayed for mercy and he was healed, as it is written: "Now Elisha fell ill with his illness from which he was to die"* (2 Kgs 13:14). *By inference,* one can derive that *he* had previously *fallen ill* with *other illnesses* from which he did not die.[86]

Strack and Billerbeck continue with a lengthy paragraph about sickness and death entering the world. They go on to cite a midrash that declares the war between Abraham and the four kings of Genesis 14, which is the first war mentioned in the Bible, to be the earth's first war.

> TanchụmaB Lech Lecha § 7 (32B): "Their sword will pierce their own heart" (Ps 37:15): this refers to the four kings, Amraphel and his companions (Gen 14), for until now there had not been any war in the world, and they came and made a beginning with the sword; as it says, "And it happened in the days of Amraphel when they began to wage war" (so Gen 14:1, 2 is cited). God said to them, "You godless, you have made a beginning with the sword; the sword shall pierce the heart of these men (i.e., your heart), as it says, 'Their sword will piece their own heart' (Ps 37:15)." Immediately Abraham rose up against them and killed them, as it says, "And he split up against them in the night" (Gen 14:15).—Since there is no mention of military battles before Gen 14 in Scripture, it is inferred that the battle mentioned in

86. English from The William Davidson digital edition of the Koren Noé Talmud.

> Gen 14 was the first war that raged on the earth. ‖ For further examples, see TanchB Noach § 20 (23B); Chayei Sara § 5 (59B).[87]

Several errors are committed by Strack and Billerbeck and those who cite them to support the claim that for the Rabbis, what is *not* said in the Torah is just as crucial for Rabbinic exegesis as what *is* said. Strack and Billerbeck refer to this maxim as a "principle." As previously mentioned, they provide a Latin formulation: *quod non in thora non in mundo*. However, is there such a principle in Rabbinic exegesis, as they claim?

(c) Problems with Strack and Billerbeck's Analysis

To begin, Strack and Billerbeck claim this concept of Rabbinic exegesis is a *Grundsatz* = Principle. A "principle" is *used to refer to a rule or standard. Again, no specific principle, rule, or standard exists, saying,* "What is not in the Torah is not in the world." *Some Christian commentators question this claim or statement (see above-quoted commentators). Moreover, in no manner can section 7:3B be categorized as a principle. The writers provide several examples from the Talmud and Midrash about* "Neither a Beginning of Days Nor an End of Life." The examples are about (1) old age, (2) suffering, (3) sickness, (4) curable sickness, and (5) the first war.

In addition, Strack and Billerbeck point out that Esther had neither father nor mother (Esther 2:7 and the Midrash 93B; see *A Commentary on the New Testament from the Talmud & Midrash*, p. 694). However, Jewish literature does not claim that she had no beginning. Instead, the Midrash unequivocally states Esther was an orphan. *Esther's father died during her mother's pregnancy, and the latter died during childbirth* (*Esth. Rabbah* 6:5; BT Megillah 13a). Therefore, she had a father and mother.

In addition, there are multiple examples in the Bible with "omissions" that, by analogy, contradict the alleged principle. However, they are frequently ignored and omitted by commentators.[88] Examples include the following cases:

1. There is no mention of Melchizedek being married; therefore, should readers presume he was not married?

87. Strack and Billerbeck, *A Commentary on the New Testament from the Talmud & Midrash*, Volume 3, 1304/1808 (2021 Longarino translation).

88. See Hahn, *Kinship by Covenant*, 301; Kilcrease, *Self-Donation of God*, 89n62; Thompson, *Hebrews*, 147.

2. There is no mention of Melchizedek performing sacrifices; therefore, should readers presume he never performed sacrifices?
3. There is no mention of Melchizedek having a beard; therefore; should readers presume that he was clean-shaven?
4. There is no mention of Melchizedek changing his clothes; therefore, should readers presume that he never did?
5. There is no mention of Melchizedek falling sick; therefore, should readers presume that he was never ill?

Moreover, Strack, Billerbeck, and many other Bible commentators fail to engage with the traditional Jewish rules of exegesis (hermeneutics). These rules are (1) the Seven Rules of Hillel (Baraita at the beginning of Sifra and Avot de-Rabbi Nathan 37), (2) the Thirteen Rules of Rabbi Ishmael, and (3) the Thirty-Two Rules of Rabbi Eliezer (or Eleazar) ben Jose. Nowhere does the specific principle 'that which is not in the Torah, is not in the world' appear in these texts. Notably, Strack and Billerbeck discuss and enumerate these rules of interpretation in their text. However, Strack, Billerbeck, and other commentators neglect to engage with these rules in their discussion of Hebrews 7:3. Scott Hahn argues that this hypothesis originates from the Strack-Billerbeck commentary on the New Testament and that it *is not a genuine rabbinical interpretive technique*.[89]

Strack, Billerbeck, and many commentators fail to explain to their readers the difference between *aggadah*, *haggadah*, and *halakah* as it relates to "Neither a Beginning of Days Nor an End of Life." They do not engage with this specific topic or the genre of Midrash. Nevertheless, Strack and Billerbeck frequently provide their readers with examples of *aggadah* rather than *halakah*. Moreover, in the Introduction to Volume 1, they extensively interact and engage with these topics. Craig Koester cites Strack and Stemberger, saying, "Rabbinic sources argue from silence most often in *haggadic* or homiletic exegesis rather than the halakhic or legal exegesis."[90] Rabbi Abraham Joshua Heschel says, "Aggadah is the expression of man's ceaseless striving that often defies all limitations."[91] The examples S-B cited from the Talmud (BM 87a) exemplify *aggadah*!

89. Hahn, *Kinship by Covenant*, 301.

90. Koester, *The Anchor Yale Bible*, 348n217. Here he cites Instone-Brewer, "Introduction to the English Translation," xxi–xli.

91. Heschel, "Halakhah and Aggadah."

Definitions of *aggadah* abound in the literature. Philip Birnbaum provides the following definition:

> AGGADAH, or *Haggadah* (narration), includes everything in Talmudic literature that is *not* of a legal nature, such as descriptions of historical events and legends, proverbs and aphorisms that illustrate moral duties, and scientific data concerning medicine, mathematics, astronomy, physiology, botany and other branches of knowledge.[92]

The Jewish commentary Chabad.org observes:

> *Aggadah:* (lit. "lore or narrative"); the portions of the Talmud and Midrash which contain homiletic expositions of the Bible, parables, stories, maxims, etc., in contradistinction to Halachah.[93]

The Encyclopedia Judaica explains:

> The term *aggadah* itself is notoriously difficult to define . . .
> The *aggadah* comprehends a great variety of forms and content. It includes narrative, legends, doctrines, admonitions to ethical conduct and good behavior, words of encouragement and comfort, and expressions of hope for future redemption. Its forms and modes of expression are as rich and colorful as its content. Parables and allegories, metaphors and terse maxims; lyrics, dirges, and prayers, biting satire and fierce polemic, idyllic tales and tense dramatic dialogues, hyperboles and plays on words, permutations of letters, calculations of their arithmetical values (*gematria*) or their employment as initials of other words (*notarikon*)—all are found in the *aggadah*. "Whatever the imagination can invent is found in the *aggadah*, with one exception: 'mockery and frivolity'" (Zunz), the purpose always being to teach man the ways of God.[94]

In Volume 3 of his Introduction to *Commentary on the New Testament from the Talmud and Midrash*, David Instone-Brewer clarifies the distinction between *halakah* and *haggadah*:

> Halakah consists of the debates in a classroom or in a court that are recorded carefully because they become the basis for future debates that eventually become fixed rulings. The rest of rabbinic traditions come under the heading of haggadah—consisting

92. Birnbaum, *A Book of Jewish Concepts*, 16.
93. Chabad.org, "Aggadah."
94. Skolnik, "Aggadah or Haggadah," 454.

> of Scripture commentaries, wise sayings, and stories. Portions of haggadic material occur within the Talmud just as halakhic excerpts are cited in commentaries.[95]

Moreover, many apologists, commentators, and theologians neglect to inform to their readers that many commentators consider the Epistle to the Hebrews, specifically Hebrews 7:3, to be a midrashic analysis (genre). In contrast, Attridge writes:

> The present chapter consists of an explanation of the significance of that verse and its characterization of Christ's priesthood. Formally *the chapter is another midrash* on a scriptural text, like those encountered earlier in Hebrews [cf. 2:5–9 and 3:7—4:11], although different interpretative techniques are in evidence.[96] (Italics added)

In a similar vein, William Lane states in *Hebrews 1–8*:

> *Homiletical Midrash. Homiletical midrash* refers to the interpretation of the biblical text in the event of preaching. Its function was to bring the text into the experience of the congregation. It involved making the Scriptures contemporary so that they could no longer be regarded as a record of past events and sayings but a living word through which God addressed the audience directly. Hebrews provides a series of illustrations of this dynamic approach to Scripture (see on 2:5–9; 3:7—4:13; 6:13–20; 7:11–25; 8:7–13; 10:5–10, 15–18, 35–39; 12:5–13, 25–29). So important is this approach to the OT text in Hebrews that it is given extended treatment in the following section, discussing Hebrews and Judaism . . .
>
> The writer elaborated upon this thesis through the interpretation of Scripture and by the appeal to the reality of the Christian experience. The development in Hebrews conforms to the Judaic tradition of *homiletical midrash*, in which key phrases of an extended quotation from Scripture are taken up and expounded for the congregation (e.g., 2:5–9; 3:7b–4:11; 8:6–13; 10:15–18; 12:26–29). This approach to Scripture, which was developed in the homiletical tradition of the synagogue, served to bring the text into the experience of an audience through preaching.[97] (Italics added)

95. Instone-Brewer, "Introduction to the English Translation," xxi–xli.

96. Attridge, *Hebrews: A Commentary,* 186.

97. Lane, *Hebrews* 1–8, cxxvii; cf. Cockerill, "The Melchizedek Christology," 290–307; Manson, *The Epistle to the Hebrews*, 12.

In contrast, Steyn refers to parts of the Epistle to the Hebrews as a commentary, exposition interpretation.[98]

Many commentators avoid frank discussions about exegesis and eisegesis, neglecting to clarify the all-important difference between the two. So, what is the difference? Claude Mariottini, a retired Professor of Old Testament at Northern Baptist Seminary, explains:

> Eisegesis is the approach to Bible interpretation where the interpreter tries to "force" the Bible to mean something that fits their existing belief or understanding of a particular issue or doctrine. People who interpret the Bible this way are usually not willing to let the Bible speak for itself and let the chips fall where they may. They set off with the up-front goal of trying to prove a point they already believe in, and everything they read and interpret is filtered through that paradigm. Stated another way, they engage in what the Bible refers to as "private interpretation."[99]

Jay G. Williams, writing in the journal *Theology*, puts it more succinctly:

> Exegesis is legitimate interpretation which "reads out of" the text what the original author or authors meant to convey. Eisegesis, on the other hand, reads into the text what the interpreter wishes to find or thinks he finds there. It expresses the reader's own subjective ideas, not the meaning which is in the text.[100]

Readers must consider whether the author of Hebrews employs exegesis or eisegesis when interpreting Genesis 14:18–20 and Psalm 110. For example, Attridge notes, "The writer of Hebrews brings a '*playful exegetical argument* to demonstrate the superiority of Melchizedek and, by implication, Christ to the Levitical priests.'"[101] (Italics for emphasis)

(d) "Without Father, Mother, or Genealogy": Is this a Literal or Figurative Description and What Does it Mean?

An important question for readers is whether the author of Hebrews intends for Hebrews 7:3 to be understood figuratively or literally. Steyn suggests that the author of Hebrews was either unaware of or did not

98. Steyn, "A Quest for the Assumed LXX," 24, 116, 131, 136, 217, 222.

99. Mariottini, "Republicans v. Democrats."

100. Williams, "Exegesis-Eisegesis," 218.

101. Attridge, *Hebrews: A Commentary*, 1265.

accept the tradition presented in *2 En*och. It states that Nir, the son of Lamech, was Melchizedek's father, and Sothonim was his mother. He writes:

> There is another interesting account, particularly regarding Melchizedek's miraculous birth, in the pseudepigraphical apocalyptic book of *2 En.* 71–72 (ca. late 1st cent. A.D.). This is the far-fetched story of a child who is born at age three and fully clothed. Nothing in this regard is found in Heb 7. In fact, the author of Hebrews makes exactly a point that his father and mother and his beginning is unknown (Heb 7:4 sic high priest)[102]

Unpacking this loaded verse, readers must ask whether the author meant figuratively or literally that Melchizedek was:

1. without a father, without a mother
2. without genealogy
3. having neither beginning of days nor end of life
4. made *like unto* the Son of God
5. abiding as a priest continually.

F.F. Bruce states unequivocally:

> When Melchizedek is described as having "neither father nor mother, without genealogy," and having "neither beginning of days nor end of life, it is not suggested that he was a biological anomaly or an angel in human guise. Historically, Melchizedek appears to have belonged to a dynasty of priest-kings in which he had both predecessors and successors."[103]

Instead, he elaborates that Melchizedek "is a fitting type of Christ" and "made conformable to the Son of God." William Lane points out a possibility that "the writer is developing a hellenistic mythological concept of a supra-human figure endowed with a mysterious heavenly origin."[104] He elaborates that the author of Hebrews provides no hint that Melchizedek is regarded in mythological terms.

Craig R. Koester minces no words, declaring, "Hebrews' insistence that Melchizedek has no father, mother or genealogy (Heb. 7:3) runs counter to tendencies in Jewish exegesis."[105] He elaborates:

102. Steyn, "A Quest for the Assumed LXX," 220, 225.

103. Bruce, *The Epistle to the Hebrews*, 159–60.

104. Lane, *Hebrew* 1–8, 165.

105. Koester, *The Anchor Yale Bible*, 339.

> Second, the author makes an argument from silence. Since the Bible makes no mention of Melchizedek's parentage, the author contends that Melchizedek has no mother, no father, and no genealogy (7:3a). Remarkably, this could actually *discredit* Melchizedek, since someone 'without father' would have been considered illegitimate, someone 'without mother' would probably have been a foundling or a child of a woman of very low status, and a person 'without 'without genealogy' would have been disqualified for service as a priest (NOTES on 7:3). From a human point of view, the author's claims seem to contradict the call to 'see how great' Melchizedek is (7:4).[106]

Donald Hagner, too, is blunt in his analysis:

> The statement in verse 3 that Melchizedek was "without father or mother or genealogy, and has neither beginning of days nor end of life" sometimes has misled readers into assuming that Melchizedek was eternal and thus represented an appearance of the preincarnate Christ to Abraham. These words merely mean, however, that in contrast to typical kings, for whom we generally possess careful documentation, in the case of Melchizedek, we have no records of his genealogy, birth, or death . . . The effect of all the information available about Melchizedek is to give the impression that he is without beginning or end, and thus to underline that his priesthood is without end.[107]

Philip Hughes agrees with Bruce and other scholars:

> The description *without father or mother or genealogy*, accordingly, should not be taken literalistically to mean that Melchizedek had no parents or family, nor does the statement that he had *neither beginning of days nor end of life* intend us to understand him as an eternally existent being who experienced neither birth nor death. The point is that these assertions apply positively to Christ, not to Melchizedek. The significance of the biblical silence is that it marks Melchizedek out as a type who in these respects resembles the Son of God, who alone exists everlastingly, from eternity to eternity. Surrounded by this silence, Melchizedek is the figure, but Christ is the reality. The incarnate Son, it is true, insofar as he was one with us in our humanity, had a human mother and a human genealogy (cf. Mt. 1:1ff.; Lk. 1:26ff.; 3:23ff.; Rom. 1:3), and a human birth as well as a human

106. Koester, *The Anchor Yale Bible*," 348.

107. Hagner, *Encountering the Book of Hebrews*, 99–100.

> death (of which our author has much to say). But as the Son of God he is eternally the same and his years will never end (Heb. 1:12; 13:8).
>
> The silence of Genesis 14 regarding the origin and termination of Melchizedek's life and any priestly succession is typological, too, in that it gives the impression of a continuous and uninterrupted priesthood, which again finds its fulfilment in the messianic antitype, who, in accordance with the declaration of Psalm 110:4, *continues a priest for ever.* His priesthood, as our author will shortly explain, is characterized by "the power of an indestructible life" (v. 16); it does not pass from him to others "because he continues for ever" (v. 24).[108]

Matthew Emadi, writing in *The Southern Baptist Journal of Theology*, concurs with Bruce and Hughes. He states:

> According to Hebrews 7:3, Melchizedek is "without father or mother or genealogy, having neither beginning of days nor end of life, but being similar to the Son of God, he remains a priest for all time" (7:3). The language of this verse does not have to be taken to mean that Melchizedek was pre-existent (without beginning of days) and that he never died (without end of life). In that case, we would assume that the author of Hebrews believed that Melchizedek was either the pre-incarnate Christ, still alive on earth somewhere, or taken into heaven without seeing death. Instead, Hebrews 7:3 is simply a description of the manner in which Melchizedek appears and disappears in the Genesis narrative. Melchizedek has no genealogical record—no record of father, mother, birth, or death. His undefined ancestry is stunning since every significant person in Genesis has a genealogical history. Unlike the Levites, his priesthood is not attached to a specific tribe and unlike the Levites, he holds his office of priesthood permanently.[109]

Paul Davidson elaborates on the significance of verse 3 for his readership. He writes:

> What qualifies Jesus to be a member of Melchizedek's priesthood? Because he is like Melchizedek, "without father, without mother, without genealogy, having neither beginning of days nor end of life" (Hebrews 7:3). He is eternal and immortal, unlike other priests. Thus, Christians are able to live under a new

108. Hughes, *A Commentary on the Epistle to the Hebrews*, 248–49.

109. Emadi, "You Are Priest Forever," 75–76.

law mediated by a new high priest in a temple superior to the one on earth.

This concept is developed further in Hebrews 7.

Gerald Kennedy poses an interesting question:

> Why did he veil his origin and his demise and that of the Sacred Word with scarcely four verses? Since we are unable to fathom the mind of God, we are unable to answer the questions which we pose for ourselves . . . However, in light of the verse three b, we are given some enlightenment by St. Paul for he writes that Melchisedech was "likened to the Son of God." In the design of Providence, the author of Genesis omitted mentioning his family background and the matters of his birth and death because the Holy Spirit so willed it . . . While it is true that St. Paul took advantage of the silence of Sacred Scripture regarding these things, he must have had a motive for doing so . . . It would seem more logical to conclude that he was inspired in order to provide a more complete picture of the type in view of the antitype.[110]

Jerome Neyrey, S.J., focuses on the Graeco-Roman background relating to the language and concepts in Hebrews 7:3. He writes:

> Paraphrased in terms of Greek philosophy, the author states three things of Melchizedek: he is (1) ungenerated, (2) uncreated in the past and imperishable in the future, and (3) eternal or immortal . . . The author of Hebrews inflated the character of Melchizedek in 7:3 beyond anything found in Scripture or midrash, so as to make comparable statements about Jesus, who is unquestionably acclaimed a divine figure in Hebrews. Thus the author supplies specific content to his acclamation of Jesus as a deity, for like true gods he is fully eternal.[111]

Neyrey's inquiry focuses on the phrase "without father or without mother or genealogy." He says that references to this phrase occur less frequently in the literature. However, Neyrey's research has uncovered evidence from ancient Greek sources that a true deity can be "both 'without father' and 'without mother.'" Moreover, he adds that it is not unusual to find a claim that a deity is self-begotten.[112] In any case, Matthew 1 and Luke 1 refute the claim made in Hebrews 7:3 that Melchizedek resembles the Son of God in not having a father or mother. According to

110. Kennedy, "St. Paul's Conception of the Priesthood," 84.
111. Neyrey, "Without Beginning of Days," 440.
112. Neyrey, "Without Beginning of Days," 444.

these gospel passages, Jesus had a mother, Mary. Moreover, Melchizedek is depicted in Hebrews 7:3 as having never been "born" or "begotten" and being ever-present. Once again, this is at variance with what the gospels tell us about Jesus.

(e) "Like unto the Son of God": What Does This Phrase Mean?

The phrase "like unto" or "resembling" the Son of God is significant and requires clarification. Brown observes, "It is not Jesus who resembles Melchizedek, but Melchizedek who resembles the Lord Jesus."[113] Adrian Giogiov writes:

> Melchizedek derives his pattern from the preexistent Christ, not Christ derives his pattern from Melchizedek. 'It was Melchizedek who was like the preexistent Son of God, and not Christ who was like Melchizedek' (Trentham 1972: 52). Hebrews 7:3 clearly states that Melchizedek was 'made like unto the Son of God'. It is not saying that the Son of God was made like unto Melchizedek.

The explanation depends on the theological assumption that Jesus, as the Son of God, was preexistent. This assertion is neither verifiable nor falsifiable.

Continuing in verse 3, the author makes Melchizedek eternal. King Melchizedek, unlike Jesus, is eternal and immortal. However, according to the Christian Bible, Jesus had a beginning (he was "begotten") and an end: "he gave up the ghost" (Luke 23:46). Bruce Demarest explains: "The fact of the absolute eternity of the Melchizedekian order of the priesthood was stated by the author in ch. 5:10 and 6:20 and is now worked out in detail in chapter 7 (vss. 1–3, 8, 16, 17, 21, 24, 25, 28). Thus, the *eternity* of the priestly dignity of Melchizedek and his antitype Christ constitutes the single great theme of Hebrews 7."[114] Since only God has no "beginning of days," it is clear that the author is making this king equal to God. In a detailed article in *The Catholic Biblical Quarterly*, Neyrey elaborates:

> When Hebrews describes Melchizedek as having "neither beginning of days nor end of life," it speaks a language in which true deities were commonly described, namely, full eternity both in the past and imperishability in the future. True deities

113. Brown, *The Message of Hebrews*, 129.

114. Demarest, "Hebrews 7:3: A Crux Interpretum," 12.

> are defined in contrast with mortals; they are uncreated and eternal, whereas mortals come into being and pass out of existence. Hence, gods must be truly eternal, eternal in the past and imperishable in the future. This concept, while clear and consistent, is expressed in the literature in many different linguistic configurations.[115]

Neyrey proceeds to enumerate eight characteristics of a true god, including various forms of eternity in the past and imperishability in the future. He concludes by saying, "They testify to popular, widespread *topoi* on the deity's full eternity. Hence, when Heb 7:3 speaks of a figure as having 'no beginning and no end,' this formula immediately and necessarily suggests that such a figure must be divine, a true god."[116]

Jane Allison elaborates:

> Using the Alexandrian style of exegesis, the author now makes use of the silence of scripture with regard to Melchizedek's death to infer that he has never died but has become a figure of the eternal priest. For us it is a difficult and convoluted step . . . It is no more than a step used in the typology to prefigure Jesus, who has been raised to God's right hand through his resurrection and is now the supreme and eternal priest. For the author, the silence of Genesis 14 at this point justifies the use he is making of Psalm 110.[117]

In a similar vein, George Guthrie observes:

> It is when the writer bases his exposition on the silence of Scripture that his method of exegesis seems strangest to modern readers. Because there is no mention of the origin or death of Melchizedek in the Genesis account, the writer deduces that *He is without father or mother or genealogy*."[118] (Italics in the original.)

Neyrey goes on to explain the phrase 'remaining forever' (7:24) when referencing Jesus. The author's usage of this phrase is crucial in its relationship to the priesthood. This statement about Jesus' "permanent priesthood" perfectly contrasts with that of the Levitical priesthood. Neyrey says they are "prevented by death from remaining in office" (7:23;

115. Neyrey, "Without Beginning of Days," 441.

116. Neyrey, "Without Beginning of Days," 445.

117. Allison, "A Study of the Priestly Christology of the Epistle to the Hebrews," 103.

118. Guthrie, *The Tyndale New Testament Commentaries*, 156.

see 7:15–16). Therefore, "remaining forever" is the opposite of perishing or dying.

Neyrey continues by saying:

> And, so when the author describes Melchizedek as 'remaining forever' (7:3), this too, must be understood in terms of some sort of deathlessness, imperishability, unchangeableness, and eternity, all characteristics of a true god . . .
>
> When the author of Hebrews says of the figure in 7:3 that he "remains forever," he is using a commonplace or *topos* [topics] about the future eternity of a true god.[119]

Neyrey concludes, "When the descriptions of Melchizedek in Heb. 7:3 are understood against this background, they immediately and cogently suggest that we are hearing popular and common descriptions of a true god."[120] His article is required reading. The theological claims in Hebrews 7 are unverifiable and are *arguments from silence*. Numerous commentators openly acknowledge or discuss the author employing this approach in Hebrews 7: 14, 20, and elsewhere.[121]

Many Christian commentators misapply Genesis 14:18–20 and Psalm 110:4 due to the genealogical context.[122] Nowhere in the Hebrew Bible does it say Melchizedek had no parents. Not even the Jewish commentator Philo made the claim that Melchizedek had no parents. In contrast, Hebrews 7:3 reads, "He is without father or mother or genealogy, having neither beginning of days nor end of life, but resembling the Son of God he continues a priest forever" (ESV). Moreover, the author provides no supporting evidence for his claim that Melchizedek (1) had no biological parents, (2) no genealogy, (3) no beginning, (4) neither a beginning of days nor an end of life, (5) but resembling the Son of God, and (6) he continues as a priest forever. These claims are *ad hoc*, unverifiable, and tantamount to an argument from silence. However, Matthew 1 and Luke 1–2 report (a) Jesus had a mother and (b) a genealogy.

Allison clarifies the significance of lacking a genealogy. She writes:

119. Neyrey, "Without Beginning of Days," 445–46

120. Neyrey, "Without Beginning of Days," 448.

121. Allison, "A Study of the Priestly Christology of the Epistle to the Hebrews," 103; Attridge, *Hebrews: A Commentary*, 187; Granerød, "Melchizedek in Hebrews 7," 195, 201.

122. Sigal, *The Jew and the Christian Missionary*, 104–6, 284–85.

> Moreover, the first priest was clearly non-Levitical and this fact is used to legitimize the non-Levitical descent of Christ which may have been an acute stumbling block for the Jewish Christians to whom he writes. This partly explains the stress in chapter 7 on Melchizedek's lack of genealogy. Melchizedek has nothing at all of the familial requirements for priesthood and can therefore foreshadow one who does not have them either.[123]

Melchizedek was *not* part of a succession of many priests, and neither was Christ.

Koester points out a negative aspect of the phrase "without genealogy." He notes:

> The lack of a known genealogy was a liability for Israel's priests, who were to be descendants of Levi (Num 3:10, 15–16) through proper marriages (Lev 21:7, 13–15; Ezek 44:22; Josephus, *Ag. Ap.* 1:30–36). Those who could not demonstrate their genealogy were disqualified (Ezra 2:62; Neh 7:63–65; 2 Chron 31:17–19; Josephus, *Ant.* 11.71).[124]

The next phase in verse 3 that deserves attention is "*but resembling the Son of God*" (ESV). Guthrie elaborates, "The word translated resembling (*aphomoiomenos*) occurs only here in the New Testament. It is a suggestive word, used in the active of 'a facsimile copy or model' and in the passive of 'being made similar to.'"[125]

Koester writes, (1) "the verb 'made like' indicates a close relationship" and (2) "The direction of thought is important: the Son of God is not like Melchizedek; rather, Melchizedek is like the Son of God, who is the principal reality (Bengel)."[126] The claim that Melchizedek resembles the Son of God by being a priest forever is a theological opinion and unverifiable. Bible translations vary:

> King James (AV or KJV): Without father, without mother, without descent, having neither beginning of days, nor end of life; *but made like unto the Son of God*; abideth a priest continually.
>
> New King James Version (NKJV): without father, without mother, without genealogy, having neither beginning of days nor end of life, *but made like the Son of God*, remains a priest continually.

123. Allison, "A Study of the Priestly Christology of the Epistle to the Hebrews," 101.

124. Koester, *The Anchor Yale Bible*, 343.

125. Guthrie, *The Tyndale New Testament Commentaries*, 157.

126. Koester, *The Anchor Yale Bible*, 343.

> English Standard Version (ESV): He is without father or mother or genealogy, having neither beginning of days nor end of life, *but resembling the Son of God* he continues a priest forever.
>
> International Standard Version (ISV): He has no father, mother, or genealogy, no birth date recorded for him, nor a date of death. *Like the Son of God*, he continues to be a priest forever.

In a similar vein, Mason translates the passage, '*was made to resemble the Son of God*' (Heb. 7:3).[127] Hahn comments that if the author of Hebrews equates Melchizedek with Shem, the resemblance lies in the duration of their shared ministry. "Melchizedek-Shem serves for centuries, Jesus for eternity."[128] However, observant readers will notice that the author omits to mention that in this respect, Melchizedek does *not* resemble the Son of God.

A notable contradiction exists here. Paul Ellingworth comments, "[b]ut unlike Melchizedek, his [Jesus'] descent from Judah is common knowledge."[129] However, the author of Hebrews states categorically that Jesus has a genealogy: "For it is evident that our Lord was descended from Judah, and in connection with that tribe Moses said nothing about priests" (Heb. 7:14, ESV). However, the author says earlier, "He is without father or mother *or genealogy*, having neither beginning of days nor end of life" (Heb. 7:3, ESV). In addition, the lines of Mary and Joseph are in Matthew 1 and Luke 2. Through Joseph's lineage, Jesus descended from King David (Luke 3:23–38). The typical apologetic is that Joseph adopted Jesus, and Joseph was from the tribe of Judah. However, the onus is on apologists to prove that Joseph adopted Jesus. Nowhere in the New Testament does it provide overt evidence that Jesus was adopted.

However, another rationalization centers on a levirate marriage (Deut. 25:5–6). In this specific situation, his deceased brother's widow (sister-in-law) produces a child for his deceased sibling. Significantly, the Torah requires that the firstborn child of the levirate marriage be a part of the genealogy of the man who died childless. The problem with this apologetic is obvious. A levirate marriage has nothing to do with the situation dealing with Jesus.

Another distracting argument is that when a man dies without a son and only has daughters, his family line can continue through his

127. Mason, *You Are a Priest*, 202.

128. Hahn, *Kinship By Covenant*, 303.

129. Ellingworth, *Epistle to the Hebrews*, 365.

daughters. This situation occurred when Zelophehad's daughters petitioned Moses in Numbers 27 (Num. 27:4–8). Moses received instructions stating that a father's name and lineage could be established through his daughter, and her inheritance would become part of her husband's tribe if she married outside of her father's tribe. However, this situation has no relevance to Jesus.

The last phrase in verse 3 is crucial. '*What did the words "priest forever after the order of Melchizedek" mean to the psalmist who wrote them?*'" On four occasions, the author refers to Jesus as "a priest forever after the order of Melchizedek":

> Heb. 5:6 as he says also in another place, "You are a priest forever, after the order of Melchizedek" (ESV).
>
> Heb. 5:10 being designated by God a high priest after the order of Melchizedek (ESV).
>
> Heb. 6:20 where Jesus has gone as a forerunner on our behalf, having become a high priest forever after the order of Melchizedek (ESV).
>
> Heb. 7:17 For it is witnessed of him, "You are a priest forever after the order of Melchizedek" (ESV).

William Lane elaborates on this key concept:

> The term τάξις here and in 5:10; 6:20; 7:11, 17 is commonly understood in the sense of "order" or "succession" (RSV: "after the order of Melchizedek"; NEB: "in the succession of Melchizedek"). In the strict sense of the term, however, there is no succession to Melchizedek (cf. 7:3, 8). Two priests, Melchizedek and Christ, do not make up a succession. Nor does the writer of Hebrews emphasize the idea of rank (cf. Moffatt, "with the rank of Melchizedek"). He uses the term τάξις to convey the same meaning as when it is said that Melchizedek is "like the Son of God" (7:3) or that Christ is "like Melchizedek" (7:15).[130]

Once again, readers come to the crucial and essential words that have generated so much controversy, the expression in Psalm 110:4b, commonly translated as "You are a priest for ever after the order of Melchizedek." It was common in the ancient world for a king to be referred to as a priest. The idea that Melchizedek's priesthood was "lasting" or "everlasting" is perhaps connected to his progeny, as it was in the

130. Lane, *Hebrews* 1–8, 109.

Assyrian kingship ritual.[131] The king's sons were also seen as priests, and thus, it could be said that (through the king's family line) he was a "lasting priest" or an "eternal priest."

The word "forever" in Hebrews 7:3 stands on the shoulders of Psalm 110:4. The crucial Hebrew word, *olam*, is translated as "forever." Gerald Sigal elaborates:

> The Hebrew term *le 'olam*, commonly rendered in English as "forever" is not necessarily always synonymous with "eternal." It is frequently used with the meaning "for a very long time," or "for an indefinite period," or as in the verse under discussion [Psalm 110:4], to indicate the normal life-span of an individual (cf. Exodus 21:6). Thus, "You are a priest forever" means that David discharged certain priestly functions during his lifetime.[132]

In *The Anchor Bible Dictionary*, Harold W. Attridge remarks that the author of Hebrews cites Psalm 110:4 (Hebrew 7:17), "the use of which verse is unattested elsewhere in the NT or in other early Christian literature not dependent on Hebrews."[133] Writing in the *Westminster Theological Journal*, M.J. Paul offers the following thoughts for consideration:

> The words *'al- dibrātî are* difficult to translate. Other places where this expression is used do not contribute much towards a better understanding of it. In Job 5:8 the meaning of *dibrat* is "cause" "lawsuit." And in Eccl 3:18 and 8:2 the meaning is "with regard to," "because of," and in Eccl 7:14 "so that." The LXX has: *kata tēn taxin;* the Vg: *secundum ordinem;* Aquila and Symmachus: *kata logon;* the Syriac version: *badmūteh,* "in the likeness of." So the old translations differ slightly from each other, but not very much. Some modern translators propose different solutions . . . M. J. Dahood gives—as is his custom—a very radical change: "You are a priest of the Eternal according to his pact. His legitimate king, my lord, according to your right hand." All these new solutions are not very convincing. It seems best to adhere to the Masoretic tradition, affirmed by the ancient versions.[134]

131. Dick quotes an Assyrian enthronement ritual in which it is said "May your priesthood and the priesthood of your sons be favorable." See Dick, "The Neo-Assyrian Royal Lion Hunt," 251.

132. Sigal, *The Jew and the Christian Missionary*, 105.

133. Attridge, *Hebrews: A Commentary*, 101.

134. Paul, "The Order of Melchizedek," 202–3.

Hahn suggests an alternative translation for the common phrase, "priest forever." "Accordingly, we suggest . . . 'continually.' Melchizedek was not immortal but remained a priest for the duration of his life."[135]

> Now this chapter will deal with what is meant by this order of Melchizedek. Sometimes it is said that the specific meaning of this phrase lies in the union of the functions: You king, are a priest for ever, as was the matter by Melchizedek. Against this interpretation the fact must be taken into account that the expression "after the order of Melchizedek" is connected only with the priesthood. It appears to be a qualification of this as opposed to other forms of priesthood such as the Levitical priesthood. Therefore, some exegetes stress the words "in eternity." Then *v* 4 says: Your priesthood shall last eternally, as was the case with Melchizedek. But the difficulty of this explanation is that, in the OT, Aaron's priesthood is connected with eternity as well. In Exod 29:9 Moses is ordered to ordain Aaron and his sons: "the priesthood shall be theirs by a perpetual statute." Exod 40:15 speaks about "a perpetual priesthood throughout their generations." The same is expressed in Num 25:13 and 1 Sam 2:30. In these four instances the qualification "perpetual" or "eternal" is connected with the generations and not with one person. Should the words "in eternity" express something about the specific character of the Melchizedek priesthood, it follows that the notion of eternity is concerned with a single person: this priest-king shall be priest for ever, If the descendants are included in the eternal aspect of his priesthood then there is no difference between his and Aaron's priesthood.[136]

Next, Paul engages with the expression "after the order of Melchizedek." After noting that this phrase is only connected with the priesthood, he points out that commentators stress the words "in eternity." However, this fact creates a fundamental contradiction. Paul mentions that in the Hebrew Bible, "Aaron's priesthood is connected with eternity as well." Several verses support this argument:

1. Exod. 29:9 and you shall gird Aaron and his sons with sashes and bind caps on them. And the priesthood shall be theirs by a statute forever. Thus you shall ordain Aaron and his sons.

135. Hahn, *Kinship By Covenant*, 303.

136. Paul, "The Order of Melchizedek," 203.

2. Exod. 40:15 and anoint them, as you anointed their father, that they may serve me as priests. And their anointing shall admit them to a perpetual priesthood throughout their generations.
3. Num. 25:13 and it shall be to him and to his descendants after him the covenant of a perpetual priesthood, because he was jealous for his God and made atonement for the people of Israel.
4. 1 Sam. 2:30 Therefore the Lord, the God of Israel, declares: 'I promised that your house and the house of your father should go in and out before me forever,' but now the Lord declares: 'Far be it from me, for those who honor me I will honor, and those who despise me shall be lightly esteemed.' (ESV)

Paul elaborates:

> In these four instances the qualification "perpetual" or "eternal" is connected with the generations and not with one person. Should the words "in eternity" express something about the specific character of the Melchizedek priesthood, it follows that the notion of eternity is concerned with a single person: this priest-king shall be priest for ever. If the descendants are included in the eternal aspect of his priesthood then there is no difference between his and Aaron's priesthood.[137]

(f) Invoking Melchizedek to Explain How Jesus, a Member of the Tribe of Judah and Could be a Priest

Readers will undoubtedly recall that David belonged to the tribe of Judah. *Therefore, neither he nor his posterity could ever be Levitical priests.* The reason is simple: God ordained that the Levitical priesthood was restricted exclusively to the tribe of Aaron (Levi). Crucially, "David or one of his descendants might only become a priest of a priesthood other than that of Aaron."[138] For example, C.E. Armerding suggests that there may have been several coexisting "orders" of priesthood in ancient Israel.[139] Of course, this hypothesis is unverifiable and unfalsifiable. Nevertheless, readers will be cognizant of the reality that there presumably existed many different "types" of priests within the numerous kingdoms,

137. Paul, "The Order of Melchizedek," 203–4.
138. Paul, "The Order of Melchizedek," 204. Italics added.
139. Amerding, "Were David's Sons Really Priests?" 75–86.

city-states, states, villages, and tribes in the ancient Near East during the time of Abram.

Notably, Melchizedek was not a descendant of Aaron (from Levitical line), yet he was a priest. Therefore, according to Scripture, Melchizedek was a priest of a priesthood *other* than that of Aaron. If Melchizedek belonged to some other type of priesthood, what was it? If Jesus belonged to some other type of priesthood, what was it? In reality, believers in Jesus are placing their faith in a mystery and an argument from silence.

Readers should recall that, according to Matthew and Luke, Jesus did *not* have a biological father. Fitzmyer asks, "How could Melchizedek be called *kohen*, 'a priest', and a 'priest of the Most High God', when there was no record of his genealogy in the OT?"[140] Hebrews answers this question by claiming that Melchizedek was without a father, mother, or genealogy. Therefore, he could become a priest of a priesthood *other than Aaron by using exegetical gymnastics and engaging in theological contortionism.* These exegetical gymnastics were the invention of the author of Hebrews, who did so by deploying an argument of silence. Walter Brooks, writing in the *Journal of Biblical Literature,* reconstructs the author's argument:

> Jesus' priesthood is based on a life that cannot end ([Heb.] 7:16), on a life that makes him the fulfillment of the Melchizedek type. The phrase . . . [*kata dynamis akatalytos zoe* = "*according to the power of an indestructible life*"] suggests that the priesthood of Jesus, in which our author is interested, is not the priesthood of Jesus' earthly life but that priesthood into which he entered at the moment of the resurrection when he triumphed over death, and entered into an "indestructible," hence endless life . . .
>
> Jesus then is an eternal priest from the moment of his resurrection-exaltation because he possesses from that moment a life that does not end . . . The priesthood of Christ, however, is not of this world but of the eternal world where he is "a minister in the sanctuary and the true tent, which is set up not by a man but by the Lord" (8:2).[141]

The theological gymnastics and contortionism contained in the above passage by Brooks require careful deconstruction:

1. How does Brooks know Jesus' priesthood is based on a life that cannot end?

140. Fitzmyer, "Melchizedek in the MT, LXX, and the NT," 66.

141. Brooks, "The Perpetuity of Christ's Sacrifice," 206–7.

2. How does Brooks know Jesus is a priest "in the same way as" Melchizedek?
3. How does Brooks know Melchizedek's priesthood is superior to that of Levi?
4. How does Brooks know Jesus experienced a resurrection?
5. How does Brooks know Jesus became an eternal priest from the moment of his resurrection-exaltation?
6. How does Brooks know Jesus possesses from the moment of his resurrection-exaltation a life that does not end?
7. How does Brooks know the priesthood of Christ is not of this world?
8. How does Brooks know Jesus is a priest forever and his sacrifice must correspond to his priesthood?

Most of Brooks' statements are unverifiable claims contradicted by academics or those on the opposite side of the religious aisle. Readers must decide if they accept Brooks' interpretation of Scripture.

On a side note, many first-century Jewish people would have questioned the claims of Jesus to be the Messiah. He did not fit the biblical requisites or the expected mold. The Bible requires direct patrilineal descent from David to become a Jewish king. Here, too, from the perspective of skeptics and detractors, the author of Hebrews employs biblical gymnastics in an ingenious endeavor to explain how Jesus can be both the Messiah and high priest, even if he has no patrilineal lineage.

(g) The Priesthood of Jesus: A Superior Priesthood?

Another crucial point to understand relates to a secondary reason why the author and most Christians believe Jesus' priesthood is superior to the Levitical priesthood. Bible commentators offer various rationales for this belief. A good summary of these rationales is in the writings of Robert Bellarmine, SJ (1542–1621), an Italian Jesuit and a cardinal of the Catholic Church. He received canonization as a saint in 1930. Bellarmine was also named a Doctor of the Church, one of only thirty-seven. Additionally, he was one of the most influential figures in the counter-reformation movement. In his classical *Commentary on the Psalms*, he identifies five reasons why the priesthood of Melchizedek was superior to that of Aaron:

1. Melchizedek succeeded no one, and no one succeeded him.
2. Melchizedek was both a king and a priest; Aaron was only a priest.
3. Melchizedek sacrificed bread and wine; Aaron sacrificed sheep and oxen.
4. Melchizedek was a priest of humanity; Aaron was a priest of the Israelites.
5. Melchizedek required neither a tent nor a tabernacle nor a temple for sacrifice; Aaron did.[142]

Mason writes, "Furthermore, Jesus' priesthood is eternal, his atoning sacrifice is final and all-sufficient, and his sanctuary is true and abiding."[143] This argument is patently fallacious:

1. If Jesus is the final and all-sufficient sacrifice, then (i) why will the sacrificial system be restored in the messianic age, as instructed by God through the prophet Ezekiel, and (ii) why will "the Messiah"—named "the Prince"—bring a sin sacrifice on behalf of himself and the nation (Zech. 14:21; Isa. 56:7; 60:7; Jer. 33:17–18; Ezek. 43:22–23; 45:17; Hos. 3:3–4; Zeph. 3:10; Zech. 14:21; Mal. 3:1–4)?
2. Jesus could not have died on the cross for *another* person's sin(s) (Ezek. 18:20). Scripture states that "The soul who sins will die. The son will not suffer for the iniquity of the father, nor will the father suffer for the iniquity of the son. The righteousness of the righteous man shall be upon him, and the wickedness of the wicked shall be upon himself" (ESV).
3. Jesus could *not* have been a final and all-sufficient sacrifice (offering) because of his multiple blemishes. He was:
    a. beaten by the men who were guarding him before his trial with the Jewish leadership (Luke 23:63);
    b. spit upon during his trial (Mark 14:65; Matt. 26:67);
    c. beaten and slapped while in the custody of the chief priests (Mark 14:65; Matt. 26:67, 68; John 18:22);

142. Bellarmine, *A Commentary on the Psalms*, 354. Note: Psalm 109, verse 4]; modified from Kennedy, "St. Paul's Conception of the Priesthood," 95.

143. Mason, *You Are a Priest*, 39; see also 191.

d. flogged and scourged as commanded by Pilate before his crucifixion by the soldiers (Mark 15:15; Matt. 27:26; John 19:1);

e. crowned with thorns (Mark 15:17; Matt. 27:29; John 19:2) that presumably punctured his scalp;

f. spit upon after a thorn of crowns was placed on his head (Mark 15:19; Matt. 27:30); either hit on the head with a staff (Mark 15:16; Matt. 27:30) or struck in the face (John 19:3); and

g. flogged before being sentenced by Pilate (John 19:1) and again after sentencing after the release of Barabbas (Matt. 27:26).

Mason argues that Jesus showed solidarity with God's people (2:5–18). Moreover, he was willing and prepared ('made perfect') to be their compassionate high priest by suffering and experiencing all aspects of the human condition short of the commission of sin (4:14–5:10).[144] This argument is unverifiable, being merely a theological belief and the opinion of the writer. Readers must ask themselves several questions. How was Jesus made the perfect candidate to be the people's compassionate, high priest by suffering and experiencing all aspects of the human condition? If Jesus is fully God and a member of the Trinity (which is unverifiable), why would he need to experience all aspects of the human condition? Would not Jesus have been already perfect? According to Christian theology, Jesus—being one of three persons of the Godhead, yet possessing the fullness of God's nature—was *omniscient.* Therefore, Jesus—being God—did not need to experience what people experienced. He would already know it. Theologians counter that it was the "Son," not the Father or the Holy Spirit, who needed to experience what the people experienced. Readers must decide if this Trinity apologetic is credible.

In a review of Hebrews, Mason provides five examples of Jesus being superior even to things ordained by God. (1) Jesus is superior to the *angels* who delivered the law (1:1–14; cf. 2:2). When, where, and to whom did the angels deliver the law? (2) He is superior to *Moses*, who received and taught *the law* (2:1–4). (3) Jesus is superior to *the law* (nomos) that Moses received and taught. Notably, in contradiction, the Hebrew Bible is unequivocal. The law (*nomos*) Moses received and taught is perfect and eternal (Deut. 31:1; Ps. 19:8; 119:70–72; Prov. 6:23). (4) He is superior to the *priests* who mediated for Israel under the law (7:11–28). Earlier in this chapter, this claim was refuted multiple times. Jesus was not a

144. Mason, *You Are a Priest*, 194.

"priest" (and never said he was a priest, let alone a priest in the manner of Melchizedek), his death could not have taken away sin (since he was blemished and his execution was performed by the wrong people, i.e., the Romans, and at the wrong location, i.e., not in the Temple; i.e., ceremonial), and he did not mediate for Israel. (5) Jesus was a *superior sacrifice.* Jesus was not and could not have been a superior sacrifice. First, Jesus was not from the tribe of Aaron or Levi (hereditary). Furthermore, he was blemished (physical). Third, the means of his crucifixion and death violated the Torah. In addition, the means of his blood offering violated the requisites specified by the Torah. In brief, Jesus failed to meet the priesthood's hereditary, physical, and ceremonial requisites.

Christian theology focuses on typology (types). Types are imaginary, not real. The readers of this book are not a "type." Within the Hebrew Bible, the concepts of "types" does not exist. Significantly, allegory is not "types." Types imply some predictive element or conscious 'foreshadowing.' That is not part of Jewish interpretation.[145]

Melchizedek was *not* a Jewish priest. He was Salem's King, and his priesthood pre-dated Abraham's covenant with God. Therefore, how could a non-Jewish priesthood have anything to do with the Jewish people? The Messiah must be from the tribe of Judah (not Levi). No Jewish priest can also be the rightful Messiah (no person cannot belong to two tribes) without being directly from the tribe of Judah through David and Solomon via patrilineal descent. The anonymous author of Hebrews 7:11 argues that the priesthood of Aaron has been done away with, yet Exodus 40:1–15 states that the Aaronic priesthood is eternal. Some commentators say that the King of Salem bringing bread and wine to Abram foreshadows the Last Supper (and perhaps the Eucharist). However, during Passover, bread is forbidden. In addition, these commentators claim that the wine foreshadows Jesus' blood on the cross. However, the Torah forbids the consumption of blood (Gen. 9:2–4; Lev. 3:17; 7:26–27; 17:10–12, 14; 19:26; Deut. 12:16; 23; 15:23). In Jewish tradition (Ned. 32b), Melchizedek is looked down upon because he blessed Abram *before* blessing God (14:17–20).

The New Testament's Epistle to the Hebrews presents Melchizedek as one who is 'likened to but not equated with' Christ Jesus.[146] Kistemaker emphasizes this point by stating, "Note that Melchizedek is compared

145. Shulman, "Melchizedek as a Type of Moshiach."

146. Bird, "Typological Interpretation Within the Old Testament," 46.

with the Son of God, not the Son of God with Melchizedek."[147] This reality raises several questions. How similar is Melchizedek to Jesus? Is it 95 percent, 90 percent, 80 percent, 70 percent, or 60 percent? Are the similarities between Melchizedek and Jesus physical or spiritual in nature? If they are spiritual, to what degree? Are Melchizedek's office and cultic actions comparable to those of Jesus? If so, to what extent? How does the author calculate and quantify these percentages?

Readers must also consider a question that Christian apologists and Bible commentators often overlook: In what ways is Melchizedek *unlike* Jesus? The differences between the two may outweigh the selected similarities that are highlighted.

At this point, readers might conclude that the functions of Melchizedek's offices closely correspond to or set the pattern for those carried out by the Messiah, who will fill these offices in a later period, which is centered on the concept of the *parousia* (second coming). However, this argument rests on an unverifiable claim. Moreover, there is no connection between Jesus and Melchizedek in the context of redemptive history.

In a dated dissertation, Methodist Reverend Paul Hydon (S.T.B.) identifies numerous problems that readers of Hebrews need to confront:

> Jesus simply does not qualify for a technical, professional and ceremonial priesthood under any circumstances. How then can the author call Jesus a priest and expect anyone who knows priests or knows Jesus to accept him as such, when by all the known standards of priesthood, Jesus does not qualify in the slightest degree?

No one other than the author of the Epistle to the Hebrews of all the early Christian writers has suggested that Jesus might be thought of as a priest. It simply never occurred to them the dissimilarity is so great. This is evidence of the lack of resemblance of Jesus to a priest . . .

> The author is aware of this initial handicap to his case. He admits frankly that Jesus cannot be a priest after any professional order. He makes no effort to fit Jesus into priestly garments to which he is not entitled and which he cannot legally wear . . .[148]

147. Kistemaker, *Exposition of the Epistles to the Hebrews*, 186.

148. Hydon, "The Priesthood of Jesus as Presented by the Epistle to the Hebrews," 152–53.

Hydon poses a rhetorical question: "To what priesthood can he and does he belong?" Jesus must belong to another priesthood since a priest cannot be alone. He must belong to a system. The answer is in Psalm 110.

> Therefore, the author casts around for another priesthood for which Jesus can qualify as a member. The priesthood after the order of Melchizedek seemed made for the order for his purposes . . . It was a priesthood without professional, technical or ceremonial requirements, the only kind of a priesthood which Jesus could belong. The author uses this Melchizedek priesthood as a deus ex machina [(Latin: "god from the machine") a person or thing that appears or is introduced into a situation suddenly and unexpectedly and provides an artificial or contrived solution to an apparently insoluble difficulty.] to resolve the dilemma in which he finds himself."[149]

Hydon devotes the following forty pages to elaborating this thesis. In the final chapter, he makes a striking confession about Hebrews. His words require thoughtful consideration:

> The whole argument rests on assumptions, however, and the use of proof text, which is not sound exegesis or good logic. Even if it could be proved that Jesus is a member of the priesthood after the order of Melchizedek, this does not prove that he could fulfil the priestly services of removing barriers that separate men from God and gaining access for men to God . . .
>
> It becomes evident, therefore, upon examination that the material which the author adduces as proof of his claim that Jesus is a priest is not logical proof but religious confession. It is a "profession of belief" not an expression of reason.[150]

HEBREWS 7:4

> 4 See how great this man was to whom Abraham the patriarch gave a tenth of the spoils! (ESV)

The author of Hebrews 7:4 adds, "See how great this man was to whom Abraham the patriarch gave a tenth of the spoils!" (ESV) Readers should

149. Hydon, "The Priesthood of Jesus as Presented by the Epistle to the Hebrews," 158.

150. Hydon, "The Priesthood of Jesus as Presented by the Epistle to the Hebrews," 198–99.

note that the author employs the name Abraham for Abram. The name Abraham is inaccurate: *in the Genesis 14 narrative mentioning Melchizedek, Abram's name has not yet been changed to Abraham. That happens in Genesis 18. According to the author of Hebrews, Abram/Abraham gave* a tenth *of his spoils* to Melchizedek. F.F. Bruce comments, "The superior greatness of Melchizedek appears in two important aspects: he accepted tithes from Abraham and bestowed his blessing on Abraham."[151] *As many commentators have noted,* the author's argument in verse 4 hinges on one crucial point. Because Melchizedek received an alleged tribute from "Abraham," the father of the Jewish nation, this allegedly demonstrates the superiority of Melchizedek's priesthood to the Levitical line (which came out of the loins of Abraham). (See Gen.14:18–20.) Gerald Kennedy expresses the argument briefly: "If Abraham recognized the superiority of Melchisedech, why should not the Levitical priests who were within his loins as descendants also recognize Melchisedech's superiority?"[152] William Lane *makes the following pertinent comment on Melchizedek*: "Basic to the argument is Abraham's payment of a tithe to him (v 2a; Gen 14:20), which provides historical verification for the greatness of the Salemite priest."[153]

(a) Did Melchizedek Give a Tithe to Abram?

The author of Hebrews assumes that it was Abram who gave a tithe to Melchizedek, but the text of Genesis 14 is ambiguous, and it could have been the other way around. Readers must remember that the Genesis text regarding the gifting and the reception of the tithe is ambiguous. The Hebrew Bible does not explicitly mention whether Abram (later known as Abraham) paid a tithe to Melchizedek in the Genesis narrative (Gen. 14:17–24). However, some interpretations and perspectives suggest that Abram may *not* have paid a tithe to Melchizedek for various reasons. An online search including ChatGPT, Gemini, and Grammarly reveals numerous reasons why, in reality, Abram may *not* have paid a tithe to Melchizedek. The list that follows is an edited and abbreviated summary of these reasons:

151. Bruce, *The Epistle of the Hebrews*, 162.

152. Kennedy, "St. Paul's Conception of the Priesthood," 88.

153. Lane, *Hebrews* 1–8, 167.

1. *No Explicit Mention*: The Genesis account does not explicitly state that Abram paid a tithe to Melchizedek. Some argue that if he did, it would likely have been mentioned.
2. *No Command from God*: There is no explicit command from God for Abram to give a tithe to Melchizedek. Tithing becomes a more formalized practice later in the biblical narrative.
3. *Voluntary Offering*: The interaction between Abram and Melchizedek may have been more of a voluntary offering or a gesture of goodwill rather than a structured tithe.
4. *Unique Circumstances*: The circumstances surrounding Abram's encounter with Melchizedek (rescuing Lot and receiving a blessing) were unique and may not fit the conventional tithe framework.
5. *Pre-Mosaic Law*: Tithing becomes more explicit in the Mosaic Law (Lev. 27:30–32). Since Abram predates the giving of the law, the concept of tithing may not have been established in the similar manner.
6. *Gifts and Booty*: Abram offered a tenth of the spoils of war (booty) to Melchizedek. Some argue that this may have been a one-time offering of gratitude rather than a regular tithe.
7. *Melchizedek's Priesthood*: Melchizedek is often regarded as a priest of the Most High God. Since Abram was already in a covenant relationship with God, some argue that he may not have been required to tithe to Melchizedek.
8. *Different Covenant Dynamics*: The covenant dynamics between Abram and God were unique, and the tithing rules may not have applied in the same manner as they did under the later Levitical priesthood.
9. *Abram's Blessing*: Melchizedek's blessing on Abram (Gen. 14:19–20) may have been seen as a sufficient exchange, and a formal tithe might not have been required.
10. *Silence on Continuation*: The Bible does not record a continued practice of Abram paying tithes to Melchizedek. This absence may suggest that it was a specific event rather than an ongoing practice.
11. *Symbolic Gesture*: Some interpretations suggest that Abram's giving a tenth to Melchizedek was a symbolic gesture rather than a formal tithe. It may have symbolized acknowledgment of Melchizedek's unique status or a recognition of God's sovereignty.

12. *Lack of Instruction*: Since there is no explicit instruction or command from God for Abram to tithe to Melchizedek, some argue that it may not have been a required practice in this particular instance.

(b) Even if Abram Gave Melchizedek a Tithe—Does that Make Melchizedek Greater?

Even supposing that Abram gave a tithe to Melchizedek, this act alone does not demonstrate Melchizedek's superiority. While some Bible commentators and theologians interpret this act as a sign of Melchizedek's superiority to Abram, others argue that there are several alternative explanations, including the following hypotheses: (1) the act exemplified Abram's character traits of generosity, graciousness, hospitality, humility, impartiality, and leadership/diplomatic skills (foreseeing and avoiding a potential future conflict). Gammie's literature review suggests these verses were composed to show that Abram was a man of nobility, generosity, magnanimity, and reverence;[154] (2) Abram was paying Melchizedek a tariff for crossing his land; (3) it was a simple customary act at the time; (4) Abram believed Melchizedek was an angel who had helped him defeat his enemies and release Lot; or (5) Genesis 14:18–20 is an apologetic or literary interpolation (a position argued by many scholars).

The list of possible hypotheses can be expanded even further by utilizing ChatGPT, Gemini, and Grammarly, whose edited proposals are listed below:

1. *Cultural Practice*: Tithing was a common cultural practice in the ancient Near East and was not exclusive to religious contexts. Abram might have given a tithe to Melchizedek as a customary act rather than an acknowledgment of superiority.
2. *Sign of Respect*: Tithing can also be viewed as a sign of respect and recognition of Melchizedek's priestly role rather than an indication of superiority. Abram may have been honoring Melchizedek's position without implying superiority to it.
3. *Recognition of God's Role*: Abram may have given Melchizedek a tithe as a way to acknowledge God's role in his victory. It could have

154. Gammie, "Melchizedek: An Exegetical Study of Genesis 14 and the Psalter," 47.

been a symbolic act of recognition of God's blessing rather than a declaration of Melchizedek's superiority.

4. *No Explicit Statement*: The Bible does not explicitly state that Melchizedek was superior to Abram based on the tithe. The narrative may not have been intended to convey hierarchical relationships between the two.
5. *Unique Circumstances*: The encounter between Abram and Melchizedek occurred in a specific context—after Abram's victory in battle. It might have been a unique situation and not necessarily reflective of an ongoing hierarchical relationship.
6. *Limited Information*: The biblical account provides limited information about Melchizedek's background, making it challenging to draw definitive conclusions about his superiority over Abram.
7. *Abram's Covenant with God*: Abram had a covenant relationship with God, and his obedience to God's commands often guided his actions. The tithe to Melchizedek could be seen within the broader context of Abram's relationship with God.
8. *Priestly Role Only*: Melchizedek is identified as a priest of God Most High, but the narrative does not elaborate on other aspects of his authority or superiority. His role may have been primarily limited to the priestly function.
9. *Abram's Recognition of God's Blessing*: The tithe could have been Abram's way of acknowledging God's blessing in his life, and Melchizedek was the priestly figure present at that moment.
10. *Symbolic Gesture*: Tithing may have been a symbolic gesture without implying a permanent hierarchical relationship. It could be a one-time act with specific significance.
11. *Silence on Melchizedek's Origin*: The Bible remains silent on Melchizedek's genealogy and background. Without a clear understanding of his origin, it is challenging to establish his superiority over Abram based solely on the tithe.
12. *Distinct Roles*: Abram and Melchizedek may have had distinct roles in God's plan, and the tithe could represent an acknowledgment of the complementary nature of their roles rather than a hierarchical relationship.

13. *Melchizedek's Blessing of Abram*: After receiving the tithe, Melchizedek blessed Abram. This act could be interpreted as recognizing God's favor toward Abram rather than asserting of Melchizedek's Superiority.[155]

14. *Precedent in the Bible*: Tithing is not always associated with acknowledging superiority. In other parts of the Bible, people gave tithes without implying submission or inferiority.

15. *Interpretive Diversity*: Biblical scholars and theologians interpret this passage in different ways. Views on the relationship between Abram and Melchizedek vary, and it is essential to consider different perspectives on this topic.

In summary, interpreting the tithe Abram presumably gave Melchizedek requires careful consideration of the cultural, historical, and theological context. While some readers may see it as a sign of Melchizedek's superiority, alternative explanations emphasize cultural practices, symbolic gestures, and the specific circumstances surrounding the event. Readers must ask themselves: does the author of Hebrews make a convincing case in arguing that the fact that Melchizedek accepted tithes from Abram demonstrates that he was greater than Abram?

In addition, readers should be aware that the descriptive term *great* is ambiguous. We must inquire into how Melchizedek was objectively great *and* in what ways he was not. Scripture reports that he was a king and priest. However, there were many king-priests in the ancient Near East when Abram was alive. Moreover, in what category is Melchizedek being judged greater? On a scale of zero to 100, how does Melchizedek's greatness compare to Abram's? The text makes no attempt to answer this question. Here, the author of Hebrews bases his case on unverifiable and unsustainable evidence: an ambiguous passage in Genesis 14:20, which reports that Abram gave Melchizedek one-tenth of the spoils.

F.F. Bruce comments, "And if Melchizedek was greater than Abraham, his priesthood (our author argues) must be greater than a priesthood

155. Kistemaker, *Exposition of the Epistle to Hebrews*, 189, comments that it is fitting that Abraham give a tithe to Melchizedek because "Abraham saw he was God's representative" and "Melchizedek functioned as God's mouthpiece." By extension, presumably Abraham's offering is a logical response to this reminder of divine favor. Kistemaker argues Melchizedek is greater than Abraham. Madsen asks, why did Melchizedek bless Abram, whose God was not the same as his god. (p. 47)

which traces its descent from Abraham."[156] As previously discussed, there exist numerous potential reasons why Abram may have given the tithe, if he gave any at all. Furthermore, to the contrary (see above), even if Abram paid a tithe, it is still not proof that Melchizedek was great, let alone greater than Abram. As a side note, Mitchell remarks on Hebrews 7:4, "It is only here in the NT that Abraham is called a patriarch."[157] However, that word is crucial to Hebrews. As William Lane explains, "the patriarch," placed at the end of the sentence for emphasis, "underscores Abraham's stature as the progenitor of Israel (4 Macc 7:19; 16:23; Acts 7:8–9; cf. Riggenbach, 186). But, Abraham is exalted in v 4 only to emphasize the exalted status of Melchizedek even more."[158]

Bruce is basing his opinion on his interpretation of Hebrews 7:7, which is addressed in the response below. Moreover, he fails to consider how Abram is superior to Melchizedek. He also provides no rationale for why Melchizedek would be viewed as inferior to Abram. In the following verses, the author of Hebrews attempts to demonstrate Melchizedek's superiority over Abram.

(c) Twelve Arguments Suggesting that Abram was Superior to Melchizedek

The comparison between Abram (later named Abraham) and Melchizedek regarding greatness is theological and interpretative. The author of Hebrews argues that Melchizedek is superior to Abram because (1) Abram presumably paid a tithe to Melchizedek, (2) Melchizedek blessed Abram, and (3) Melchizedek lives forever. Now, it is time to investigate a competing hypothesis. How was Abram superior to Melchizedek? To argue that Abram is greater than Melchizedek requires careful consideration of aspects of his life and role in religious history. The Bible portrays Abram and Abraham in many ways as a great figure. The following edited and condensed list is derived from ChatGPT, Gemini, and Grammarly:

1. Abraham is often referred to as the "father of faith." His unwavering trust in God and willingness to follow divine commands, such as the willingness to sacrifice his son, Isaac, demonstrate a level of

156. Bruce, *The Epistle to the Hebrews*, 161–62.

157. Mitchell, *Sacra Pagina: Hebrews*, 140.

158. Lane, *Hebrews* 1–8, 168. (He cites: Riggenbach, *Der Brief an die Hebräer*. 3rd ed. KNT 14. Leipzig: Deichert, 1922.)

faith that has profoundly impacted the development of monotheistic religions. This deep faith sets Abraham apart and underscores his importance in religious history.

2. Abraham is considered the progenitor of the Israelites and, through his descendants, the lineage of the Messiah. In Christianity, Jesus, as the Christ, fulfills the Messianic promise to Abraham, further elevating Abraham's significance in the religious narrative.
3. The covenant God established with Abram, promising him numerous descendants and the land of Canaan, is a central theme in the Bible. This covenant is foundational to the identity of the Jewish people, and its significance extends to Christianity and Islam. The covenant establishes Abraham as a critical figure in the divine plan for humanity.
4. Abraham is described as the friend of God (2 Chron. 20:7; Isa. 41:8; James 2:23). This intimate relationship underscores Abraham's closeness and favor with God, further emphasizing his significance in the religious narrative.
5. Abraham's journey of faith is a recurring theme in the Bible, and his willingness to leave his homeland and follow God's direction him is a testament to his obedience and trust. This act of leaving everything familiar behind, known as the "call of Abraham," marks a pivotal moment in the biblical narrative. It signifies Abraham's readiness to embrace the unknown based solely on his faith in God's promises, showcasing a level of commitment and reliance that sets him apart.
6. The concept of circumcision as a sign of the covenant between God and Abraham further emphasizes his unique status. This ritual, instituted by God as a perpetual covenant, signifies a physical and spiritual mark of separation for Abraham and his descendants. The enduring significance of circumcision in Judaism highlights Abraham's lasting influence on the religious practices of his descendants.
7. The incident of Abraham's willingness to sacrifice his son Isaac, known as the *Akedah*, further emphasizes his greatness. Abraham's obedience and willingness to follow through with such a difficult command illustrate unparalleled devotion and submission to the divine will. This event has profound theological implications, especially in Christianity, where its interpretation foreshadows Jesus' sacrifice.

8. The New Testament further emphasizes Abraham's greatness, particularly in the writings of the apostle Paul. In Romans 4 and Galatians 3, Paul expounds on the importance of Abraham's faith and its connection to the Christian doctrine of "justification by faith alone." Abraham becomes a key figure in Paul's theological arguments, illustrating how his faith foreshadowed the justification that comes through Christ.
9. Recognizing Abraham as a prophet in Islamic tradition adds another layer to his greatness. In Islam, Abraham, known as Ibrahim, is revered as one of the greatest prophets, and his story is in the Qur'an. His unwavering commitment to monotheism, trials, and role in building the Kaaba in Mecca contribute to his significance in the Islamic faith, affirming his enduring impact across multiple religious traditions.
10. The inclusivity of Abraham's blessings is a notable aspect of his greatness. In Genesis 12:3, God promises Abraham, "I will bless those who bless you, and whoever curses you I will curse, and all peoples on earth will be blessed through you." This expansive vision of blessing all peoples emphasizes Abraham's role as a source of blessing for humanity. The universal nature of this promise distinguishes Abraham as a figure whose impact transcends tribal or cultural boundaries, making him a symbol of God's benevolence to all of humanity.
11. Abraham journeyed as a nomad, establishing sacrificial altars (Shechem, Bethel, and Hebron) and holy sites around the future land of Israel. In contrast, Melchizedek remained in one place, Jerusalem.
12. Abraham offers burnt animal sacrifices, while Melchizedek offers Abram bread and wine.

In conclusion, Abram or Abraham's greatness is a multifaceted tapestry woven with threads of faith, obedience, compassion, righteousness, leadership, and intercession. The various episodes and attributes associated with Abraham in the biblical narrative, as well as his recognition of different religious traditions, collectively contribute to his elevated status. These additional aspects deepen the reader's understanding of his character and highlight the enduring impact of his legacy across various dimensions of human experience and spirituality. While Melchizedek holds a unique role as a mysterious priest and king, Abraham's comprehensive impact on the unfolding narrative of religious history establishes him as a figure of unparalleled significance.

(d) Ten Arguments Suggesting that Melchizedek was Inferior to Abram

The author of Hebrews argues that Melchizedek was superior to Abram, later named Abraham. However, a central weakness in this argument is the failure to consider any counterarguments. Skeptics and detractors pose the question: could Melchizedek actually be inferior to Abram and Abraham? The following edited list of arguments that support Melchizedek's inferior status has been compiled from ChatGPT, Gemini, and Grammarly. Readers are encouraged to give these arguments thoughtful consideration:

1. *Less Prominent in Scripture*: Abraham is a central figure in the Bible, while Melchizedek appears sparingly. Some people might argue that this reality suggests a difference in importance.
2. *Melchizedek's Lack of Prominence in Later Scriptures*: Melchizedek is not frequently referenced in subsequent biblical texts, unlike Abraham, who continues to play a significant role in the narrative.
3. *Melchizedek's Lack of Prophetic Role*: Abraham is portrayed as a prophet, receiving direct messages and prophecies from God. On the other hand, Melchizedek does not appear in a similar prophetic role.
4. *No Promised Descendants*: Abraham receives a Divine promise of numerous descendants, while Melchizedek does not receive a similar promise. This lack of future influence might be a sign of inferiority.
5. *Abraham's Covenant Seal*: Abraham receives the covenant seal of circumcision as a physical sign of the covenant. Melchizedek is not associated with a similar tangible symbol.
6. *Not Mentioned in Covenant*: The Abrahamic Covenant, a crucial element in biblical theology, is not directly linked to Melchizedek. This reality could be seen as a sign of Melchizedek's inferior status.
7. *Abraham's Iconic Sacrifice of Isaac*: The willingness of Abraham to sacrifice his son Isaac is a profound and iconic moment in the Bible,

showcasing his faith and obedience in a way that has no parallel in Melchizedek's narrative.

8. *Abraham's Establishment of Altars*: Throughout the biblical narrative, Abraham is depicted building altars as a means of worship and covenant affirmation. Melchizedek is not depicted engaging in a similar practice, reflecting an inferior status.
9. *No Mention of Melchizedek's Faith*: While Abraham's faith is highlighted frequently in the Bible, there is limited information about Melchizedek's faith or relationship with God. This absence might allude to his spiritual deficiencies.
10. *Abraham's Interaction with the Divine Messenger*: In some interpretations, Abraham's encounter with the divine messenger in Genesis 22 is a pivotal moment in his spiritual journey. Melchizedek is not explicitly linked to a similar divine encounter that reflects an inferior status.

In conclusion, Melchizedek's perceived inferiority is multifaceted. Unlike Abram or Abraham, he does not demonstrate faith, obedience, compassion, righteousness, leadership, prophecy, or biblical prominence. The lack of "positive" attributes associated with Melchizedek (an argument from silence) in the biblical narratives collectively contributes to his inferior status. In contrast, Abraham's greatness extends beyond individual episodes, encompassing a rich tapestry that inspires believers across different faith traditions. To illustrate these attributes, Abram/Abraham followed God's order to leave his homeland and father's household (Gen. 12:1), he rescued Lot from four kings (Gen. 14), at the age of 99, he circumcised himself (Gen. 17:24), he pleaded with God to save Sodom (Gen. 18:16–33), he offered Isaac to God as a sacrifice (Gen.22), and he agreed to send Hagar and Ishmael away (Gen. 21). Readers must note that these interpretations can vary widely. The significance and roles of Abram, Abraham, and Melchizedek are subject to diverse theological perspectives and scholarly interpretations.

HEBREWS 7:5

> 5 And those descendants of Levi who receive the priestly office
> have a commandment in the law to take tithes from the people,

> that is, from their brothers, though these also are descended from Abraham. (ESV)

The author of Hebrews is correct when he writes, "And those descendants of Levi who receive the priestly office have a commandment in the law to take tithes from the people, that is, from their brothers, though these also are descended from Abraham." The Torah is unmistakable on this point. The Levitical priests receive tithes from "the people," "their brothers," for their service in the priestly office (Num. 18:21–24). However, this ordained reality does not prove that Melchizedek was superior to Abram. In fact, the Levites were *not* superior to the other members or tribes of Israel. God ordained that they had a differentiated function, but "different" does not entail "greater." Additionally, readers should note that the *kohen*, being from the tribe of Levi, received tithes because God dictated that the descendants would *not* own any land (Num. 18:20; Deut. 10:8–9; 18:1–8; Josh. 13:33). Lastly, Paul Ellingworth points out a paradox: "Those whom the Levitical priests tithe are descendants of Abraham, and so by implication members of God's people, but Melchizedek is not."[159]

HEBREWS 7:6

> 6 But this man who does not have his descent from them received tithes from Abraham and blessed him who had the promises. (ESV)

Verse 6 continues the point made in verse 5. The author correctly reports that Melchizedek was not a descendant of Levi. The author continues that the tithe Melchizedek received was more important than the tithe collected by the Levitical priests. The argument centers on Melchizedek *not* being a fellow Israelite, and his priesthood predates the law of Moses. Consequently, when Abram voluntarily gave Melchizedek a tithe, that action allegedly proved that Melchizedek was the greater figure.

Once again, readers must note that this topic is subject to academic debate. The Hebrew text's ambiguity and lack of clarity have been known since the time of Jerome, who interpreted it to mean that Melchizedek gave a tithe *to* Abram. Moreover, Genesis 14:20 is dubious, as it is a possible interpolation. Next, the author writes that Melchizedek blessed Abram. Chan points out that Melchizedek views Abram's victory as a

159. Ellingworth, *Epistle to the Hebrews*, 361.

result of God's blessing. God gave him the victory (Gen. 14:20).[160] Similarly, Emadi comments, "Melchizedek's blessing acknowledges God as the one who "delivered" (מגן) Abraham's enemies into his hand (Gen 14:20b)."[161] This statement is also subject to academic debate, since the verse it quotes is a possible interpolation.

HEBREWS 7:7

> 7 It is beyond dispute that the inferior is blessed by the superior. (ESV)

Both the Hebrew and Christian Bibles refute this statement. The author of Hebrews conveniently refuses to engage or interact with any of the numerous biblical verses that demonstrate when blessings are from those in lower authority (status) or power to the higher:

> Gen. 47:7 Then Joseph brought in Jacob his father and stood him before Pharaoh, and Jacob blessed Pharaoh. (ESV)
>
> Genesis 47:11 And Jacob blessed Pharaoh and went out from the presence of Pharaoh. (ESV)
>
> 2 Sam. 8:10 Toi sent his son Joram to King David, to ask about his health and to bless him because he had fought against Hadadezer and defeated him, for Hadadezer had often been at war with Toi. And Joram brought with him articles of silver, of gold, and of bronze. (ESV)
>
> 2 Sam. 14:22 And Joab fell on his face to the ground and paid homage and blessed the king. And Joab said, "Today your servant knows that I have found favor in your sight, my lord the king, in that the king has granted the request of his servant." (ESV)
>
> 1 Kgs 1:47 Moreover, the king's servants came to congratulate our lord King David, saying, 'May your God make the name of Solomon more famous than yours, and make his throne greater than your throne.' And the king bowed himself on the bed.
>
> 1 Kgs 8:66 On the eighth day he sent the people away, and they blessed the king and went to their homes joyful and glad of heart for all the goodness that the Lord had shown to David his servant and to Israel his people. (ESV)

160. Chan, *Melchizedek Passages in the Bible*, 41.

161. Emadi, "You Are Priest Forever," 67.

> Ruth 2:4 And behold, Boaz came from Bethlehem. And he said to the reapers, "The Lord be with you!" And they answered, "The Lord bless you." (ESV)
>
> Ruth 2:19 And her mother-in-law said to her, "Where did you glean today? And where have you worked? Blessed be the man who took notice of you." So she told her mother-in-law with whom she had worked and said, "The man's name with whom I worked today is Boaz." (ESV)
>
> John 12:12–13 The next day the large crowd that had come to the feast heard that Jesus was coming to Jerusalem. So they took branches of palm trees and went out to meet him, crying out, "Hosanna! Blessed is he who comes in the name of the Lord, even the King of Israel!" (ESV)

It is noteworthy that Strack and Billerbeck *refute* the argument made by the author of Hebrews 7:7. They write:

> *This statement is not in line with the Jewish view.* [Italics for emphasis]
>
> Babylonian Talmud Megillah 15A: R. Eleazar (ca. 270) said that R. Hanina (ca. 225) said, "Never let the blessing of an ordinary person hidyot (= idiōtēs) be small in your eyes; for see, two ordinary people blessed two greats of the generation (of the age), and it was fulfilled in them. And these (the greats) were David and Daniel. David: Araunah blessed him, as it is written, 'Araunah said to the king, "May Yahweh, your God, be gracious to you!"' (2 Sam 24:23) Daniel: Darius blessed him, as it is written, 'May your God, whom you consistently worship, save you!' (Dan 6:17)."[162]

George Buchanan, writing *To the Hebrews*, points out another contradiction: "There are blessings which the inferior gives to the superior, such as the anonymous woman in a crowd who said to Jesus, 'Blessed is the womb that bore you, and the breasts that you sucked' (Luke 11:27)."[163] In a similar vein, Koester writes, "Yet it is not 'without any dispute' that the lesser is always blessed by the greater, since servants or the people sometimes blessed a king (2 Sam 14:22; 1 Kgs 1:47; 8:66)."[164]

However, unlike most commentators, Johnson applies a critical analysis to verse 7:

162. Strack and Billerbeck, *Kommentar zum Neuen Testament*, 695; Strack and Billerbeck, *A Commentary on the New Testament*, 1395 of 1809.

163. Buchanan, *To the Hebrews*, 121.

164. Koester, *The Anchor Yale Bible*, 344.

> Commenting on this exchange, Hebrews states as an incontestable principle (lit. "apart from all denial") that "the lesser is blessed by the greater." If he is thinking of the relationship of Moses and Aaron to the people Israel, then the principle holds in general, at least with respect to their social positions. But Scripture itself shows that there are contrary cases, in which the lesser blesses the greater (see 2 Sam 14:22; 1 Kgs 1:47; Job 31:20). The case here is less that Hebrews can site a standard principle than that Hebrews sees in this specific instance that the greater blesses the lesser which is shown, parenthetically, by the tribute paid by Abraham.[165]

Citing the saying, "less is blessed of the better" [i.e., blessings are always given from a higher authority or power to a lower one], as if it were some general rule or principle, is self-defeating, as it is false. In the Bible, people bless God, and God blesses people (Ps. 66:8; Luke 1:64; 2:28; 24:53). It is notable that Melchizedek blesses God: "and blessed be God Most High, who has delivered your enemies into your hand" (Gen. 14:19, ESV)! Blessings work both ways. In addition, scholarly controversy exists regarding the text's authenticity, with some arguing that it is an interpolation.

HEBREWS 7:8

> 8 In the one case tithes are received by mortal men, but in the other case, by one of whom it is testified that he lives. (ESV)

In his comments on Hebrews 7:8, Paul Ellingworth presents a syllogism that he opines is implicit but clear:

> Christ is a priest for ever.
> Christ is a priest like Melchizedek.
> Therefore, Melchizedek is a priest for ever.
> Corollary: he is alive.[166]

In Hebrews 7:8, the focal point is on the word *lives*. Commentators interpret this word as meaning "eternal." Strack and Billerbeck refer their readers back to Hebrews 7:3B. The author of Hebrews compares the *relative duration* of the Levitical priesthood to Melchizedek's. In the case of the Levites, they are mortals who receive tithes. However, Melchizedek is

165. Johnson, *Hebrews: A Commentary*, 180.

166. Ellingworth, *Epistle to the Hebrews*, 368.

eternal and did not die ("by one of whom it is testified *that he lives*"). This claim is an argument of silence. Significantly, nowhere is it stated that Melchizedek lost his priestly office due to death. The author of Hebrews and Christian Bible commentators posits that since the Hebrew Bible (Genesis 14) does not report the death of Melchizedek, he is considered immortal and everlasting (i.e., "that he lives"). Johnson's analysis is concise and decisive. "But we should observe that Scripture does not actually say that Melchizedek goes on living. That was a deduction drawn by the author from hints in the text, or rather, not in the text, since it provided for 'neither beginning of days nor an end of life' so 'he remains a priest forever (7:3).'"[167] Readers must ask themselves, does this argument make sense? For example, the Bible is silent about other aspects of his life:

1. No mention is made about Melchizedek being married; therefore, he was unmarried.
2. No mention is in the Bible that Melchizedek performed sacrifices; therefore, he did not perform any sacrifices.
3. No mention is in the Bible that Melchizedek was anointed; therefore, he was never anointed.
4. No mention is made of Melchizedek being bald; therefore, he had a full head of hair.
5. No mention is in the Bible about Melchizedek having tattoos; therefore, he never had tattoos.

A lengthy list of speculations about his life, which range from the ridiculous to the absurd, can be offered without a means of verification or falsification.

Simon Kistemaker comments:

> In this section (7:1–10) the author stresses the principle of life with reference to Melchizedek and to Levi. Melchizedek is portrayed as a person "without beginning of days and end of life" (7:3) and as one "who is declared to be living (7:8). Because of his likeness to the Son of God and because he thus is a type of Christ. *Melchizedek lives on scripturally although not historically.* (Italics added) The author of Hebrews bases his theological observations on the scriptural references to Melchizedek.[168]

167. Johnson, *Hebrews: A Commentary*, 180.

168. Kistemaker, *Exposition of the Epistle to the Hebrews*, 190.

HEBREWS 7:9 AND 7:10

> 9 One might even say that Levi himself, who receives tithes, paid tithes through Abraham, 10 for he was still in the loins of his ancestor when Melchizedek met him. (ESV)

The author of Hebrews argues that Levi was Abram's great-grandson and had not yet been born or conceived (i.e., he was "still in the loins of his ancestor") when Abram met Melchizedek. Again, the author makes a doubtful assertion when remarking that Abram paid tithes to Melchizedek. Crucially, Abram later became the father of the Jewish nation. However, the author regards an ancestor as containing all his descendants within himself. William Lane elaborates:

> Here it indicates the writer clearly recognized his statement that Levi had paid a tithe to Melchizedek was not literally true, because at the moment in primal history when Abraham met Melchizedek Levi was as yet unborn. Nevertheless, the statement that Levi had himself paid the tithe was true in an important sense, indicated by the expression δι' Ἀβραάμ, "through Abraham," which immediately follows. The corporate solidarity that bound Israel to the patriarch implied that Levi was fully represented in Abraham's action. Therefore, Levi's status relative to Melchizedek was affected by Abraham's relationship to that personage."[169]

However, the book of *Jubilees* only recounts a part of Genesis 14. Luke Timothy Johnson writes, "But in contrast to Hebrews, Jubilees understands the story to say that Melchizedek gave tithes to Abraham—and the Hebrew can be read that way."[170] Readers must be the final judge of whether this exegesis of the Bible makes sense.

HEBREWS 7:11

> 11 Now if perfection had been attainable through the Levitical priesthood (for under it the people received the law), what further need would there have been for another priest to arise after the order of Melchizedek, rather than one named after the order of Aaron? (ESV)

169. Lane, *Hebrews* 1–8, 170.

170. Johnson, *Hebrews: A Commentary*, 181.

In verses 11 to 19 of Hebrews 7, the author attempts to illustrate the imperfections of the Aaronic priesthood. First, he rhetorically inquires, if perfection were attainable through the Levitical priesthood, what further need would there be for another priest to arise after the order of Melchizedek? Koester comments that "'If' introduces an unreal condition."[171] Herbert Bateman elaborates that the author tells his readers two things: "(1) the Levitical priesthood did not bring perfection and (2) there was a need for a different kind of priest."[172]

Bateman goes on to explain the term "perfection."

> We also need to define the word "perfection" (τελείωσις). "Perfection" does not mean faultless or to be "without flaws." "Perfection" in Hebrews concerns a person's relationship with God. So the author tells us that Levitical priests, no matter what they did, no matter how many sacrifices the offered, no matter how many prayers they prayed, Levitical priests were unable to fix or establish a person's relationship with God. So the author tells us there was need. There was a need for a "different" priest.[173]

In this passage, Bateman makes a point that requires understanding: *The author of Hebrews is expressing his opinion.* Readers must be cognizant of the fact that the author is (1) anonymous, (2) a believer, (3) writing an exhortatory text, and (4) advocating supersession *or the belief that Christianity is the fulfillment of Biblical Judaism* (see Heb. 8:13). Grindheim is explicit. He references a source that "among the New Testament writings, Hebrews has to be considered to be the most supersessionist of all."[174] Then, he rejects that source:

> This view is not in evidence in Hebrews, as the letter presupposes that God has only only people throughout history, a people that includes Abel, Enoch, Noah, Abraham and Israel's ancestors, the judges, the prophets, and probably the Maccabean martyrs as well. This people reaches its completion with the inclusion of all those who believe in Jesus (11:4–40).[175]

Pamela Eisenbaum says the following about Hebrews:

171. Koester, *The Anchor Yale Bible*, 353.
172. Bateman, "Jesus, God's Different Priest (Hebrews 7:11)."
173. Bateman, "Jesus, God's Different Priest (Hebrews 7:11)."
174. Eisenbaum, "Ritual and Religion, Sacrifice and Supersession," 345.
175. Grindheim, *The Letter to the Hebrews.*

> By contrast, mature Christianity came to seen as the incarnation of Christ as a rupture with the past insofar as Christ was the culmination of God's relationship with humanity in general and Israel in particular. Ultimately Christianity, as the religion that developed around worship of Christ, understood itself as having replaced not just the covenant between Israel and God, but Judaism as a religion. Hebrews is the foundation of this idea that Christianity has "replaced" Judaism.
>
> Supersessionist theology inscribes Israel as an obsolete, illegitimate religion, and in the New Testament this idea is articulated no more plainly than in Hebrews. Drawing on Jeremiah's reference (31:31) to "a new covenant" (Heb *brit hadashah*; Gk *diathēkē kainē),* the author of Hebrews calls the Mosaic Law "only a shadow of the good things to come (10.1) and insists that "in speaking of 'new covenant,' he has made the first one obsolete. And what is obsolete and growing old will soon disappear (8:13). Such language helped foster the view that Judaism was an inferior religion, at best a precursor to Christ.[176]

Karen Jobes explains that perfection refers to "the completion of Christ's work to usher in the eschatological ages."[177] However, this explanation rests on assumptions that require further elaboration:

1. Christ was the Messiah before he suffered but came to perfection in that role only through his death, resurrection, and ascension.
2. His role in God's redemptive plan as Messiah was perfected only when he suffered and died on the cross.
3. His obedient suffering brought his role as the Messiah to *completion* or *fulfillment.*
4. In other words, Jesus has brought God's redemptive plan to its *perfection.*

Jobes' analysis stands on a foundation of sand. It makes numerous faulty assumptions, violates the Hebrew Bible, and employs eisegesis rather than exegesis: (1) From a Jewish standpoint, Jesus cannot be the Messiah because he does not have patrilineal descent from David (being born from a virgin); (2) Adoption would not make Jesus from the line of David; (3) The Hebrew Bible does not permit vicarious atonement; (4) The suffering and death of an innocent and righteous person can neither

176. Eisenbaum, "The Letter to the Hebrews," 461–62.

177. Jobes, *Letters to the Church.*

wipe away a person's sins nor redeem another from their sins. Scripture states that "the soul who sins is the one who will die. The son will not share the father's guilt, nor will the father share the son's guilt. The righteousness of the righteous man shall be upon him, and the wickedness of the wicked shall be upon him" (Ezek. 18:20, ESV); (5) Jesus' body was blemished and improperly "sacrificed" (e.g., on account of his scourging and means of death via crucifixion, the slaughterers being the Romans, and the location of the offering being outside the Temple); (6) Since God can forgive, there is no need for the 'sacrifice' of which Christianity speaks. God is almighty and pardons all people of their sins, only requiring that they repent (see Mark 1:14–15; Matt. 4:17; Luke 10:25–28); and (7) There were many "exhaustive" or verifiable prophecies which Jesus failed to fulfill (e.g., the resurrection of the dead, world peace, no weapons of war).

Donald Hagner explains the concept of perfection from a Christian viewpoint. He states, "By this perfection/completion is meant the full realization of the goal of God's plan of salvation."[178] He later adds, "The word 'perfection'(*teleiosis*) here, as elsewhere in Hebrews, does not mean 'without flaws,' but has to do with 'arriving at a desired end' or 'reaching a goal.' (quoting Ellingworth, 371) That 'desired end' refers to the type of relationship established between God and his people under the new covenant."[179] Readers must ask a crucial question: did the average person, probably illiterate, with limited knowledge of the Hebrew Bible (if any) have the capacity to understand the meaning of perfection advocated by modern Bible commentators? To be certain, native Greek speakers would not have knowledge of the Hebrew Bible (not the Septuagint).

Hagner's interpretation is rejected by those who do not accept the argument that a new covenant exists. Scripture is clear: the covenant, law, or Torah will not be replaced or superseded by another instruction from God, and neither is it difficult.

> Exod. 31:16 Therefore the people of Israel shall keep the Sabbath, observing the Sabbath throughout their generations, *as a covenant forever*. (ESV)
>
> Exod. 40:15 and anoint them, as you anointed their father, that they may serve me as priests. And their anointing shall admit

178. Hagner, *Encountering the Book of Hebrews*, 101.

179. Hagner, *Encountering the Book of Hebrews*, 265; cf. Koester, *The Anchor Yale Bible*, 353.

them *to a perpetual priesthood throughout their generations.* (ESV)

Deut. 4:2 *You shall not add to the word that I command you, nor take from it,* that you may keep the commandments of the Lord your God that I command you. (ESV)

Deut. 12:1 These are the statutes and rules that you shall be careful to do in the land that the Lord, the God of your fathers, has given you to possess, *all the days that you live on the earth.* (ESV)

Deut.12:32 Everything that I command you, you shall be careful to do. *You shall not add to it or take from it.* (ESV)

Deut. 13:1–6 1 *All this word which I command you, that shall ye observe to do; thou shalt not add thereto, nor diminish from it.*
2 If there arise in the midst of thee a prophet, or a dreamer of
dreams—and he give thee a sign or a wonder, 3and the sign or
the wonder come to pass, whereof he spoke unto thee—saying:
'Let us go after other gods, which thou hast not known, and let
us serve them'; 4thou shalt not hearken unto the words of that
prophet, or unto that dreamer of dreams; for the LORD your
God putteth you to proof, to know whether ye do love the LORD
your God with all your heart and with all your soul. 5After the
LORD your God shall ye walk, and Him shall ye fear, and His
commandments shall ye keep, and unto His voice shall ye hearken, and Him shall ye serve, and unto Him shall ye cleave. 6And
that prophet, or that dreamer of dreams, shall be put to death; because he hath spoken perversion against the LORD your God, who brought you out of the land of Egypt, and redeemed thee out of the house of bondage, to draw thee aside out of the way which the LORD thy God commanded thee to walk in. So shalt thou put away the evil from the midst of thee. (JPS 1917)

Deut. 30

11 "For this commandment that I command you today is not
too hard for you, neither is it far off. 12 It is not in heaven, that
you should say, 'Who will ascend to heaven for us and bring it to
us, that we may hear it and do it?' 13 Neither is it beyond the sea,
that you should say, 'Who will go over the sea for us and bring
it to us, that we may hear it and do it?' 14 But the word is very
near you. It is in your mouth and in your heart, so that you can
do it. 15 "See, I have set before you today life and good, death
and evil. 16 If you obey the commandments of the Lord your
God that I command you today, by loving the Lord your God, by walking in his ways, and by keeping his commandments and his statutes and his rules, then you shall live and multiply, and

> the Lord your God will bless you in the land that you are entering to take possession of it. (Deut. 30, ESV)
>
> Prov. 30:5–6
>
> 5 Every word of God proves true; he is a shield to those who take refuge in him. 6 *Do not add to his words*, lest he rebuke you and you be found a liar. (ESV)

Koester also comments on the Greek word *teleiosis* and the issue of God's purpose being completed. To his credit he surveys the literature and provides his readership with an opposing reference point:

> The initial statement places the issue at its most fundamental level: Did the Levitical priesthood ultimately accomplish God's purposes (7:11a)? The author assumes that the answer is no, and his view runs counter to the dominant tendencies in Jewish sources. Writing before the destruction of the Temple. Philo called the Levitical priesthood "that perfect priesthood by which mortality is commended to and recognized by God" (*Sacrifices* 132; Moses 2.5; *Special Laws* 1.80). Writing in Rome decades after the Temple's destruction, Josephus argued that in the Law, God established the most perfect form of community life by assigning "the administration of its highest affairs to the whole body of priests" (Ag. Ap. 2.184–88). Hebrews, however, contends that God did not complete his purposes through the Levitical priesthood.[180]

The author of Hebrews is presenting a red herring. No person ever claimed that perfection was attainable through the Levitical priesthood. Moreover, there was no need for someone different, like Melchizedek, to arise to establish a relationship between God and his people. Unlike the order of Melchizedek, the purpose of the Aaronic priesthood is detailed explicitly in the Hebrew Bible. God willed and ordained the Levitical priesthood system. Johnson comments, "The section is bracketed by the language of perfection, *beginning in 7:11 with a condition contrary to fact*, and ending in 7:19 with a flat assertion that the law perfected nothing." (Italics for emphasis)[181] Readers must judge whether the author suggests that God erred in establishing the Aaronic priesthood.

180. Koester, *The Anchor Yale Bible*, 358–59.

181. Johnson, *Hebrews: A Commentary*, 183–84.

HEBREWS 7:12

> 12 For when there is a change in the priesthood, there is necessarily a change in the law as well. (ESV)

The author is advocating supersession, both here and elsewhere (Heb. 8:13). Theopedia.com provides a handy definition:

> Supersessionism is the traditional Christian belief that Christianity is the fulfillment of Biblical Judaism and therefore that Jews who deny that Jesus is the Jewish Messiah fall short of their calling as God's Chosen people.
>
> Supersessionism, in its more radical form, maintains that the Jews are no longer considered to be God's Chosen people in any sense. This understanding is generally termed "replacement theology."[182]

Therefore, the Aaronic priesthood and the laws found within the Torah can be changed. F.F. Bruce explains, "If the Aaronic priesthood was instituted for a temporary purpose, to be brought to an end when the age of fulfilment dawned, the same must be true of the law under which that priesthood was introduced."[183] Bruce minces no words: "Its supersession is here seen to be implied in the acclamation of Messiah as a priest after the order of Melchizedek."[184] However, God's instructions within the Torah are unequivocal. No person can add or subtract from the Torah (Deut. 4:2; 12:32). Koester confirms this, writing, "*For when there is a change in the priesthood.* This runs counter to the idea that the Levitical priesthood was permanent (Exod 40:15; Num 18:19; 25:13)."[185] In addition, the detractors of supersession counter that the God of the Bible is a covenant-keeping God.

HEBREWS 7:13

> 13 For the one of whom these things are spoken belonged to another tribe, from which no one has ever served at the altar. (ESV)

182. "Supersessionism."
183. Bruce, *The Epistle to the Hebrews*, 166.
184. Bruce, *The Epistle to the Hebrews*, 167; cf. Manson, *The Epistle to the Hebrews*, 114.
185. Koester, *The Anchor Yale Bible*, 355.

At this point, the author of Hebrews confronts a dilemma. Under the "old order," Jesus had no right to be a priest, let alone the high priest. In addition, the Messiah had to be a direct descendant of the tribe of Judah. However, God prescribed that the priesthood *must* be from the tribe of Levi. A person only has one biological father, who determines an individual's tribal affiliation. If Jesus had been born from a virgin, there would have been no father and no patrilineal line. However, in Luke 3:23–38, Jesus' lineage through Joseph (his presumed *adopted father*) is through the tribe of Judah.

To circumvent this obstacle, the author of Hebrews claims Jesus was not from the order of Levi but from a different order: that of Melchizedek. It is important to remember that Melchizedek allegedly had no mother, father, or genealogy. By claiming Jesus was from the order *of* Melchizedek, the author and apologists remove the requirement that the Messiah must be from the tribe of Judah and a priest from the tribe of Levi. Therefore, the author has to invent an explanation of how Jesus can be both Messiah and priest. In a similar vein, Nadine Fishbeck comments, "Jesus was not eligible during his lifetime to be a priest because he was not a descendant from the tribe of Levi. Therefore, the author appropriates the 'order of Melchizedek' as an alternative and legitimate option to the Levitical priesthood."[186] Skeptics will likely conclude that "necessity is the mother of invention."

It is essential to understand that the author of Hebrews' argument violates the precise meaning of the Hebrew Bible. Readers must ask themselves: can the author of Hebrews, even if he is well-meaning, override the unequivocal instruction of God with a literary or theological invention? F.F. Bruce employs theological gymnastics, claiming that the priesthood "is not exercised on earth: it belongs to the eternal order, not to the material world."[187] This argument from silence contradicts the Hebrew Bible, is ad hoc, and is unverifiable. Moreover, in the eyes of skeptics and detractors, it rests on a foundation of sand—Genesis 14:18–20—and conveniently (or deliberately) omits Psalm 110:5–7.

186. Fishbeck, "The High-Priestly Christology of the Letter to the Hebrews," 50.

187. Bruce, *The Epistle to the Hebrews*, 168.

HEBREWS 7:14

> 14 For it is evident that our Lord was descended from Judah, and in connection with that tribe Moses said nothing about priests. (ESV)

Hebrews begins bluntly with the phrase, "it is evident that our Lord." The author employs the Greek *Kyrios* (Strong 2962). The use of *kyrios* in the New Testament is a topic of debate among modern scholars. Often, this word is employed to designate attributes of God. The website blueletterbible.org provides some examples:

I. he to whom a person or thing belongs, about which he has power of deciding; master, lord

   a. the possessor and disposer of a thing

      ii. the owner; one who has control of the person, the master

      iii. in the state: the sovereign, prince, chief, the Roman emperor

   d. is a title of honor expressive of respect and reverence, with which servants greet their master this title is given to: God, the Messiah.[188]

The great unknown is how first-century listeners (Greeks) would have understood this word: whether it referred to a human master or an exalted figure (God or the Messiah).[189] If the latter, the author claims that "Jesus is our God." Harold W. Attridge writes, "Our author no doubt refers to the widely accepted Davidic descent of Jesus."[190] Christian Bibles incorporate an uppercase "L" which indicates divinity (ASV, CEB, ESV, KJV, NASV, NIV, NRS, RS). Judaism, Islam, and "nontraditional" Christians (Biblical Unitarians, Christadelphians, and Jehovah's Witnesses) repudiate the idea that Jesus is God.

The author of Hebrews continues his line of thought emphasizing that Jesus descended from the tribe of Judah. Readers must remember

188. "G2962- Kyrios"; Boyarin, *The Jewish Gospels*, 25–71. Readers must note that Jewish thought is not monolithic.

189. Traditional Judaism rejects the thinking that the Messiah is God.

190. Attridge, *Hebrews: A Commentary*, 201. Then he cites Matt. 1:1; 9:27; 15:22; Mark 10:47; Luke 1:32; 2:4; 18:38; John 7:42; Acts 12:22–23; Rom. 1:3; 2 Tim 2:8; Rev. 22:16.

that Judah is a non-priestly tribe.[191] Moreover, in verse fourteen, he is patently at odds with other passages in the New Testament. For Jewish people, the family line is determined *exclusively* by patrilineal descent: "and on the first day of the second month, they assembled the whole congregation together, who registered themselves by clans, by fathers' houses, according to the number of names from twenty years old and upward, head by head" (Num. 1:18, ESV). However, according to Matthew 1:23, Jesus was born from a virgin. Jesus, therefore, could not trace his lineage from Judah without a biological father. Luke 3:23–38 exclusively provides Joseph's lineage, tracing it back to Judah and ultimately to Adam himself. He says nothing about Mary's; even if he did, it would not be relevant for identifying Jesus' tribe.

HEBREWS 7:15

> 15 This becomes even more evident when another priest arises in the likeness of Melchizedek, (ESV)

The author of Hebrews says, "when another priest arises," referencing Jesus. However, another priest cannot arise in the likeness of Melchizedek and be from the Aaronic line *if* he lacks a mother, father, or genealogy. Moreover, the other priest could not be Jesus. The author claims in the prior verse that Jesus *is* from the tribe of Judah (Heb. 7:14), and Luke 3:23–38 details his genealogy through Joseph. Jesus either has a genealogy (Heb. 7:14; Luke 3:23–38), or he does not. The author elaborates in the following verses.

HEBREW 7:16

> 16 who has become a priest, not on the basis of a legal requirement concerning bodily descent, but by the power of an indestructible life. (ESV)

The Levitical priesthood is determined by one's genealogy, as dictated by the law (Torah, *nomos*). Therefore, the author of Hebrews is compelled to draw a significant implication from the change in the priesthood from Levitical to Melchizedek: a law change (see Hebrews 7:12). The author

191. Ellingworth, *Epistle to the Hebrews*, 376.

argues that Melchizedek's position as high priest was *not* dependent on ancestry. Coincidently, neither was Jesus' position. Instead, the author argues that the new priesthood is marked by indestructible life (i.e., eternal life). This claim contradicts the Torah, which states that God ordains a priest or the high priest, who comes exclusively from the line of Levi/Aaron.

Koester discusses several problems. (1) "One problem is that Jesus was subject to death, how is his life 'indestructible'?" (2) If Jesus *did* possess an indestructible life, "The problem is that this suggests that Christ did not die in the way that others die, even though Hebrews stresses the reality of Christ's suffering and death (2:14–15; 4:15; 5:7–8)."[192] He goes on to review some possible solutions. However, the last part of the verse, which declares that the "other priest" of Hebrews 7:15 has an indestructible life, is unverifiable. In the following verse, the author attempts to provide biblical proof.

HEBREWS 7:17

> 17 For it is witnessed of him,
> "You are a priest forever,
> after the order of Melchizedek." (ESV)

Koester writes, "*For it is attested that you are a priest forever.* Attestation comes from the Scriptures (Ps 110:4; Heb 5:6, 10; 6:20)."[193] On three occasions, Koester utilizes the author of Hebrews to confirm the author of Hebrews. This apologetic is weak, ineffective, and irrelevant. The fourth occurrence is Koester's eisegesis of the verse in Psalm 110. Skeptics and detractors contend that there is no evidence that Jesus or Melchizedek are priests forever. The claim is unverifiable. Koester and other passionate believers in Christianity are making a theological claim.

William Lane comments that the formula 'for he has borne witness that,' "introduces the quotation of Ps. 110:4 to support the assertion that Jesus possesses a life that can never be destroyed."[194] The author argues that verse 4 proves that Melchizedek was a priest forever. He continues, "The quotation proves why Jesus' life qualifies him as a priest. It indicates

192. Koester, *The Anchor Yale Bible*, 355.
193. Koester, *The Anchor Yale Bible*, 355.
194. Lane, *Hebrews* 1–8, 184.

that an authentic priesthood independent of the Levitical order exists and that it is characterized as a perpetual priesthood."[195] In other words, he is indestructible (verse 16) and immortal. F.F. Bruce comments, "But the Christians' high priest is immortal; having died once for all and risen from the dead, he discharges his ministry on his people's behalf in the power of a life which can never be destroyed."[196] Bruce elaborates, adding, "The law which established the Aaronic priesthood is called a 'carnal commandment' (AV/KJV, ERV/ARV) because it is 'a system of earth-bound rules'(NEB); it is concerned with the externalities of religion—the physical descent of the priests, a material shrine, animal sacrifices, and so forth."[197]

In contrast, skeptics and detractors dispute the claims that Jesus (1) died once and for all, (2) has risen from the dead, and (3) has a life that can never experience destruction. They point out that these three claims are all unverifiable. How do Christians know Jesus "died once and for all" or that he "has a life which can never be destroyed"? The claim that Jesus "has risen from the dead" (the resurrection) is based on reports in the Christian Bible that a resurrected Jesus was seen, heard, and touched by his disciples after his death. However, these reports were composed by believers in the resurrection about thirty to sixty years *after* Jesus' crucifixion. There is no way to verify them independently. Consequently, Christian Bible commentators and theologians are guilty of arguing in circles: Jesus has risen because "the Christian Bible says so."

Returning to the first part of Hebrews 7:17, skeptics and detractors inquire about the identity of the witnesses who make the declaration. Paul Ellingworth says that in this context, the author "as usual refers to the witness of scripture . . . implying 'God' or 'scripture' as the subject."[198] Bible commentators claim that the author of the Psalm is David, the Holy Spirit, or even God the Father. However, detractors argue that the New Testament contains stories about stories and demonstrates an evolving storyline, with embellishment and aggrandizement, or some posit that the narratives are inventions. Therefore, they challenge the reliability or outright historicity of the narratives (in the Gospel) reflecting an evolving oral tradition.

195. Lane, *Hebrews* 1–8, 184.

196. Bruce, *The Epistle to the Hebrews*, 169.

197. Bruce, *The Epistle to the Hebrews*, 169.

198. Ellingworth, *Epistle to the Hebrews*, 380.

As we have already discussed, Jesus could not have been a Levitical priest because he was not of the line of Levi or Aaron. Therefore, the author of Hebrews asserted that he was to be "after the order of Melchizedek." This claim was essential in responding to potential first-century Jewish doubters who were knowledgeable of the Hebrew Bible and the patrilineal requisite to be a priest or the Messiah. Assuming the author was aware of the controversy surrounding the lack of a paternal line, this reality may have necessitated the invention of the idea that Melchizedek did not have a father or genealogy. This counter-apologetic argument is based from silence, which is neither verifiable nor falsifiable.

Another factor to consider is the dating of the Epistle to the Hebrews, Mark, Matthew, and Luke. If Hebrews were composed before these three gospels, then the author would have had no means of knowing about a genealogy except through an evolving oral tradition. We cannot say for certain if the author had access to members of Jesus' family.

HEBREWS 7:18

> 18 For on the one hand, a former commandment is set aside because of its weakness and uselessness (ESV)

Koester comments, "Yet since God gave the Law, Hebrews assumes that he also has the right to alter it."[199] He goes on to provide robust evidence to refute this assertion:

> Hebrews says that the Law was changed because of its weakness (7:18), but the author does not support this claim by arguing that the Jewish people *felt* the Law to be ineffective—The Psalms say that "the law of the lord is perfect, reviving the soul" (Ps 19:7) and call "blessed" those who delight in in the Law (Ps 1:1–2) . . . To say categorically that the Law made nothing "complete" (7:19a) is more provocative than explanatory."[200]

Interestingly, James says in his letter, "But the one who looks *into the perfect law* [*nomon*; 3551 *nómos* – *law*. 3551 (*nómos*) is used of: a) the Law (Scripture), with emphasis on the first five books of Scripture], the law of liberty, and perseveres, being no hearer who forgets but a doer who acts, he will be blessed in his doing" (James 1:25, ESV).

199. Koester, *The Anchor Yale Bible*, 355.

200. Koester, *The Anchor Yale Bible*, 361.

F.F. Bruce explains, "The declaration 'You are a priest for ever, after the order of Melchizedek' thus announces the abrogation of the earlier law which instituted the Aaronic order."[201] Paul Ellingworth discusses several synonymous terms, including (1) setting aside, (2) cancellation, (3) repeal, (4) abolition, and (5) abrogation.[202] This argument is challengeable on three grounds. Firstly, both the Hebrew and Christian Bible acknowledge that the Torah cannot be changed (see above). Secondly, the Torah categorically rejects the author's opinion that a commandment of God is weak and useless. Thirdly, the author advocates a form of *supersession*, with a "New Covenant" superseding the old, which is refuted by the Hebrew Bible.

HEBREWS 7:19

> 19 (for the law made nothing perfect); but on the other hand, a better hope is introduced, through which we draw near to God. (ESV)

The author contrasts "the law" with "a better hope." Notably, the Hebrew Bible does not report that the law (*nomos*) made everything perfect. Instead, the Hebrew Bible repeatedly declares that the law is readily obtainable, good, and a gift from God (Deut. 31:1; Ps. 19:8; 119:70–72; Prov. 6:23). Contrary to what the author of Hebrews maintains, the Hebrew Bible says:

> 11 "For this commandment that I command you today is not too hard for you, neither is it far off. 12 It is not in heaven, that you should say, 'Who will ascend to heaven for us and bring it to us, that we may hear it and do it?' 13 Neither is it beyond the sea, that you should say, 'Who will go over the sea for us and bring it to us, that we may hear it and do it?' 14 But the word is very near you. It is in your mouth and in your heart, so that you can do it. (Deut. 30:11–14, ESV)

And, as the author of Proverbs declares:

> Her ways [the Torah's] are ways of pleasantness, and all her paths are peace. She is a tree of life to those who lay hold of her; those who hold her fast are called blessed. (Prov. 3:17–18, ESV).

201. Bruce, *The Epistle to the Hebrews*, 169.

202. Ellingworth, *Epistle to the Hebrews*, 380.

Pamela Eisenbaum elaborates by saying, "*The Law made nothing perfect*, Although Hebrews sees the Torah as given by God, it cannot be *perfect*, because its human institution does not exist in the material realm."[203]

To his credit, F.F. Bruce acknowledges, "This is not to say that faithful men and women in the Old Testament times did not enjoy peace of conscience and a sense of nearness to God; the Psalter provides evidence enough that they did."[204] He goes on to cite Psalm 32:1 and 73:28. However, Bruce insists: "Access to God is our author's grounds for claiming that the gospel has achieved that perfection which the law could never bring about."[205] However, Bruce appears to overlook Deuteronomy 30:11–14 and Proverbs 3:17–18, which contradict his assertion.

HEBREWS 7:20

> 20 And it was not without an oath. For those who formerly became priests were made such without an oath, (ESV)

The author continues by saying that the LORD made a Divine oath declaring He would not change His mind (Ps.110:4). Here, the author of Hebrews employs theological gymnastics. While it is true that the establishment of the Aaronic priesthood was not made by God swearing an oath, the author omits to mention that its inauguration was a divine command.

There are multiple instances in Exodus where the Bible reports the command, "Then, he said to Moses" (The Covenant Confirmed, 24:1; Offerings for the Tabernacle, 25:1; Atonement Money, 30:11; Basin for Washing, 30:17; Anointing Oil, 30:22; Incense 30:34; Bezalel and Oholiab to Make Artistic Designs, 31:1; and The Sabbath, 31:12). At other times, God's commands find expression in the word(s) "Make," followed by the specification: The Ark 25:10, Atonement Cover, 25:17; The Table, 25:23; The Lampstand, 25:31; The Tabernacle 26:1; The Curtains 26:7; The Frames 26:15; The Crossbars 26:26; A Curtain, 26:31; The Altar of Burnt Offerings, 27; The Courtyard 27:8; The Ephod, 28:6; the Breastpiece, 28:15; Other Priestly Garments, 28:31; and The Altar of Incense,

203. Eisenbaum, "The Letter to the Hebrews," 474.

204. Bruce, *The Epistle to the Hebrews*, 169.

205. Bruce, *The Epistle to the Hebrews*, 170.

30:1. God did not swear an oath in any of these cases. What He issued was a Divine command/instruction. The author of Hebrews is playing a semantic word game by employing the word "oath." In addition, the author of Hebrews deliberately ignores verses five and six in Psalm 110 (see below). These verses refute the claims of the author.

HEBREW 7:21

> 21 but this one was made a priest with an oath by the one who said to him:
> "The Lord has sworn
> and will not change his mind,
> 'You are a priest forever.'" (ESV)

In verse 21, the author quotes Scripture (Ps. 110:4), which states that a Divine oath was made. This claim is the third time in Hebrews 7 where the author stresses that Jesus is a priest "forever (7:3, 17, 21), quoting Psalm 110:4 as an authority for his conviction."[206] The oath contains three elements: (1) The Lord swore an oath, (2) the Lord will not change His mind, and (3) the priest will be a priest forever. Readers should ask themselves whether the Bible universally supports the statement that "the Lord will not change His mind"?

Koester engages this subject. His examination of the Bible finds that the claim that God never changes His mind is not absolute. "God sometimes changed his mind in order to do good (Exod 32:14; Jer 18:8; Joel 2:13–14; Amos 7:3, 6; Jon 3:9–10), although his judgments could be unrelenting (1 Sam 15:29; Jer 4:28; Zech 8:14)."[207]

William Lane elaborates, "Through his death, exaltation, and installation as heavenly priest, Jesus provides security that the new and better covenant will not be annulled."[208] However, as previously discussed, the phrase "priest forever" has several possible meanings. Both the author of Hebrews and Bible commentators overlook the following verses (Ps. 110:5–6), which preclude the possibility of Jesus being the Messiah or a high priest. The Lord's [YHWH] oath includes the following points:

1. God will crush kings

206. Brown, *The Message of Hebrews*, 132.
207. Koester, *The Anchor Yale Bible*, 363.
208. Lane, *Hebrews 1–8*, 188.

2. God will execute judgments among the nations
3. God will shatter chiefs [rulers] over the wide earth.

In contrast, (a) Jesus was rejected by his people and by his disciples; (b) he was humiliated and crucified by the Romans; (c) Israel remained under Roman subjugation; and (d) about forty years later, the Second Temple was destroyed, with the Jewish people either murdered or forced into slavery.

Notably, "the author of the Epistle to the Hebrews claims that Jesus is a priest. This argument is a unique and original claim since no other New Testament document calls him a priest, and none of Jesus' contemporaries apparently thought of him in this manner."[209]

Hydon elaborates on the significance of Hebrews 7:21, quoting Psalm 110:4.

> The author is aware of the technical, professional and ceremonial requirements of priesthood. He recognizes, too, that Jesus could never be a priest according to any such professional priestly order. He admits frankly that Jesus is not a priest after the order of Aaron. Since he needs to belong to some order of priesthood, he makes him a priest after the order of Melchizedek on the strength of a quotation from Psalm 110:4 which calls the Messiah such a priest. Since Christians hold Jesus to be the Messiah, he must therefore be a Melchizedek priest. The Melchizedek priesthood allows the author to say "by interpretation" that Jesus belongs to an order of priesthood, and that this order is superior to the order of Aaron because eternal, prior to that of Aaron, deferred to by it, and permanent.[210]

HEBREWS 7:22

> 22 This makes Jesus the guarantor of a better covenant. (ESV)

To reiterate, Jesus allegedly becomes a guarantor "through his death, exaltation, and installation as a heavenly priest."[211] Brown points out that the word *surety* or *guarantor* (*engyos*) "makes its only New Testament

209. Hydon, "The Priesthood of Jesus," abstract.
210. Hydon, "The Priesthood of Jesus," abstract.
211. Bruce, *The Epistle to the Hebrews*, 171.

appearance in this verse."[212] However, God is good and merciful. Since God can forgive, Jesus does not need to offer his blood on the cross, as Christian theology asserts (1 Cor. 15:3–4). God is almighty and pardons all people for their sins, only requiring that they repent (Deut. 30:1–62; 2 Chron. 7:14; Prov. 28:13; Isa. 55:6–7; Ezek. 18:27–30; 33:11). No vicarious atonement is requested or required.

> Isa. 55:7 Let the wicked forsake his way, and the unrighteous man his thoughts: and let him return unto the Lord, and he will have mercy upon him; and to our God, for he will abundantly pardon. (ESV)

F.F. Bruce adds, "And since it is Jesus who is acclaimed as priest after the order of Melchizedek, it is Jesus whose superior dignity is thus confirmed."[213] This statement expresses the opinion that Jesus is a priest after the order of Melchizedek, so therefore, he must be superior. That line of thought was refuted above. Moreover, there is no evidence that Jesus is the guarantor of a better covenant. Here, the author is expressing an unverifiable opinion.

Brown comments, "In his merciful goodness God deigned to enter into a covenant with us through the work and merit of his Son."[214] However, both Jews and Christians alike acknowledge that God willed the "initial covenant" with the people of Israel. Therefore, the author of Hebrews implies that God was in error when He composed His covenant to Israel. However, the Hebrew Bible is unequivocal: the covenant is eternal and good. In addition, the Hebrew Bible testifies that a sinner cannot be "saved" through the work or merit of another person: "The soul who sins is the one who will die. The son will not share the father's guilt, nor will the father share the son's guilt. The righteousness of the righteous man shall be upon him, and the wickedness of the wicked shall be upon him" (Ezek. 18:20, ESV).

HEBREWS 7:23

> 23 The former priests were many in number, because they were prevented by death from continuing in office. (ESV)

212. Brown, *The Message of Hebrews*, 133.
213. Bruce, *The Epistle to the Hebrews*, 171.
214. Brown, *The Message of Hebrews*, 133.

F.F. Bruce elaborates:

> It has already been pointed out (vv. 16f.) that our Lord's indissoluble life makes it possible for him to fulfil to the letter the words "You are a priest *for ever*." If these words were applied to a dynasty of priests, "for ever" could be understood only of a hereditary succession of indefinite duration. The Aaronic priests were indeed appointed on the hereditary principle (not, of course, on the basis of Ps. 110:4); but none of them could enjoy the priestly dignity in perpetuity) . . . eighty-three high priests officiated from Aaron to the fall of the Second Temple in A.D. 70.[215]

F.F. Bruce is correct. There were many priests, and the priests were mortal. Consequently, their deaths prevented them from continuing in office. Paul Hydon comments, "It has been shown, therefore, that neither the author's method nor his material conforms to the usual technical standards of argument and disputation. From the standpoint of strict, formal reasoning his proof is not valid."[216] Moreover, what the author of Hebrews fails to acknowledge is that this priestly system is precisely the way God willed and designed His program to operate. In addition, God Himself instituted the priesthood. Therefore, the author criticizes God and challenges His omniscience.

HEBREWS 7:24

> 24 but he holds his priesthood permanently, because he continues forever. (ESV)

F.F. Bruce comments, "But to our author the death of the high priest (or of any other priest) means that he is no longer available to those who counted upon him to intercede for them with God."[217] In contrast, it is alleged that Jesus will always be able to intercede on behalf of the people with God. Donald Hagner elaborates, "But because Christ 'continues forever' (v. 24), his priesthood is permanent ('You are a priest forever' [Ps 110:4])."[218] The inconvenient truth is that the statement in verse 24

215. Bruce, *The Epistle to the Hebrews*, 172; cf. Josephus, *Complete Works of Josephus*, see *Ant.* 20.227.

216. Hydon, "The Priesthood of Jesus," abstract.

217. Bruce, *The Epistle to the Hebrews*, 173.

218. Hagner, *Encountering the Book of Hebrews*, 104; cf. Brown, *The Message of*

is ad hoc, unverifiable, and wishful thinking. There is simply no way of knowing that Jesus holds this priesthood permanently. This belief is a matter of faith.

Moreover, it is impossible to verify that he continues to live. Detractors argue that the author is making a theological claim. If Jesus died, then his priesthood was not permanent. Finally, we should note that God specifically designed the Levitical system with the built-in feature (which the author of Hebrews regards as a defect) that the high priest was mortal and unable to serve the people perpetually. Readers must ask themselves whether the author of Hebrews knows better than God.

HEBREWS 7:25

> 25 Consequently, he is able to save to the uttermost those who draw near to God through him, since he always lives to make intercession for them. (ESV)

Verse 25 expresses a theological belief without any supporting evidence. Koester says that "on a human level, people recognized that requests that were brought before a sovereign would be most favorably received if submitted by someone close to the throne . . . According to Hebrews, Jesus the Son of God is now seated at God's right hand, which is a good place from which to make requests."[219] Being seated on the right-hand side symbolizes favoritism or a seat of honor, not a physical location. There are multiple examples of individuals being given a right-hand seat in the New Testament: Rom. 8:34; Eph. 1:20; Col. 3:1; 1 Pet. 3:22; Mark 12:36; Matt. 22:44; Luke 20:42; Acts 2:34; Heb. 1:3; 8:1; 10:12; 12:2. Skeptics and detractors will counter that there is no convincing evidence that Jesus is "seated at the right hand" and that this assertion is an unsubstantiated and unverifiable claim.

The author of Hebrews argues that Jesus can save and "the spiritual deliverance has an unlimited duration."[220] Skeptics and detractors counter that (1) there is no convincing evidence Jesus can save anyone, (2) there is no evidence that people must draw near to God through him (Jesus), (3) his actions are irrelevant, (4) his death on the cross at the hands

Hebrews, 134–35.

219. Koester, *The Anchor Yale Bible*, 366.

220. Bateman, "Jesus, Our Eternal Intercessor (Hebrews 7:25)."

of the Romans violated the requirements of the Hebrew Bible for an acceptable offering, (5) vicarious atonement by an innocent person for the sins of a guilty sinner violates the teaching of the Hebrew Bible, (6) there is no convincing evidence that Jesus will live forever (being eternal), and (7) being dead, Jesus cannot make intercession for anyone. It should be noted that there is no convincing evidence that Jesus makes eternal and permanent intercession on behalf of the people.

Skeptics and detractors also contend that Jesus' death on the cross was *not* a one-time sacrifice for the sins of humankind (see Heb. 9:27). Firstly, the Hebrew Bible refutes the author's claim (suggestion) that Christ's sacrifice annulled, repealed, and ended all other sacrifices (Zech. 14:21; Isa. 56:7; 60:7; Jer. 33:17–18; Ezek. 43:22–23; 45:17; Hos. 3:3–4; Zeph. 3:10; Mal. 3:1–4). Secondly, Adelbert Denaux, a Catholic professor in exegesis of the New Testament, Biblical Theology, and Biblical Greek, acknowledges that "In early Judaism, few doubted the importance of the priesthood," and he adds that it was "considered to be a divine institution, affirmed by the Law (Exod 25–31, 35–40; Lev 1–10, 16–17, 21–24; Num 3–4, 8, 15–19)." He also notes that even in the Qumran community, they widely shared this belief:

> They nevertheless expected the restoration of the divinely-built Temple and of the sacrifice in the future age (4QFlor 1:1–6; 11QTa XXIX:8–10) . . . Jewish writings of the first century BCE expected a priest to come in final times (e.g., *T. Levi* 18:6;11QMelch' 1QM XVIII; 1QSa 2) (Schiffman, 1992). No fulfilment worthy of this name could set aside any of the essential elements of God's design, and priestly meditation and the sacrificial system was certainly one of these essential elements."[221]

Thirdly, the author of Hebrews makes an unsubstantiated and unverifiable claim about how people can approach God. Contrary to the author's assertion, God, through His mercy, saves people without going through an intermediary (e.g., Jesus) or requiring the sacrifice of an innocent person. It bears repeating that God was the designer of the Levitical system, with all of its alleged built-in deficiencies, including the fact that the high priest was mortal and unable to perpetually serve the people.

God's instructions on this point—as well as those of Jesus—are clear and unequivocal:

221. Denaux, "Jesus Christ, High Priest and Sacrifice," 113; Vanhoye, *Structure and Message of the Epistle to the Hebrews*, 14–15.

> Deut. 30:11–14 11 "For this commandment that I command you today is not too hard for you, neither is it far off. 12 It is not in heaven, that you should say, 'Who will ascend to heaven for us and bring it to us, that we may hear it and do it?' 13 Neither is it beyond the sea, that you should say, 'Who will go over the sea for us and bring it to us, that we may hear it and do it?' 14 *But the word is very near you. It is in your mouth and in your heart, so that you can do it.* (ESV)
>
> Luke 10:25–28 25 And behold, a lawyer stood up to put him to the test, saying, "Teacher, what shall I do to inherit eternal life?" 26 He said to him, "What is written in the Law? How do you read it?" 27 And he answered, "You shall love the Lord your God with all your heart and with all your soul and with all your strength and with all your mind, and your neighbor as yourself." 28 And he said to him, "You have answered correctly; do this, and you will live." (ESV; cf. Mark 10:17–22; Matt. 19:16–22; Luke 18:18–23)[222]

Skeptics and detractors are unconvinced that the author of Hebrews is correct when he writes that Jesus "is able to save to the uttermost those who draw near to God through him." They can quote verses from the Christian Bible (Matt. 3:2; 4:17; Mark 1:14–15) which suggest otherwise:

> Matt. 3: John the Baptist Prepares the Way
>
> 1 In those days John the Baptist came preaching in the wilderness of Judea, 2 "Repent, for the kingdom of heaven is at hand."
>
> Matt. 4: Jesus Begins His Ministry
>
> 17 From that time Jesus began to preach, saying, "Repent, for the kingdom of heaven is at hand."
>
> Mark 1: Jesus Begins His Ministry
>
> 14 Now after John was arrested, Jesus came into Galilee, proclaiming the gospel of God, 15 and saying, "The time is fulfilled, and the kingdom of God is at hand; repent and believe in the gospel."

These verses do not mention the need for people to approach God through a mediator. The instructions are clearly stated and easy to understand.

Skeptics and detractors argue that the original message—as taught by John the Baptist (the first to preach this concept) and Jesus—was clear and unequivocal: repent. The word repent means "to return." It can

222. It is important note that Jesus also presents alternatives: Matthew 10:32–33; 28:18; Mark 16:16; John 3:36; 5:21–23; 8:24; 10:9; 17:1–2.

either refer to returning to God or a person changing their former ways of thinking and acting. Neither John the Baptist nor Jesus *initially* taught that (1) Jesus must die on the cross for the sins of humanity, (2) Jesus' death on the cross is a one-time sacrifice for the sins of humankind, (3) only believing in Jesus' death and resurrection can ensure eternal salvation, or (4) Jesus will eternally be an intercessor on behalf of humankind. Therefore, the verses cited above counter the claim that Jesus "is able to save to the uttermost those who draw near to God through him."

Mark's (1:15) words "believe in the gospel" (or "the good news") have multiple possible meanings. They could not refer to the four gospels because they had not been composed. Commentators offer numerous explanations of "the good news" being either (1) the message that the future King of the Kingdom of God was already present among them, (2) faith in Jesus, as well as what he said, (3) the teaching that Jesus died for our sins and then experienced a physical bodily resurrection; (4) the news of God's salvation in Jesus, (5) the gospel proclaimed by Jesus or the gospel about Jesus, or (6) the news of God manifesting himself in Jesus Christ. James R. Edwards writes:

> Likewise, the gospel, as it is proclaimed by and present in Jesus, can remarkably be summarized in a single indicative: the diving blessing is present in "the kingdom of God," and the human obligation in two simple imperatives, "repent" and "believe."[223]

Many Christian commentators argue that Jesus was implying that the kingdom of heaven is now available today in the Person of the King.[224] These commentators debate (1) whether the time element refers to the present or future, or both; (2) the location of the kingdom (earth or heaven); (3) whether the kingdom is a state of mind that the believer experiences or a state of affairs on earth, and (4) the meaning of the word "repent." Regardless, they all agree it must *come* with the ministry of Jesus. However, this interpretation is merely a Christian theological belief and opinion. In fact, the Hebrew Bible refutes this belief, which is why it is unacceptable to many detractors, to the consternation of adamant Christian believers. Establishing or refuting a theological claim (Hebrews, Mark, or Matthew) is difficult if the author's original meaning is no longer known.

223. Edwards, *The Gospel According to Mark*, 48.

224. There is no genuine distinction between the Kingdom of Heaven and the Kingdom of God.

HEBREWS 7:26

> 26 For it was indeed fitting that we should have such a high priest holy, innocent, unstained, separated from sinners, and exalted above the heavens. (ESV)

In verses 26 through 28, the author asserts that Jesus, the high priest, is superior due to his character. The author also makes several unsubstantiated and unverifiable claims about Jesus. In the Gospels, Jesus never assigns himself the title or claims to be a priest.[225] Hebrews 5:5 is precise: "So also *Christ did not exalt himself to be made a high priest*, but was appointed by him who said to him" (ESV). Therefore, Jesus did not assume the high priest's office until the Father called on him to do so. As a proof text, the author of Hebrews quotes Psalm 2: "The supreme qualification of Jesus to be a high priest is that he is the unique Son."[226]

Skeptics and detractors find these arguments unconvincing. (1) There is no evidence that God appointed Jesus as a high priest. (2) Just because the author claims that Psalm 2:7 refers to Jesus does not mean that assertion is correct. He is merely providing his opinion. Detractors—especially Jewish counter-missionaries—refute the notion that Psalm 2:7 could have referred to Jesus. (3) An incomprehensible and unfathomable problem arises with the Trinity: each member of the Trinity is entirely divine, possessing all attributes of God. (a) If the Son is fully God, as are the Father and the Holy Spirit, (b) the three are co-omniscient, co-omnipotent, co-omnipresent, and co-eternal, and (c) the three are distinct "persons," there exists a "mystery." Christian theology posits that the Triune God does not have three separate 'minds" or "wills." The Godhead is one essence. One God exists in three distinct "persons" but is of one Divine nature and, therefore, of one will and mind. How, then, can the author claim that Jesus, the Son, did not assume the high priest's office until the Father called on him to do so? This question involves metaphysics that exceed human comprehension and are subject to diverging interpretations (arguments from authority or *argumentum ab auctoritate*). (4) In the gospel narratives, the disciples do not call Jesus a priest. (5) The author is proclaiming his understanding and opinion. The source of his information is unknowable and unverifiable.

225. Schrock, "5 Ways We See Jesus Serve as a Priest."

226. Hagner, *Encountering the Book of Hebrews*, 13.

Moreover, there is no way of verifying whether the three adjectives employed to describe Jesus in Hebrews 7:26 (holy, innocent, unstained) are aptly attributed to him. The word "holy" means "separate." The author does not elaborate on how Jesus is holy. Brown says, "Christ lived a holy life? it was set apart completely for God's work and so was fully pleasing to the Father."[227] What "separates" Jesus from other human beings is a matter of academic and theological debate: Jesus' relationship with human beings or his moral purity. Does the author mean Jesus was *holy* throughout his entire life? People can be separated into a wide range of categories that can be selectively identified (e.g., sinners and non-sinners). Even if he is correct in his assertion that Jesus was holy, how would the author of Hebrews know this alleged fact since there is no evidence that he met Jesus or had information about the first thirty years of his life?

The author is also adamant that Jesus is innocent without identifying what he is innocent of. Does the author mean that Jesus was innocent throughout his life? If so, how can he confirm this claim? The author declares that Jesus is unstained. Koester says, "Hebrews argues that Christians have a high priest who remains undefiled even though he has 'tasted death on behalf of everyone (Heb 2:9)."[228] This statement is an unverifiable opinion.

Brown claims, "He lived an *unstained* life; nothing remotely impure ever marred its sinless beauty."[229] Koester identifies several possible categories of defilement: (1) physical, (2) moral, (3) sexual impurity, and (4) from the taint of death.[230] Evaluating the author's claim is difficult if his terminology is not defined. Moreover, does the author mean that Jesus was unstained throughout his life? Even if he is correct, how would the author know this alleged fact since there is no supporting evidence that the author met Jesus or had information about his first thirty years of his life? If the author refers to the idea that Jesus was sinless (never sinned), how does he know that Jesus never sinned?

Moreover, how could anyone know that Jesus was unstained throughout his life (from the age of majority i.e., thirteen)? Donald Hagner provides a Christian apologetic: "The problem with the faulty reasoning on Christ's sinlessness is that it fails to face the mystery and

227. Brown, *The Message of Hebrews*, 136.

228. Koester, *The Anchor Yale Bible*, 367.

229. Brown, *The Message of Hebrews*, 336.

230. Koester, *The Anchor Yale Bible*, 367.

paradox of the incarnation head-on."[231] Skeptics and detractors will contend that apologists require people to suspend doubt, logic, and the words of the Hebrew Bible and to accept several unfathomable mysteries on blind faith: the Trinity, the Divinity of Jesus, God's appointing Jesus to be the heir of all things through whom he also created the worlds; the Incarnation; the virgin birth, the resurrection, and the ascension of Jesus to heaven at the right hand of God. The author of Hebrews presents a theological belief.

The author claims Jesus is separated from sinners. F.F. Bruce argues that although Jesus came to earth "in the likeness of sinful flesh," he lived among sinners, received sinners, ate with sinners, and was known as the friend of sinners. Nevertheless, he is set apart from sinners, being "in a different class from sinful men." Koester refers to this description as "qualitative separation."[232] Bruce is writing as an apologist and theologian. Koester identifies a second aspect of the meaning: "Spatial separation." He declares, "It means that by his exaltation Jesus was removed from the place of sinners," and he cites Luther, Attridge, Braun, and Ellingworth to support his claim.[233] This statement is a theological claim without any means of verification. Readers must ask whether these words make sense. Once again, Koester's claim lacks supporting evidence.

The author of Hebrews also declares that Jesus is "exalted above the heavens." Brown explains: "he passed through the heavens to the throne of God."[234] This statement is hyperbolic, lacks supporting evidence, and is unverifiable. From the perspective of skeptics and detractors, the inconvenient truth is that verse 26 contains a list of descriptions of Jesus written by a believer for believers and intended to be exhortatory for those in doubt. The author's claims are unverifiable and serve a theological agenda.

F.F. Bruce provides several reasons why Jesus is a superior priest:

1. Jesus poured out his heart in earnest prayer. This argument is irrelevant. Moreover, if Jesus is God, he is pouring out his heart to God (himself, being a member of the three-person Godhead). This argument is based on the dogma of the Trinity,

231. Hagner, *Encountering the Book of Hebrews*, 77.

232. Koester, *The Anchor Yale Bible*, 367.

233. Koester, *The Anchor Yale Bible*, 367.

234. Brown, *The Message of Hebrews*, 336.

described as a mystery. On the contrary, the Trinity is a false doctrine (refuted by Christian Scripture and theologians).

2. Jesus learned suffering and how hard the path to obedience could be. However, if Jesus is God, how could he learn something new? Again, apologists will refer to Jesus' "human" aspect, arguing that God incarnate learned in his human nature.
3. Jesus offered up his life as a sin offering. This claim of a human-vicarious death violates God's explicit instructions in the Hebrew Bible. Moreover, the manner of the sacrifice violated the Torah on several vital points (e.g., whether the sacrifice was unblemished, who offered the sacrifice, where the sacrifice was offered, and how the sacrifice was offered).[235]

HEBREWS 7:27

> 27 He has no need, like those high priests, to offer sacrifices daily, first for his own sins and then for those of the people, since he did this once for all when he offered up himself. (ESV)

Bruce discusses the claim that Jesus did not need to present a daily or yearly sacrifice for the people's sins. He provides two explanations: (1) Jesus provided a permanently valid sin offering (with no need for repetition) on behalf of the people when he offered up his own life on the cross. It is a one-time sacrifice because Jesus was a "perfect and efficacious" offering. (2) Jesus was "holy, free from guile and defilement."[236] Koester concurs, saying, "On the basis of these statutes, Hebrews assumes that the priests regularly sinned. Jesus alone was sinless."[237] Brown agrees: "Our high priest is by contrast pure and spotless, *made perfect for ever*, that is, completely efficacious."[238]

Gerald O'Collins and Michael Keenan Jones expand on the writing of the authors mentioned above:

> Nevertheless, the author of Hebrews is concerned to insist that the *entire life* of Jesus was without sin (4:15) and that, while

235. Bruce, *The Epistle to the Hebrews*, 176–79.
236. Bruce, *The Epistle to the Hebrews*, 177.
237. Koester, *The Anchor Yale Bible*, 367.
238. Brown, *The Message of Hebrews*, 137.

> tested by suffering, he behaved with unshaken obedience (5:7–8; 13:12). As High Priest he never needed to offer sacrifices of expiation for his own sins (7:27). When the pre-existent Son came, he came to do the will of God (10:5–7); he proved himself to be 'holy, blameless, undefiled' (7:26) and so at the end could offer himself to God 'without blemish' (9:14). This was a blameless, priestly life that involved, from beginning to end, completing the race of faith perfectly (12:1–2). Christ remains the unsurpassable source and model of faith for others.[239]

In response, Luke Timothy Johnson points out that verse 27 is factually false:

> The author declares that in contrast to the high priests, Jesus had no need to offer sacrifices every day first for himself and then for the people. The factual problem is not the offering for the self and for the people (see 5:3), but the use of the term "every day" (*kath' hēmeran*). The requirement for the high priest to offer such a double sacrifice was only yearly, on the Day of Atonement (see 9:7).[240]

In addition, skeptics and detractors find the following objections powerful and convincing: (1) The death of Jesus on the cross contradicts the Hebrew Bible. (2) An innocent person cannot die (vicarious atonement) for the sins of the guilty. (3) No proof exists that Jesus was a perfect and efficacious offering. (a) The Christian Bible provides limited snapshots of his life from about thirty. There is no information about Jesus' life from the age of adulthood/maturity (thirteen) to the age of thirty. Moreover, we have only limited information, perhaps favorably composed and edited, about his remaining years (an argument from silence). (b) In addition, the word "perfect" requires elaboration. His body (if we are referencing the body) would have experienced blemishing during his trial, scourging, and crucifixion. Consequently, it would be ritually impure. On the other hand, if we are referring to Jesus' ethics and morals, they are also unverifiable. (4) There is insufficient evidence for the claim that Jesus was "holy, free from guile and defilement." It bears repeating that the Christian Bible provides only snapshots of his life and that the authors of the Gospels and the composer of Hebrews had no means of knowing everything that Jesus thought, said, or did. The author is expressing a personal belief.

239. O'Collins and Keenan, *Jesus Our Priest*, 61.

240. Johnson, *Hebrews: A Commentary*, 195.

F.F. Bruce continues with his apologetic argument that Jesus is superior: he "made purification for sins" (1:3), he was appointed "to make atonement for the people's sins" (2:17), it is the function of the high priest to "offer gifts and sacrifices for sins" (5:1), and "the Lord offered up himself" (7:27).[241] Here, Bruce is employing Hebrews to substantiate Hebrews.

Donald Hagner focuses on the phrase "once for all." This phrase occurs several times in Hebrews, employing two Greek words, *hapax* and *ephapax*, with the same meaning. They are in Hebrews 7:27; 9:12, 26, 28; and 10:10. He continues by saying the affirmation of "once and for all" points to the "weakness and provisional character of the Levitical priesthood and to the sufficiency and finality of Christ's sacrificial death on the cross."[242]

However, the Hebrew Bible is unequivocal. *The Messiah will restore the sacrificial system* (Zech. 14:21; Isa. 56:7; 60:7; Jer. 33:17–18; Ezek. 43:22–23; 45:17; Hos. 3:3–4; Zeph. 3:10; Zech. 14:21; Mal. 3:1–4) *as well as the practices of the Sabbatical Year (Shmitah) and reestablish the law of the Jubilee.* For instance, "in those days," referring to the future time, Jeremiah 33:18 declares, "and the Levitical priests shall never lack a man in my presence to offer burnt offerings, to burn grain offerings, and *to make sacrifices forever*" (ESV).

Once again, by contrast, the Christian Bible repeatedly declares that Jesus is the *final* sacrifice for all time and that there will *no longer* be any future need to return to the animal sacrificial system. For example, Paul writes in Romans 6:10: "The death he died, he died to sin, once for all . . ." (See also Heb. 10:10, 18.) If Jesus is the final sacrifice, then (1) why will the sacrificial system be restored in the messianic age, as instructed by God through the prophets Isaiah, Jeremiah, Ezekiel, Hosea, Zechariah, and Malachi, and (2) why will "the Messiah"—named "the Prince"—*bring a sin sacrifice on behalf of himself and the nation*?

> Ezek. 45:22 On that day the prince shall *provide for himself* and all the people of the land a young bull for *a sin offering*. (ESV)

Skeptics and detractors question why the author of Hebrews ignores Ezekiel 45:22.

Verse 27 concludes with the words "when he offered up himself." Donald Hagner continues, "The shocking fact that in this case the high

241. Bruce, *The Epistle to the Hebrews*, 178

242. Hagner, *Encountering the Book of Hebrews*, 105.

priest offers up *himself* as a sacrifice should not be missed."[243] Koester elaborates, saying:

> Levitical priests offered animals, but Christ offered himself, thereby making a superior sacrifice (9:13–14). Early Christians recognized that it was not only important that Christ died, but that he voluntarily 'gave himself for our sins' (Gal 1:4; cf. Mark 10:45; 1 Tim 2:6; Tit 2:14; John 10:11, 18; cf. 1 John 3:16).[244]

Notably, since Abraham voluntarily offered Isaac during the *Akedah* (and Isaac offered no resistance), human sacrifice has been viewed as unacceptable. Moreover, the Hebrew Bible is clear: a person cannot offer their life to atone for the sins of another (Ezek. 18:20). Coincidentally, Josephus says, "Now Isaac was twenty-five years old."[245] Rabbinic tradition claims that Isaac was thirty-seven years old.[246] In *Apologetic Press*, Dave Miller's literature review says, "We conclude that as the several lines of evidence converge, they point to Isaac being a young man—not a young boy."[247] Therefore, Abraham offered to give up his son as a young man as a burnt offering, and Isaac, a young man, offered himself as a burnt offering without requiring an explanation of God's purpose.[248] The shocking fact that in this case, Isaac, a young man, offers up himself as a sacrifice should not be missed.

Ezekiel 18:20 states that the soul who sins is the one who will die. The son will not share the father's guilt, nor will the father share the son's guilt. The righteousness of the righteous man shall be upon him, and the wickedness of the wicked shall be upon him. Therefore, the death of an innocent and righteous person can neither wipe away a person's sins nor redeem another from their sins.

In addition, Jesus did not state in the four Gospels that he would die to save humankind from sin. When approached by a man who asked what he could do to gain eternal life, Jesus told him to keep the commandments (Matt. 19:16, 17); in other words, it was sufficient to obey God's Law. Furthermore, even if Jesus were altruistic and willing to

243. Hagner, *Encountering the Book of Hebrews*, 105.

244. Koester, *The Anchor Yale Bible*, 368.

245. Josephus, *Antiquities* 1.13.2

246. E.g., Ibn Ezra, *Ibn Ezra's Commentary on the Pentateuch*; Genesis 22.5.1

247. Miller, "How Old Was Isaac?"

248. Genesis 22:1 informs readers that the purpose of the *Akedah* was to serve as a test.

exchange his life for the sins of humanity, his noble gesture would have been invalid and unacceptable. Despite the author's claim, no one can receive a pardon for their sins through another's death.

Finally, the author of Hebrews fails to mention arguments that refute the claim that believing in Jesus' vicarious death, burial, and resurrection is sufficient to remove a person's sins. Instead, he focuses on Jesus being the paschal lamb and the belief that "without the shedding of blood, there can be no remission of sin" (Heb. 9:22). As we have already discussed, the Hebrew Bible provides numerous verses where the prophets redirect the emphasis away from sacrifice, by stressing God's desire for obedience, repentance, righteousness, justice, and mercy. Skeptics and detractors argue that a false understanding exists among many sincere Christian believers: if they sin against another person, Jesus will forgive them for the sin without requiring repentance or restitution. These Christians believe that grace is superior to the law and faith is superior to works. However, the New Testament contains a crucial caveat, "For as the body apart from the spirit is dead, so also faith apart from works is dead" (James 2:26, ESV).

HEBREWS 7:28

> 28 For the law appoints men in their weakness as high priests, but the word of the oath, which came later than the law, appoints a Son who has been made perfect forever. (ESV)

The design and instructions of God's law mandate that mortal men, with all of their frailties and limitations, were to serve the Jewish people and God. F.F. Bruce argues, "But the divine acclamation, given under oath, of a new and perpetual priesthood after Melchizedek's order, was designed to supersede the earlier priesthood established by the law."[249] In other words, the author of Hebrews and Bruce argue that God was in error when He designed and willed the creation and function of the priesthood. The reader must judge whether the anonymous author of Hebrews and Bruce interpret the Hebrew and Christian Bibles correctly. The reader must be cognizant that the author of Hebrews is not a prophet, and we cannot verify that he was a rabbi. It is possible (though doubtful) that he was not a member of the Children of Israel, but a pagan who came to accept Jesus. We know as little about this author as we do the enigmatic Melchizedek.

249. Bruce, *The Epistle to the Hebrews*, 179.

Finally, the author claims that God "appoints a Son who has been made perfect forever." This claim expresses an unverifiable opinion. Where is the indisputable evidence that (1) God appointed the Son (Jesus), (2) the Son (Jesus) has been made perfect, and (3) the Son (Jesus) will remain perfect forever? These claims are unverifiable theological beliefs that are derived from the Christian Bible. Therefore, skeptics and detractors point out that the Christian Bible is being used to confirm the Christian Bible.

HEBREWS 8:1–13

Hebrews chapter 8 does not mention Melchizedek. However, the author continues explaining why Jesus and the new covenant are superior to the old covenant of the Hebrew Bible. Grindheim says, "Of all the writings in the New Testament, the Letter to the Hebrews contains the most categorical statements about the abrogation of the old covenant (8:13) and the impotence of the Mosaic law (10:1)."[250] The author repeats prior ideas about the high priest, sacrifices, and the covenant when he discusses Melchizedek. (1) The old covenant was imperfect. (2) The old covenant was powerless. (3) The old covenant was obsolete. To support his reasoning, the author quotes five verses of Jeremiah 31, claiming that God would create a *new* covenant with His people. The quote comprises one-third of chapter 8.

> 8 For he finds fault with them when he says:
> "Behold, the days are coming, declares the Lord,
> when I will establish a new covenant with the house of Israel
> and with the house of Judah,
> 9 not like the covenant that I made with their fathers
> on the day when I took them by the hand to bring them out of the land of Egypt.
> For they did not continue in my covenant,
> and so I showed no concern for them, declares the Lord.
> 10 For this is the covenant that I will make with the house of Israel
> after those days, declares the Lord:
> I will put my laws into their minds,
> and write them on their hearts,

250. Grindheim, *The Letter to the Hebrews.*

and I will be their God,
and they shall be my people.
11 And they shall not teach, each one his neighbor
and each one his brother, saying, 'Know the Lord,'
for they shall all know me,
from the least of them to the greatest.
12 For I will be merciful toward their iniquities,
and I will remember their sins no more." (ESV)

Jewish commentators differ in their interpretation of Jeremiah 31:31.

Rabbi Dovid Rosenfeld (AishTorah) writes:

> Jeremiah 31:30 follows this same pattern. Although it does state that God will create a new covenant, it clearly states that it will be with the House of Israel and the House of Judah. It further continues that as part of the covenant God would place His Torah upon our hearts (v. 32). Thus, even though we had broken our original covenant with God, He will create a newer stronger one in its place—but still with Israel and again commanding us to observe His Torah. The new covenant did not abrogate the original one to keep the Torah nor was it directed towards all the nations. As vv. 34–35 continue, Israel will continue to be God's nation so long as the sun shines, the moon rises, and the surf breaks upon the coast.
>
> In addition, as is clear from the verses, this renewal of the covenant will be with both the houses of Judah and Israel (i.e., with both the southern kingdom of Judah and the northern kingdom of the Ten Tribes). This clearly did not occur in Jesus's time, when the Ten Tribes had already been dispersed. Jeremiah also states that at the time of this renewal, there will be universal knowledge of God ("for they will all know Me" (v. 33). This too did not occur in Jesus's day but is rather a reference to the End of Days.[251]

Gerald Sigal (Jews for Judaism) explains:

> Is Jeremiah's reference to a "new covenant" (Jeremiah 31:31–34) a prophecy fulfilled by the New Testament?

Answer: The term "new covenant" would be meaningless unless what Jeremiah meant by it was the renewing of the old covenant, which will thereby regain its full original vigor. The covenant of old is of eternal

251. Rosenfeld, "Jeremiah 31 and the New Covenant."

duration, never to be rescinded or to be superseded by a new covenant (Leviticus 26:44–45). The covenant between God and Israel is frequently referred to as everlasting (e.g., Genesis 17:7, 13, 19; Psalms 105:8, 10; 1 Chronicles 16:13–18).

The Christian position concerning Jeremiah's covenant is the complete opposite of what the Jewish Scriptures teach. Hebrews 8:13 states: "In that he says, a new covenant, he has made the first obsolete. Now that which is being made obsolete and growing old is near to vanishing away." In stark contrast to this statement, the Scriptures state: "The works of His hands are truth and justice; and His precepts are sure. They are established forever and ever, they are done in truth and Uprightness" (Psalms 111:7–8); "The grass withers, the flower fades; but the word of our God shall stand forever" (Isaiah 40:8).

> Jeremiah's "new covenant" is not a replacement of the existing covenant, but merely a figure of speech expressing the reinvigoration and revitalization of the existing covenant. The people of Israel possess an old covenant yet a new covenant, truly an everlasting covenant.[252]

Rabbi Tovia Singer (Outreach Judaism,) says:

> Notice how the author of Hebrews reversed the message of Jeremiah. Jeremiah 31:31 states, "I was a husband unto them . . ." Whereas Hebrews completely changes it to, "I disregarded them . . ." [Singer elaborates that the Greek phrase literally reads, "*although I disregarded them*."][253]

Rabbi Bentzion Kravitz (Jews for Judaism) writes:

> Jeremiah's New Covenant—Is There a Conspiracy to Hide the Truth?

Some Christian missionaries mistakenly believe that God broke his covenant with the Jewish people and replaced it with a "New Covenant." This is the reason they claim the New Testament supersedes the Torah.

Their mistake is based on a mistranslation of Jeremiah.

In context and based on a correct translation, Jeremiah reiterates the statement in Leviticus that although we may break the covenant, God will remain faithful to us. Jeremiah says it this way, "*I will make a new*

252. Sigal, "Is Jeremiah's "New Covenant" (Jeremiah 31:31–34) a Prophecy Fulfilled by the New Testament?"

253. Singer, *Let's Get Biblical*, 67.

covenant with the House of Israel. . .It will not be like the covenant I made with their fathers, when I took them by the hand to lead them out of the land of Egypt, a covenant which they broke, though I remained a husband to them" (Jeremiah 31:31–32).

The New Testament misrepresents Jeremiah's statement. Instead of saying that God remained a faithful "husband" to the Jewish people, the New Testament claims that God "*turned away from (or rejected) them*" (Hebrews 8:9).

This is not the only mistake made by missionaries. They falsely accuse the rabbis of hiding the truth from the Jewish people by concealing some "sensitive" passages.

There are many responses to this accusation. However, in this week portion, this conspiracy theory is blatantly refuted by the great biblical commentator Rashi. Commenting on the reaffirming words "*I will maintain My covenant with you*" (Leviticus 26:9), Rashi does not hesitate to mention Jeremiah 31 and a New Covenant.

> Rashi explains that the New Covenant will be called "new" because it will be enhanced so that not only will God keep his promise never break it, but even the Jewish people will no longer break it. This will possible because in the future, our desire to rebel against God will be eradicated, and we will serve God wholeheartedly (Ezekiel 36:26–27).[254]

Rabbi Stuart Federow explains:

> Jeremiah 31:31–34 speaks of a 'new covenant,' and the term 'covenant' means 'testament.' So, in these verses, Christians see a prophecy of their New Testament . . .
>
> Jeremiah 31:31 speaks of a 'new covenant.' But one could ask the question, 'is this new covenant a covenant which replaces any of the covenants that Gd made with the Jews beforehand? . . .
>
> The covenant that Gd made with the People of Israel through Moses, did not replace or break the covenant Gd made with Jacob, or with Isaac, or with Abraham. Every subsequent covenant that Gd makes with the Jews, re-affirms and re-establishes the covenant that Gd made with the Jews before it.
>
> The covenant that Gd made with the Jews is an eternal covenant, and it is a covenant made with them, with their descendants, and with all those who convert to Judaism. Gd's promise to the

254. Kravitz, "Jeremiah's New Covenant—Is There a Conspiracy to Hide the Truth?"

> Jews, that His covenant with them is eternal, is repeated over and over again throughout the Hebrew Scriptures . . .
>
> More importantly, that the covenant between Gd and the Jews is eternal is also found immediately following the very passage in question, of Jeremiah 31:31–, beginning with the very next verse . . .
>
> The next verses actually deny the most basic belief of Christianity, that Jesus can die for your sins:
>
>> *In those days they shall say no more, The fathers have eaten a sour grape, and the children's teeth are set on edge. But every one shall die for his own iniquity: every man that eateth the sour grape, his teeth shall be set on edge.* [Jer. 31:29–30][255]

Readers should thoughtfully reflect on Hebrews 8:8 and Jeremiah 31:31. The "new covenant" is a sacred promise explicitly made with the house of Israel and the house of Judah. It does not extend to others, despite the assertions that this covenant has been superseded and that Christianity stands as the "New Israel." This covenant does not involve a physical transfer. Instead, it will be inscribed on their hearts, creating a deeper intimacy with God. As it beautifully states, "I will put my law within them, and I will write it on their hearts. And I will be their God, and they will be my people" (31:33, ESV). Through a powerful metaphor, the Hebrew text reveals that God will "write" it on their hearts, signifying a transformative relationship.

This instruction is also in Ezekiel 36:26–27. "26 And I will give you a new heart, and a new spirit I will put within you. And I will remove the heart of stone from your flesh and give you a heart of flesh. 27 And I will put my Spirit within you, and cause you to walk in my statutes and be careful to obey my rules" (ESV). It should be noted that Christian commentators and theologians omit the last half of verse 27. It unequivocally refutes any notion of a "new covenant" replacing the Torah. The Jewish people will walk in God's statutes and carefully observe His rules. Hence, the people will be observant of the mitzvot (i.e., commandments). There is no suggestion that believing that Jesus' vicarious atonement on the cross (i.e., the crucifixion) and his resurrection will atone for the people's sins.

Moreover, Jeremiah 31:34 rejects the alleged "new covenant" proclaimed by Christian Bible commentators and theologians. This alleged new covenant cannot refer to the first century or the approximate next

255. Federow, "Jeremiah 31:31."

two thousand years. "And no longer shall each one teach his neighbor and each his brother, saying, 'Know the Lord,' for they shall all know me, from the least of them to the greatest, declares the Lord. For I will forgive their iniquity, and I will remember their sin no more." If this prophecy was correct, why would a Christian need to evangelize and "teach his neighbor and each his brother" about the Lord?

However, in Hebrews 8:13, the concluding sentence is the lynchpin. The author of Hebrews is uncompromising. "In speaking of a new covenant, he makes the first one obsolete. And what is becoming obsolete and growing old is ready to vanish away" (ESV). Therefore, the Law (Torah, *nomos*) is over. In this brief sentence, the author of Hebrews differentiates Christianity from Judaism, creating an unbridgeable gulf between the two faiths. Verse 13 directly contradicts and supersedes God's instructions. Skeptics and detractors ask (an argument from silence): why did the author refuse to engage with contradictory passages?

> Gen. 17:7 And I will establish my covenant between me and you and your offspring after you throughout their *generations for an everlasting covenant*, to be God to you and to your offspring after you. (ESV)
>
> Gen. 17:9 And God said to Abraham, "As for you, you shall keep my covenant, you and your offspring after you *throughout their generations*. (ESV)
>
> Gen. 17:19 God said, "No, but Sarah your wife shall bear you a son, and you shall call his name Isaac. *I will establish my covenant with him as an everlasting covenant* for his offspring after him. (ESV)
>
> Deut. 7:9 Know therefore that the Lord your God is God, the faithful God who keeps covenant and steadfast love with those who love him *and keep his commandments, to a thousand generations* (ESV)
>
> Deut. 32:4 The Rock, his work is *perfect*, for all his ways are justice. A God of faithfulness and without iniquity, just and upright is he. [ESV]
>
> Ps. 19:7 [8 Hebrew Bible] The law of the Lord is *perfect*, reviving the soul; the testimony of the Lord is sure, making wise the simple (ESV)
>
> Ps. 105:8–10 He remembers his covenant forever, the word that he commanded, for a thousand generations, 9 the covenant that he made with Abraham, his sworn promise to Isaac, 10 which

he confirmed to Jacob as a statute, to Israel as an everlasting covenant (ESV)

1 Chron. 16:15–17 Remember his covenant forever, the word that he commanded, for a thousand generations, 16 the covenant that he made with Abraham, his sworn promise to Isaac, 17 which he confirmed to Jacob as a statute, to Israel as an everlasting covenant (ESV)

Isa. 40:8 The grass withers, the flower fades, *but the word of our God will stand forever.* (ESV)

PAUL HYDON'S CRITIQUE OF THE AUTHOR OF HEBREWS

The Methodist minister Paul Hydon concludes his PhD dissertation in theology with a compelling and critical analysis of the anonymous author of the book of Hebrews. His thought-provoking critique is worthy of attention. The points that he discusses are rarely explored in the existing literature.

1. When . . . the author is arguing the failure of the Aaronic priesthood, his argument rests mainly upon the fact that this priesthood has failed for him and his readers. It failed to do for him and them what a priesthood should do, he claims, and there would seem to be no way of controverting his claim.
2. When he claims that this priesthood "can never make perfect them that draw nigh" [Heb. 10:1b], he means that it did not make him perfect when he tried to draw nigh.
3. When he speaks of the law as "weak" and "unprofitable," he means that it was weak and unprofitable to him. It did not perform for him what a law should perform for a believer.
4. When he states that the Aaronic priests offered "gifts and sacrifices that cannot, as touching the conscience, make the worshipper perfect, being only . . . carnal ordinances" [Hebrews 9:9b–10], he means that these gifts and sacrifices could not and did not touch his conscience and make him perfect. He did not gain forgiveness of his sins through the ministry of the Aaronic priests in offering these sacrifices. He did not feel his conscience cleansed "from dead works to serve the living God." [Heb. 9:14b]

5. When he says the Aaronic priests failed to remove the obstacles, the hindrances, the hurdles, that men meet as they strive to approach God, and which so fatally separate them from God, he means that these priests did not remove these obstacles and hindrances for him as he tried to approach God. They did not enable him or anyone else to draw nigh to God or come into the presence of God.[256]

256. Hydon, "The Priesthood of Jesus as Presented by the Epistle to the Hebrews," 202–3; cf. Denaux, "Jesus Christ, High Priest and Sacrifice," 120—21.

5

Jesus' Bodily Resurrection

> The New Testament book known as the epistle to the Hebrews contains little obvious reference to Jesus' resurrection. Modern interpreters generally account for this relative silence by noting that the author's soteriological and christological concerns have led him to emphasize Jesus' death and exaltation while ignoring, spiritualizing, or even denying his resurrection.[1]

INTRODUCTION

Some readers might object that the author of Hebrews does not explicitly mention Jesus' bodily resurrection. However, from a Christian perspective, many verses in Hebrews only make sense if its author believed that Jesus was raised from the dead.

1. Readers and listeners are told by the author that "after making purification for sins" [Heb. 1:3], referring to Jesus' sacrificial death, "he sat down at the right hand of the Majesty on high." However, if Jesus had not been raised from the dead, he could hardly have been exalted by God the Father and could hardly have sat down at the right hand of God.

1. Moffitt, "A New and Living Way," iv.

2. If the author of Hebrews believed Jesus did not rise from the dead, how can the author say of him in Hebrews 1:8, "Your throne, O God, is forever and ever"?
3. If the author of Hebrews believed Jesus is dead, never more to rise, how can the author say in Hebrews 1:10 that, whereas the natural creation "wears out like a garment" and "perishes," the incarnate Son of God "remains" and is ever "the same"?
4. If the author of Hebrews believed Jesus is still dead, how can the author say at the end of Hebrews 1:12 that his "years will have no end"? This verse would make no sense if Jesus only lived thirty-three years and then died, never to live again.
5. If the author of Hebrews believed Jesus' body was decaying in a distant grave, how can the author say in Hebrews 2:17 that this very Jesus "can help those who are being tempted"?
6. If the author of Hebrews believed Jesus is still dead, how can the author say in Hebrews 2:8–10 that Jesus is the one in whom the destiny of humankind as ruler over all of creation is ultimately fulfilled?

Christian theists point to one unambiguous, undeniable, and incontrovertible verse about the resurrection toward the end of the Epistle: "*Now may the God of peace who brought again from the dead our Lord Jesus*, the great shepherd of the sheep, by the blood of the eternal covenant" (Heb. 13:20, ESV). In addition, by his death on the cross and his subsequent resurrection, the Epistle proclaims that Jesus *became the source of eternal salvation to all who obey him.*

Skeptics, detractors, and others who adopt an alternative worldview argue that the evidence presented by many Christian theists does not provide compelling, convincing, and sufficient support for the claims made about Jesus in the Epistle to the Hebrews. Moreover, they argue that a detailed reading and critical examination of the Epistle to the Hebrews, the Hebrew Bible, and the Qur'an does *not* support the proclamation that Jesus is a high priest according to the order of Melchizedek, that he is the Messiah, or that he died for our sins and *rose from the dead on the third day.*

David Moffitt's literature review identifies several academic and theological explanations as to why the resurrection does *not* play an essential role in the author's design at face value:

1. *The "Passed Over" View*
   The event is not central for the writer because his particular soteriological concerns—and especially the elements of his priestly Christology—have led him to focus on the moments of Jesus' death and exaltation. Moffitt identifies nine commentators who support this view. Proponents include F.F. Bruce, Paul Ellingworth, and William L. Lane.

2. *The Agnostic Approach and Jesus' Resurrection as a Spiritual Ascension*
   One cannot draw any firm conclusions about the place or conception of Jesus' resurrection in Hebrews (the Agnostic approach). Proponents include William G. Loader, Craig C. Koester, and Luke Timothy Johnson. In contrast, other commentators argue that the evidence in the text indicates that Jesus ascended to the heavenly realm at the moment of his death. In this way, they avoid a possible resurrection-gap between Jesus' sacrificial death on the cross and the atoning work associated with his heavenly exaltation. Moffitt cites Hans Windisch, Otfried Hofius, Erich Grässer, Richard D. Nelson, and Kenneth L. Schenck as examples of scholars who advocate this view.

3. *No Resurrection of Jesus in Hebrews*
   Moffitt engages the opinion that some writers think the author of Hebrews has deliberately avoided applying the terminology of resurrection to Jesus. "In place of the language/concept of resurrection, they argue, stands the idea of the transition of Jesus' spirit out of the earthly realm and into heaven, or perhaps just the theological significance such an idea might imply. The author does not confuse or conceive of this transition in terms of resurrection."[2] (p. 34) Moffitt provides a list of commentators who support this view, including Georg Bertram, Ernst Käsemann, and Harold Attridge.

Moffitt concludes with the following observations (sentence numbering has been added by the author):

1. The evidence presented in the foregoing discussion attests the diversity of views regarding the presence of Jesus' resurrection in Hebrews.

2. Moffitt, "A New and Living Way," 27.

2. The overwhelming consensus in contemporary scholarship holds that the author makes little or no reference to Jesus' resurrection.
3. Disagreement arises when talking about what one can or cannot conclude from this strange silence.
4. Amid the disagreement, however, one point of unanimity lies in the primary rationale for why Jesus' resurrection is not a significant event or category for this author: to the extent that the writer's portrayal of Jesus as the great high priest intends to identify Jesus' death on the cross as the moment of self-sacrifice that ultimately atones for sin, the resurrection of Jesus is unnecessary.[3]

WHY JUDAISM REJECTS THE CHRISTIAN VIEW THAT JESUS WAS RAISED FROM THE DEAD, IN ACCORDANCE WITH THE SCRIPTURES

In Judaism, Malachi is considered the last of the Twelve Minor Prophets, which is why his writings appear at the very end of the *Nevi'im* (Prophets) in the Hebrew Bible. Jesus, whom Christians regard as a prophet, priest, and king, lived hundreds of years *after* the time of Malachi. Therefore, the Hebrew Bible could not have included the New Testament narratives of Jesus' life, death, and alleged resurrection. In addition, the Hebrew Bible offers numerous *theological* reasons why Jesus' resurrection could not have occurred, contrary to the claims made by Paul in 1 Corinthians 15:3–4.

There are no explicit and unequivocal verses in the Hebrew Bible that the Messiah (i.e., Christ) will die, be buried for three days, *and be raised on the third day for the sins of humanity*. Some Christians have proposed Matthew 16:4/Luke 11:29–30, which reports Jesus' exclusive, self-proclaimed proof of his identity: the sign of Jonah. "'An evil and adulterous generation seeks for a sign, but no sign will be given to it except the sign of Jonah.' So he left them and departed" (ESV). Jonah 1:17 reads, "And the Lord appointed a great fish to swallow up Jonah. And Jonah was in the belly of the fish three days and three nights." (ESV)

However, this alleged proof fails because Jesus' death and resurrection do not match the storyline in Jonah. Jonah was swallowed *alive*, stayed in the fish *alive*, and was later spat out *alive*. In contrast, Jesus died, was buried, remained in the tomb while dead, and was resurrected alive.

3. Moffitt, "A New and Living Way," 53.

The conditions do not match. In addition, the timescales do not match either:

> Insofar as the components of time are concerned, Christian apologists counter in Jewish tradition that part of a day counts as a whole day. Hence, Jesus fulfilled the three-day prophecy. On two grounds, this defense is lacking. First, the onus is on the apologists to unequivocally prove that concerning this specific prophecy, Jesus meant that part of a day would count as a whole day. Numerous Christian Bible commentators advocating a Wednesday or Thursday crucifixion deny the hypothesis that part of a day counts as an entire day. Second, regardless of the previous apologetic, Christian apologists could not prove that Jesus was resurrected on the third day because there were no witnesses. On Easter Sunday, visitors to the tomb found a missing corpse. The fact that the Gospels reported many events relating to Jesus' resurrection occurring on or after Easter Sunday is irrelevant. Presumably, even if there was a resurrection, it could have happened before Easter Sunday.[4]

Moreover, the Hebrew Bible explicitly warns its readers against placing any credence in signs and miracles that could lead them away from the one true God (Deut. 13:1–5, AV):

> *Deuteronomy 13:1–5 If a prophet or a dreamer of dreams arises among you and gives you a sign or a wonder, 2 and the sign or wonder that he tells you comes to pass, and if he says, 'Let us go after other gods,' which you have not known, 'and let us serve them,' 3 you shall not listen to the words of that prophet or that dreamer of dreams.* For the Lord your God is testing you, to know whether you love the Lord your God with all your heart and with all your soul. 4 You shall walk after the Lord your God and fear him and keep his commandments and obey his voice, and you shall serve him and hold fast to him. 5 But that prophet or that dreamer of dreams shall be put to death, because he has taught rebellion against the Lord your God, who brought you out of the land of Egypt and redeemed you out of the house of slavery, to make you leave the way in which the Lord your God commanded you to walk. So you shall purge the evil from your midst. (ESV)

In any case, a resurrection would prove nothing. Resurrections (i.e., resuscitations) occur elsewhere in the Hebrew Bible:

4. Alter, *Resurrection and Its Apologetics*, 151.

- Widow's son (1 Kgs. 17:17–22): Resurrected by Elijah.
- Shunammite's son (2 Kgs. 4:32–35): Resurrected by Elisha.
- Unnamed man (2 Kgs. 13:20–21): Resurrected by Elisha.

Other than Jesus, the Christian Bible reports records six instances of individuals being resurrected. These include people who were (according to the writers of the Gospels and the Acts of the Apostles) resurrected by Jesus, by God Himself, and by the apostles Peter and Paul.

New Testament (Jesus' ministry):

- Jairus' daughter (Mark 5:41): Resurrected by Jesus.
- Widow's son at Nain (Luke 7:11–15): Resurrected by Jesus.
- Lazarus (John 11:43–44): Resurrected by Jesus.
- Many saints (Matt. 27:52–53 Their tombs were opened after Jesus' death on the cross; they were then raised to life by God and appeared to people after Jesus' resurrection.

New Testament (after Jesus' resurrection):

- Dorcas (Acts 9:36–40): Resurrected by Peter.
- Eutychus (Acts 20:6–12): Resurrected by Paul.

Christian commentators and theologians could point out that, unlike Jesus, these people were *not* raised with a glorious, spiritual, and immortal body that would no longer die or experience physical decay. However, the resurrection of the saints in Matthew 27:52–53 may have been similar to that of Jesus.

WHY ISLAM REJECTS THE CHRISTIAN NOTION OF JESUS' SACRIFICIAL DEATH ON THE CROSS AND HIS RESURRECTION TO ETERNAL LIFE

The Islamic worldview is unequivocal: there was no resurrection on Easter Sunday. The Islamic view centers on their Scripture: the Qur'an. Jesus could and did *not* die as a result of crucifixion.[5] Therefore, he was not raised from the dead after being crucified. The pertinent verses from the Qu'ran (*sūra Nisa*) 4:155–158 read as follows:

5. Cockerill, "Building Bridges to Muslims or Syncretism," 332.

> 4:155 And [We cursed them] for their breaking of the covenant and their disbelief in the signs of Allah and their killing of the prophets without right and their saying, "Our hearts are wrapped." Rather, Allah has sealed them because of their disbelief, so they believe not, except for a few.
>
> 4:156 And [We cursed them] for their disbelief and their saying against Mary a great slander,
>
> 4:157 And [for] their saying, "Indeed, we have killed the Messiah, Jesus, the son of Mary, the messenger of Allah." And they did not kill him, nor did they crucify him; but [another] was made to resemble him to them. And indeed, those who differ over it are in doubt about it. They have no knowledge of it except the following of assumptions. And they did not kill him, for certain.
>
> 4:158 Rather, Allah raised him to Himself. And ever is Allah Exalted in Might and Wise.[6]

While Christians reject the Qur'an, it would be remiss not to present the theological rationale for the Muslim view that Jesus did not die due to crucifixion. This rationale is drawn directly from the Bible. What follows are the twelve *theological* reasons why Muslims reject the Christian view that Jesus was crucified and died for the sins of humanity:

1. The Islamic view of God entails that Christianity is radically mistaken in its claims about God:

    a. God is neither a body nor the essential form of a body; His presence within and unification with a human body are metaphysically impossible. Therefore, Jesus could not have been God Incarnate or died as a result of crucifixion.

    b. According to Christians, Jesus claimed to be the Divine Son of God (i.e., the second member of the Trinity). If this is correct, then he could not have died on the cross because "God is immune to death," and therefore, "You cannot kill God" (Isa. 40:28; 44:6; Jer. 10:10; 1 Tim. 1:17).

    c. If Jesus was indeed God (i.e., the second member of the Trinity), he could not have died on the cross because God cannot be human (Num. 23:19; 1 Sam. 15:29; Hos. 11:9; Job 33:12).

2. The Islamic view of sin is fundamentally at odds with the Christian view:

6. From the Saheeh International Translation.

a. Although the notion that Jesus died on the cross and redeemed all of the sins of humankind forms the basis of all Christian doctrine, the Muslim counter-position is perfectly consistent with the above-mentioned Scriptures. In essence, Muslims do not find it necessary for "God" to come down as a man and get murdered, nor is there any need for God to offer Himself as a sacrifice in order for anyone to enter heaven. The Muslim position on salvation rests upon God's infinite mercy. That is why God, through His prophets, demanded repentance for sins committed. Human beings, unlike other creatures, are endowed with free will and have the choice to accept or reject faith. Thus, sin is a byproduct of being human. Sin also enables humans to recognize their imperfections and their need for God, who is the embodiment of perfection. Through repentance, humans return to God, asking for His forgiveness and mercy. That is why repentance is the key to salvation. In the Old Testament, the words "repentance" and "forgiveness" appear hundreds of times, whereas in the New Testament, these two words appear fifty-two times.[7]

b. According to Christian doctrine, Jesus died on the cross as a sacrifice for our sins. Every human is born in original sin and will eventually commit personal sins, and therefore, someone as pure as Jesus needed to suffer crucifixion to nullify these sins. At this point, the question arises: why does anyone have to die for our sins when God, the all-merciful, could effortlessly grant us forgiveness if we asked for it? Why does He have to make someone suffer for our or someone else's sins? Isn't that unjust of Him? According to the Bible, the way to redemption is obtainable without the need for sacrifice).[8]

c. Jesus could not have died on the cross for *another* person's sin(s) (Ezek. 18:20). Scripture states that the soul who sins is the one who will die. The son will not share the father's guilt, nor will the father share the son's guilt. The righteousness of the righteous man shall be upon him, and the wickedness of the wicked shall be upon him.

7. Imran, *Christ Jesus, the Son of Mary*, 246–47.

8. Qasem, *A Closer Look at Christianity*.

d. The Christian claim that without the death of Jesus and shedding his blood, there is no redemption and remission of sin (Heb. 9:22) is a false doctrine.

e. The claim that the death of Jesus was for the atonement of our sins is a Christian theological belief. This theological claim—relating to sin—is merely an interpretation of an alleged historical event: Jesus' death.

f. Nowhere in the four Gospels does Jesus explicitly state that he would die to save humankind from sin. When approached by a man who asked what he could do to gain eternal life, Jesus told him to keep the commandments (Matt. 19:16, 17); in other words, it was sufficient to obey God's Law.

3. Justice:

   a. The death of an innocent and righteous person can neither wipe away a person's sins nor redeem another from their sins. For an innocent person to die in the place of a guilty person is an outrageous injustice.[9]

   b. "But is this just?" That is the question that our Muslim friends ask when they hear that Jesus died in place of sinners. It is not good news for them because they think it is unjust for an innocent man to die in place of the guilty.[10]

4. Allah's Goodness and Mercy:

   a. Since God can forgive, there is absolutely no need for the 'sacrifice' of which Christianity speaks. God is almighty and pardons all people of their sins provided they repent or remain steadfast in their faith as Muslims. God is kind; He is not an unmerciful judge.

   b. Allah is almighty—He can do what He likes. Allah is merciful—He forgives whom He wills.

   c. Proverbs 10:27 The fear of the LORD prolongs life, but the years of the wicked will be short. (Unless we acknowledge that Jesus did not die on the cross, we cannot have a literal interpretation of this prophecy.)

9. Troll, *Muslims Ask, Christians Answer*, 19.

10. Anyabwile, *The Gospel for Muslims*, 74.

d. Proverbs 15:29 The LORD is far from the wicked, but he hears the prayer of the righteous. (If this biblical verse is true, God must have listened to Jesus' cries and delivered him from an accursed death on the cross.)

e. Psalm 20:6 Now I know that the LORD saves his anointed; he will answer him from his holy heaven with the saving might of his right hand.

f. Psalm 28:8 The LORD is the strength of his people; he is the saving refuge of his anointed.

g. Psalm 41:2 The LORD protects him and keeps him alive; he is called blessed in the land; you do not give him up to the will of his enemies.

5. Deuteronomy 21:23 stipulates that if a man is killed for a capital offense, "his body shall not remain all night on the tree, but you shall bury him the same day, for a hanged man is cursed by God. You shall not defile your land that the LORD your God is giving you for an inheritance" (ESV):

   a. If Jesus was crucified, he was cursed because the Bible says that God curses those who are hanged from a tree.

   b. The logical conclusion of this passage in Scripture is that Jesus is accursed.

6. For many reasons, Allah would not permit crucifixion:

   a. It would be wrong for Allah to allow one of His prophets to die in shame and humiliation.

   b. If Jesus suffered and died, it would follow that God had deserted him, making him abandoned by God.

   c. How could God have abandoned so great a prophet as Jesus to His enemies? How could the Father sacrifice His Son on the cross? Ascribing such an action to god is simply blasphemy.[11]

7. In two respects, Jesus failed to fulfill the prophecy he uttered in Matthew 12:40: "For just as Jonah was three days and three nights in the belly of a giant fish, so will the Son of Man be three days and three nights in the heart of the earth" (ESV):

11. Troll, *Muslims Ask, Christians Answer*, 19.

a. Jesus was not in the tomb for three "full" days and three "full" nights, but only for one "full" day and two "full" nights, at most. According to the Bible, Jonah was in the belly of the giant fish for three days and three nights. (*The time components of the two accounts do not match.*)

b. Jonah was swallowed *alive*, stayed *alive* in the fish, and was later spit out *alive*. In contrast, Jesus died, was buried, remained in the tomb while dead, and was resurrected alive. (*The condition or state components of the two accounts do not match.*)

c. Based on this prophecy, Jesus could not have died. Why would God need to send Muhammad if the Son of God had already been crucified for the sins of humanity?

8. Muslims view the cross as a symbol of defeat, not a proclamation of divine love (see John 3:16). They seek to exalt God and not denigrate Him to the ignominy of suffering and death. For Muslims, the cross is a place of disgrace, not majesty. It is an offense both against God and the prophet of Islam.[12]

9. Muhammad:

   a. Why would God need to send Muhammad if the Son of God himself lived on earth, died as the final sacrifice for our sins, and rose again to show his power over death?[13]

   b. Muhammad, as Seal of all the Prophets, has superseded Christ.

10. Deuteronomy 18:15–18 says: "The LORD your God will raise up for you a prophet like me from among you, from your brothers—it is to him you shall listen— 16 just as you desired of the LORD your God at Horeb on the day of the assembly, when you said, 'Let me not hear again the voice of the LORD my God or see this great fire any more, lest I die.' 17 And the LORD said to me, 'They are right in what they have spoken. 18 I will raise up for them a prophet like you from among their brothers. And I will put my words in his mouth, and he shall speak to them all that I command him" (ESV). In other words, readers must ask who is more like Moses: Jesus or Muhammad.

12. Van Gorder, *No God but God*, 134.

13. Greear, *Breaking the Islam Code*, 116.

a. Muhammad, like Moses, had a natural death; the Gospels report Jesus had a violent death by crucifixion.

b. Muhammad, like Moses, died at an advanced age, whereas Jesus died at about age thirty-three.

c. Muhammad, like Moses, died married and with children, whereas Jesus died unwed and childless.

d. Muhammad, like Moses, died a leader of his people, whereas Jesus died rejected by his people.

e. Muhammad's body, like that of Moses', lies buried in the earth, whereas Jesus' body is in heaven.

f. Muhammad, like Moses, died, and none considered him a God, whereas Jesus was considered a god by some of his followers.

11. The Jewish people:

    a. The Jews, who claim to have killed Jesus in *sūrat al-nisā'* (4) 157, are doubly in error. They both schemed against the Messenger of God and arrogated to themselves God's power over life and death.

    b. "Humans can no more take a human life than they can create one. . .. God creates life, and He takes life away . . . No one can die except by God's permission" [*sūrat al 'Imran* (13) 145].

12. The Qur'an:

    a. The Qur'an, God's word, declares that Jesus did not die (*sūrat* 4:157)

    b. The Qur'an supersedes the Christian Bible.

In conclusion, Muslim theologians offer different answers to the question: what happened to Jesus before, during, and after the crucifixion? However, they all agree on one point: Muslims reject the Christian doctrine that Jesus died by crucifixion, and especially the teaching that he died for the remission of sins. The Muslim belief, relating to the remission of sins is that the sinner only needs to express sincere contrition and be faithful to Muslim laws, in order to be forgiven. In particular, an innocent person, who is certain to obtain salvation, does *not* have to die in order to eliminate the sins of others.[14]

The Islamic worldview rejects the proclamations of the Hebrews' author. Since their arguments are founded on theology, Christians must engage with them. The notion of Jesus' resurrection—which presupposes his death—is refuted by the Qur'an. Moreover, Islam categorically rejects the idea that Jesus, as a prophet, could have died via crucifixion to atone for the sins of humanity. In addition, the belief that Jesus was a high priest who died, ascended into heaven, was exalted by God, and now sits at the right hand of the Father reflects a view of Christ that is totally at odds with the words of Allah in the Qur'an.

14. Alter, *Resurrection and Its Apologetics*, 156–61.

6

A Hypothetical Jewish View of the Epistle to the Hebrews

> Proverb 27:17 instructs us that "Iron sharpens iron, and one man sharpens another" (ESV).

THE JEWISH CASE AGAINST THE LETTER TO THE HEBREWS

The Apostle Paul wrote in Romans 1:16, "I am not ashamed of the gospel." That statement is a powerful declaration of faith and commitment. It unequivocally signifies a refusal to hide or be embarrassed by one's beliefs, particularly those that are related to the Christian faith and the message of salvation through Jesus Christ. The belief of committed Christians in Romans 1:16 is respected. However, what happens when the verse is modified for those of a different faith? For example, imagine a member of the Jewish community wrote, "I am not ashamed of the Torah" or a member of the Islamic community says, "I am not ashamed of the Qur'an." This chapter and another will explore a hypothetical Jewish response: "I am not ashamed of the Torah." Its response to the author of Hebrews is unabashed, forthright, and bold. This chapter and the following provide an answer that continues to elude many Christians: why Judaism and Islam do not accept several central tenets of the Christian faith.

By now, readers will be aware that the Epistle to the Hebrews contains a multitude of assertions that are historically, exegetically, and theologically problematic from a Jewish perspective. This chapter summarizes from a Jewish point of view why the Epistle to the Hebrews should not be considered a creditworthy source and why its theological claims should be rejected. Christian apologists, Bible commentators, and theologians refute these opinions.

It is argued that the anonymity of the Epistle undermines its trustworthiness. In any case, the fact that the Epistle to the Hebrews was composed long after the biblical age of prophecy had passed means that it cannot overturn any of the Divine commands found in the Hebrew Bible, as it lacks the authority to do so. Some Christian theologians might argue that Jesus' miracles validate the Epistle's claim that he is both God and the Messiah. However, the Hebrew Bible explicitly warns believers against trusting miracle workers who attempt to entice people into worshiping anyone other than the God of Israel (Deut. 13).

Furthermore, the Epistle to the Hebrews contains over two dozen erroneous statements, calling its credibility into question. In addition, the Epistle's teachings regarding the Messiah and the need for blood sacrifice in order to obtain forgiveness of sins are fundamentally at odds with those of the Hebrew Bible. Finally, there are powerful Scriptural arguments that show that Jesus could not possibly be either God or the Messiah, as the Epistle claims he was.

Why Should Anyone Trust an Epistle Whose Author is Unknown and Who Was Not a Prophet?

The author of the Epistle to the Hebrews is anonymous. However, the scholarly consensus is that this letter was a composition for Jewish Christians. Several clues scattered throughout the Epistle suggest that the author was addressing himself to a Jewish Christian congregation and its leaders. Readers will be aware that the Epistle to the Hebrews contains a multitude of assertions that are historically, exegetically, and theologically problematic from a Jewish perspective. This chapter summarizes why, from a Jewish perception, the Epistle to the Hebrews should not be considered a credible source and that its theological claims should be rejected. Arguably, the anonymity of the Epistle undermines its trustworthiness. In any case, the fact that this Epistle was composed long after the biblical age of prophecy had passed means that it cannot overturn any of the Divine commands found in the Hebrew Bible, as it lacks the authority to do so. Some Christian theologians might argue that Jesus' miracles validate the Epistle's claim that he is God and the Messiah. However, the Hebrew Bible explicitly warns believers against trusting miracle workers who attempt to entice people into worshiping anyone other than the God of Israel.

In the concluding section of this chapter, these arguments will be illustrated through the voice of an imagined Jewish rabbi from the first century, who has scrutinized the Epistle to the Hebrews and is passionately rebuking its author for misrepresenting the foundational teachings of Judaism and the Hebrew Scriptures. Readers will have the opportunity to decide for themselves whether the rabbi's case proves to be persuasive.

While some believe Jesus was the Messiah, there remains significant ambiguity regarding the locations of these early Christians and the author of the Epistle at the time of its composition. Carson and Moo suggest that the title of this book, Hebrews, originates from an early manuscript, P46, which bore the inscription Πρὸς Ἑβραίους—(Pros Hebraíous, 'To [the] Hebrews').[1] Given these unknowns about Hebrews, commentators from both sides of the religious aisle can only tentatively offer their best hypothesis or avoid expressing opinions on the more controversial issues altogether.

The author of the Epistle to the Hebrews makes numerous theological claims that challenge and contradict the instructions in the Torah. They contend that the covenant in the Hebrew Bible is obsolete and has been replaced by a "newer covenant" (Heb. 8:13). People on both sides of the religious aisle have written entire books, encyclopedia entries, and journal articles about this topic.

In the Epistle to the Hebrews, the author supports his argument with quotations from Greek sources, some possibly Hebrew, and paraphrases of them. They often contradict the Torah and its reasoning. However, why would members of the Torah-knowledgeable first-century Jewish community accept the reasoning of an anonymous author?

In the first century, knowledgeable Jewish community members could have posed several preliminary questions to the author of Hebrews. Was the author Jewish or from a non-Jewish background? Was the author a rabbi, or did he receive an education from the rabbis like Paul? Was the author of Hebrews an apostle or a prophet? Did he know Hebrew and read the Hebrew Bible (not the Septuagint or Greek texts)? How did the author obtain the authority to reinterpret or contradict the Torah? Did

1. Carson and Moo, *An Introduction to the New Testament*, 609.

the author of Hebrews have any conception that his letter to the Hebrews would later be considered part of Scripture?

Traditional Judaism generally believed that the end of prophecy occurred around the time of the Second Temple's destruction or shortly before it, with Malachi, Haggai, and Zechariah being considered the last remaining prophets. Rabbinic Judaism holds that after these prophets, the era of prophecy came to an end. If the age of prophecy had ceased, how could the Epistle to the Hebrews override the Hebrew Bible? It is merely an expression of opinion and a commentary on the Hebrew Bible by its anonymous author.

The book of 1 Maccabees, one of the Deuterocanonical books in the Catholic and Orthodox Christian Bibles, refers to the cessation of prophecy during the Maccabean revolt (c. 167 to 160 BCE. Specifically, 1 Maccabees 9:27 mentions this fact:

> "So there was great distress in Israel, such as had not been since the time that prophets ceased to appear among them."

This passage suggests that the author of 1 Maccabees viewed the period when the book was composed as a time when prophecy had ceased to exist. The reference suggests that the people of Israel acknowledged that a significant period elapsed since the last prophets had been active.

An earlier passage, 1 Maccabees 4:43–47 describes the cleansing and dedication of the Temple, a significant event after the Maccabean revolt against the Seleucid Empire. The Seleucids desecrated the Jewish Temple in Jerusalem in the reign of Antiochus IV Epiphanes, who set up a pagan altar to Zeus in the Temple and offered unclean sacrifices. After the successful revolt led by Judas Maccabeus, the Jewish forces recaptured Jerusalem and the Temple. The rebuilding and rededication of the altar are described in 1 Maccabees 4:43–47:

> 43 and they cleansed the sanctuary and removed the defiled stones to an unclean place. 44 *They deliberated what to do about the altar of burnt offering, which had been profaned*. 45 And they thought it best to tear it down, so that it would not be a lasting shame to them that the Gentiles had defiled it. So they tore down the altar, 46 *and stored the stones in a convenient place on the temple hill until a prophet should come to tell what to do with them*. 47 Then they took unhewn stones, as the law directs, and built a new altar like the former one. (New Revised Standard Version Catholic Edition)

Attentive readers will note the rationale for the Maccabees' act of storing the stones: there were no prophets. Moreover, the books of the Maccabees, specifically 1 and 2 Maccabees, were excluded from the Hebrew Bible (the Tanakh) for several reasons rooted in historical, theological, and canonical considerations. Two considerations merit particular mention:

> *Time Period*: The events described in the books of the Maccabees took place during the 2nd century BCE after the time traditionally associated with the prophetic writings in the Hebrew Bible. By the time these books were written, many Jewish communities believed that the era of inspired prophecy had ended.
>
> *Lack of Prophetic Authority*: The Hebrew Bible strongly emphasizes prophetic authority, and the books of the Maccabees do not claim to be written by prophets. This lack of prophetic endorsement likely contributed to their exclusion.

Consequently, 1 Maccabees reflects a historical moment when the Jewish people no longer had prophetic voices to guide them. Given that the age of prophecy had ceased, these passages provide insight into why the book of the Maccabees was not included in the Hebrew Bible. Perhaps this omission is in line with the Jewish belief that prophecy ceased with the last biblical prophets around the 5th century BCE.

In conclusion, knowledgeable first-century Jewish opponents of the author would have considered the Epistle to the Hebrews a polemical text written by a devout and sincere believer in Jesus, who was attempting to convince Jewish people and fellow believers in Jesus that Christianity was superior to Judaism. All this "proves" is that the author considered his opinions correct and valid. It does not "prove" anything to anyone else. "A fool takes no pleasure in understanding, but only in expressing his opinion" (Prov. 18:2, ESV).

The reader is invited to answer the following questions:

1. Do the Vedas and Upanishads demonstrate that Hinduism is superior to mainstream Christianity?
2. Does the Qur'an prove the superiority of Islam over Christianity?
3. Does the Book of Mormon show that LDS (the Church of Latter-day Saints) is superior to mainstream Christianity?

If the answer to these questions is "no," then why should anyone regard the anonymous Epistle to the Hebrews as an example of Christianity's superiority over Judaism?

Miracles: Should People Trust Them and Will the Messiah Perform Them?

At this point, readers may wonder whether Jesus' miracles lend credence to the claim made in the Epistle to the Hebrews that Jesus is the *Mashiach* or Messiah. However, no passage in the Hebrew Bible explicitly states that the *Messiah will perform miracles*. Moreover, *even if miracles were performed, they would not* confirm someone's status *as a messiah. The Torah* clearly *warns about* those who claim to be *miracle workers*:

> If a prophet or a dreamer of dreams arises among you *and gives you a sign or a wonder, 2 and the sign or wonder that he tells you comes to pass*, and if he says, 'Let us go after other gods,' which you have not known, 'and let us serve them,' 3 you shall not listen to the words of that prophet or that dreamer of dreams. For the Lord your God is testing you, to know whether you love the Lord your God with all your heart and with all your soul. 4 You shall walk after the Lord your God and fear him and keep his commandments and obey his voice, and you shall serve him and hold fast to him. 5 But that prophet or that dreamer of dreams shall be put to death, because he has taught rebellion against the Lord your God, who brought you out of the land of Egypt and redeemed you out of the house of slavery, to make you leave the way in which the Lord your God commanded you to walk. So you shall purge the evil from your midst. (Deut. 13:1–5, ESV)[2]

God's instructions in the Hebrew Bible are explicit, even if the miracles come to pass. "If a prophet or a dreamer of dreams arises among you and gives you a sign or a wonder, and the sign or wonder that he tells you comes to pass, and if he says, 'Let us go after other gods,' which you have not known, 'and let us serve them,' 3 *you shall not listen to the words of that prophet* or that dreamer of dreams" (Deut. 13:1–3, ESV).

Curiously, the author of Hebrews omits discussing the numerous miracles associated with Jesus, which are recorded in later gospel narratives. Skeptics and detractors argue that the miracles that are attributed

2. The Christian Bible deviates from the Hebrew Bible with its verse numbering. In the Torah, the verses are 2 through 6.

to Jesus were later literary embellishments to his life, such as those in the Gospels (an argument from silence), and lack compelling and satisfactory evidence. The standard academic position is that Mark—the earliest Gospel—was composed approximately forty years after the crucifixion of Jesus. Matthew, Luke, and John were composed about fifty to sixty years after Jesus' death. If the claims of miracles were later embellishments, the author of Hebrews would have known nothing of them, and neither would any of their religious opponents.

The anonymity of the Epistle to the Hebrews, combined with the fact that a recognized prophet did not author it, raises significant questions about its credibility. While some might argue that it is a trustworthy source, a closer examination brings its claims about Jesus into question.

Firstly, the Epistle includes numerous assertions that directly contradict the Hebrew Bible on over two dozen specific points. Readers cannot overlook these inconsistencies because they undermine the foundation of its teachings. Furthermore, the depiction of the Messiah's role within the text does not align with the established biblical understanding, raising concerns about its theological reliability.

Secondly, the claim that blood sacrifice is essential for the forgiveness of sins starkly opposes the teachings found in the Hebrew Bible, which emphasizes repentance, prayer, and a personal relationship with God over ritualistic sacrifices (Joel 2:32). This critical contradiction warrants reconsideration of the Epistle's claims.

Lastly, compelling, convincing, and substantial scriptural arguments challenge Jesus' dual role as both God and the Messiah that is presented in Hebrews. The weight of these discrepancies suggests that the foundations of the Epistle rest on shaky ground, making it prudent to approach its declarations with caution and critical intent.

The Extraordinary Claims Made About Jesus in the Epistle to the Hebrews

The author of Hebrews presents the most extended polemical argument against Judaism in the Christian Bible. Pamela Eisenbaum says its anonymous author "is often perceived as the New Testament's most anti-Jewish text."[3] The author goes on to describe the exalted position of Jesus as a high priest (Heb. 3:1; 4:14–16; 5:5; 9:11–12; and indirectly in 2:17). Melchizedek appears no less than eight times in the Epistle to the Hebrews. On six

3. Eisenbaum, "The Letter to the Hebrews," 460.

occasions, there is a reference to "the order of Melchizedek" (Heb. 5:6, 10; 6:20; 7:1, 11, and 17), and twice, only his name is mentioned (Heb. 7:10, 15). The author insists that Jesus is superior to the Aaronic priesthood. The author interweaves numerous biblical verses and their interpretations to support his opinion. They argue that (1) Jesus is divine (Heb. 1:8) and (2) he is the Messiah, or Christ (Heb. 3:6; 13:8, 20–21). In addition, (3) Jesus is a priest or high priest (Heb. 3:1; 4:14–16; 5:5–10; 6:20; 7:21–26; 8:1; 9:11–12), (4) his sacrifice was superior to all past and future sacrifices (Heb. 9:11–14, 23–28), and (5) he is superior to the angels (Heb. 1:5–14), Moses (Heb. 3:3), Aaron (Heb. 5:4–6), and Joshua (Heb. 4:6–10). Moreover, the author contends that (6) the old covenant is obsolete and has been replaced by a "newer covenant" (Heb. 8:8–13). The author's knowledge of the Hebrew Bible and that of his readers is unknown. Assuming that the author knew the Torah in its original form (Hebrew) as well as in Greek (LXX or a similar version), readers will need to confront the invisible elephant in the room: if the author was so knowledgeable about the Torah, then how could he have believed the extraordinary claims he makes about Jesus, which directly contradict the Torah?

> 1 Kings 4:29–31 29 And God gave Solomon wisdom and understanding beyond measure, and breadth of mind like the sand on the seashore, 30 so that Solomon's wisdom surpassed the wisdom of all the people of the east and all the wisdom of Egypt. 31 For he was wiser than all other men. (ESV)

Solomon wrote (Prov. 18:17), "The one who states his case first seems right, until the other comes and examines him" (ESV). The anonymous author of the Epistle to the Hebrews presents a one-sided argument, which employs quotations or paraphrases from Scripture that are occasionally incorrect and his own interpretation of the Hebrew Bible to justify his opinion. However, to repeat Solomon's warning, "The one who states his case first seems right, until the other comes and examines him."

An Unreliable Source: Twenty-Eight Errors in the Epistle to the Hebrews

The Epistle to the Hebrews' lack of reliability is a topic that requires extensive investigation. A knowledgeable first-century Jewish community member could have easily pointed out that the author's letter contains numerous unsupported claims, errors, and falsehoods. The following is a list of twenty-eight selected examples:

1. Hebrews 1:2 says, "but in these last days he has spoken to us by His Son, whom he appointed the heir of all things, through whom also he created the world" (ESV). (a) The writer believed he lived in the last days (ca. 70). Yet Jewish Christians had already been waiting for nearly forty years. For those living in 2026 or later, approximately two thousand years have passed. (b) The writer erroneously tells his readers that God's heir, the Son, was the person who made the world. Consequently, Jesus is the creator, not God the Father (Gen. 1:1–1). (c) Claiming that God created the world "through" the Son implies that the Son was active *before* creation, suggesting his pre-existence and divinity. These claims are unverifiable and contradict the teachings of the Torah.
2. Hebrews 1:3 says, "He [the Son] is the radiance of the glory of God . . ." (a) In contradiction, Isaiah 48:11 says, "For my own sake, for my own sake, I do it, for how should my name be profaned? My glory I will not give to another." (ESV) (b) Claiming that Jesus is the "radiance" and "exact imprint" of God contradicts the Torah that God has no image or form (Deut. 4:15–16). (c) The claim that "after making purification for sins" implies that through his death, Jesus provided atonement for humanity. Atonement is achieved through repentance (teshuvah), prayer, righteous deeds, and, in ancient times, through animal sacrifices at the Temple in Jerusalem (Lev. 16, 17). Moreover, no human sacrifice or vicarious atonement is allowed or necessary. Ezekiel 18:20 strongly rejects the idea that one person can bear the sins of another.
3. Hebrews 2:2 says, "For since the message declared by angels proved to be reliable, and every transgression or disobedience received a just retribution" (ESV). Therefore, according to the author of Hebrews, the angels gave the Law (cf. Gal 3:19). This statement is false. In the Hebrew Bible, the Torah was given directly by God to Moses at Sinai (see Exod. 20:1; Deut. 5:4; 33:2). The idea that angels mediated the Torah is not part of Torah. Exodus 20:1 reads, "And God spoke all these words, saying . . .," which directly contradicts the author's claim.

4. Hebrews 2:10 says, "10 In bringing many sons and daughters to glory, it was fitting that God, for whom and through whom everything exists, should make the pioneer of their salvation perfect through what he suffered" (ESV). This passage suggests that Jesus was "made perfect" through suffering. (a) Given that God is perfect, how can Jesus—who was considered divine—be made perfect through suffering? (b) This verse is also theologically problematic for those who believe in Christ's inherent perfection. (c) The Hebrew Bible rejects the idea that one person's suffering or death (especially a human's) can atone for the sins of others (Ezek. 18:20). (d) Moreover, the Torah teaches that each individual relates directly to God—without a mediator. Consider Isaiah 43:11 – "I, even I, am the LORD, and besides Me there is no savior.") (e) There is no requirement or prophecy in the Tanakh that the Messiah must suffer, die, or be "perfected through suffering."

5. Hebrews 2:17 says, "Therefore he had to be made like his brothers in every respect, so that he might become a merciful and faithful high priest in the service of God, to make propitiation for the sins of the people." (a) The phrase "He had to be made like his brothers in every respect" refers to Jesus—who is God—becoming fully human, like other people. This phrase supports the Christian doctrine of the Incarnation: that God became flesh in the person of Jesus. However, the belief that God took on human form, is absolutely rejected in Judaism. God is not physical, not human, and cannot change forms (see Num. 23:19; Deut. 4:15–16). Hosea 11:9 – "For I am God, and not a man, the Holy One in your midst." (b) Within the New Testament, the doctrine that Jesus is the "high priest" is found exclusively in the Epistle to the Hebrews, which reflects the opinion of the anonymous author. The silence of Paul, the disciples, and James speaks volumes. We cannot know whether the author had access to their writings. Moreover, Jesus could not have been a priest, let alone a high priest, due to his lineage (he was not from the tribe of Aaron or Levi). Compounding matters, Hebrews 7:14 claims Jesus was from the tribe of Judah, not Levi or Aaron. (c) The verse teaches that Jesus made propitiation—atoned for sins—on the behalf of others. Atonement is not achieved by the death of a man, especially not an innocent man, for the sins of others. Each person

is responsible for their repentance. Human sacrifice is strictly forbidden (see Deut. 12:31; Lev. 18:21).

6. Hebrews 2:18 says, "For because he himself has suffered when tempted, he is able to help those who are being tempted." How can an omnipotent God be tempted? However, in direct contrast, James, the brother of Jesus, said in James 1:13, "Let no one say when he is tempted, "I am being tempted by God," for God cannot be tempted with evil, and he himself tempts no one" (ESV). We do not know (a) whether James authored the book that bears his name and (b) whether it was available to the author of Hebrews. Either way, it remains true that God—who is omnipotent—cannot be tested. (b) Christian theology holds that Jesus is both God and man, yet Jesus is said to be tempted, which implies a vulnerability to sin. In Judaism, God cannot be tempted and cannot sin. Therefore, God is exempt from human frailty. Numbers 23:19 says, "God is not a man, that He should lie, nor a son of man, that He should change His mind" and says Malachi 3:6 – "I, the LORD, do not change." The idea that a divine being suffered temptation undermines both God's immutability and divine perfection, which makes this claim theologically invalid. (c) Verse 18 implies that Jesus mediates between humans and God, assisting those who are tempted. Judaism emphasizes direct access to God without any human or supernatural intermediary. See Isaiah 45:22 – "Turn to Me and be saved . . . for I am God, and there is no other."

7. Hebrews 6:20 says, "where Jesus has gone as a forerunner on our behalf, having become a high priest forever after the order of Melchizedek" (ESV). (a) There is no evidence that Jesus was a priest or a high priest. This claim is exclusive to the Epistle to the Hebrews. The letter's author views Jesus as the great high priest of the Christian religion who performed services that were analogous to those carried out by the Levitical priests of the Hebrew Bible. The author's rationale is that he already knows Jesus cannot be a priest according to the order of Aaron due to his lineage. Therefore, he employs an ambiguous personality with an enigmatic description that bears multiple meanings: "after the order of Melchizedek." In addition, the author's claim that Jesus is a high priest forever is unverifiable. (b) Jesus cannot be the high priest because he must be from the tribe of Levi, descended from Aaron (see Exod. 28:1; Num. 3:10; Lev. 21).

Moreover, Jesus—by the New Testament's own admission—is from the tribe of Judah (see Heb. 7:14). (c) Hebrews portrays Jesus as a heavenly high priest, offering atonement once and for all. This assertion replaces the entire Levitical priesthood, the Temple service, and the sacrificial system that is given in the Torah and contradicts God's established covenant with the tribe of Levi.

8. Hebrews 7:3 says Melchizedek is a priest forever like Jesus because he is "without father or mother, without genealogy, without beginning of days or end of life." (a) Jesus had a biological mother, whose name was Mary. (b) The New Testament itself refutes this claim since it provides a genealogical record of Jesus (Matt. 1:1–17 and Luke 3:23–38). (c) Jesus began his days as a baby in Bethlehem and died on a Roman cross in Jerusalem. (d) This verse implies that Melchizedek is eternal or pre-existent, and by comparison, Jesus shares in that timelessness. In Judaism, only God is considered eternal—no human or angelic figure (including Melchizedek) is described in this manner. (e) From a Jewish perspective, Melchizedek's priesthood is not eternal. The only eternal priesthood in Judaism is the Aaronic (Levitical) priesthood, which was established by God in the books of Exodus, Leviticus, and Numbers. Hebrews 7 replaces this divinely commanded priesthood with a man-made reinterpretation of a brief narrative (e.g., Exod. 29:9—"The priesthood shall be theirs by a perpetual statute.").

9. Hebrews 7:7 says, "It is beyond dispute that the inferior is blessed by the superior" (ESV). (a) The author is wrong on this point; see Gen. 14:19; 47:10; Exod. 18: 9–12; 1 Sam. 1:24–28; 10:1; 23:16–18; 25: 23–31; 2 Sam. 14:22; 1 Kgs. 1:47; 8:66; Job 31:20. These examples from the Hebrew Bible present scenarios where those of seemingly lesser status—whether socially, hierarchically, or circumstantially—offer blessings to those considered greater. (b) The blessing Melchizedek gives to Abram is on behalf of God, not himself. The real "blesser" here is God, not Melchizedek.

10. Hebrews 7:12 says, "For when there is a change in the priesthood, there is necessarily a change in the law as well" (ESV). According to the author of Hebrews, the question of duration is more important than the hereditary status of the high priest's office. This interpretation is an invention born of necessity. In reality, the author knows full well that Jesus cannot be a priest due to his lineage. Hebrews

7:7 misreads the text by attributing divine authority to Melchizedek rather than acknowledging him as a mouthpiece for God.

11. Hebrews 7:14 says, "For it is evident that our Lord was descended from Judah, and in connection with that tribe Moses said nothing about priests" (ESV). (a) There is no evidence that Jesus descended from Judah because he had no biological father. (b) Judah was not a designated tribe from which priests were chosen. Appointing priests from another tribe is a violation of Torah law. (c) Readers must remember that the author proclaims that Jesus is not just a priest, but a high priest. As a high priest, Jesus violates Torah law. The Levitical priesthood is eternal, as per God's explicit covenant (Num. 25:13).

12. Hebrews 7:27 says, "He has no need, like those high priests, to offer sacrifices daily, first for his own sins and then for those of the people, since he did this once for all when he offered up himself." (a) If Jesus was the final sacrifice "once and for all," why would animal sacrifices be fully restored in the Messianic era? (Isa. 56:7; Jer. 33:17–18; Ezek. 43:22; 44:27–31; 45:4, 17–25; Zech. 6:12–13; 14:21) (b) The daily sacrifices (Tamid offerings) were offered by ordinary priests, not exclusively by the high priest. The high priest only made sin offerings for himself and the people on Yom Kippur once a year (Leviticus 16), not "daily." (c) Jesus is described as needing no such offering, implying he is sinless. In Judaism, no human being is without sin, and self-sacrifice is never a valid means of atonement. Ecclesiastes 7:20 – "There is no righteous man on earth who does good and never sins." (d) Human sacrifice is never permitted as a form of atonement in the Torah. (e) No one can die for someone else's sins—each person is responsible before God (Ezek. 18:20). (f) The verse claims that Jesus' self-offering was "once for all," replacing all further need for sacrificial service. The Torah describes sacrifices (especially sin offerings and burnt offerings) as eternal statutes that are tied to the Mishkan or Temple and Levitical priesthood (Exod. 29:42; Lev. 6:18).

13. Hebrews 8:9 quotes Jeremiah 31:31–32, saying, "not like the covenant that I made with their fathers on the day when I took them by the hand to bring them out of the land of Egypt. For they did not continue in my covenant, and so I showed no concern for them, declares the Lord. (ESV) (a) This quotation is patently false and a serious distortion of the Hebrew Bible. God's relationship with Israel

is eternal and covenantal, even in the face of sin. Jeremiah 31:31–32, says, "Behold, the days are coming, declares the Lord, when I will make a new covenant with the house of Israel and the house of Judah, 32 not like the covenant that I made with their fathers on the day when I took them by the hand to bring them out of the land of Egypt, my covenant that they broke, though I was their husband, declares the Lord." (b) Hebrews says: "I showed no concern for them," which implies that God abandoned Israel after they violated the Sinai covenant. The Torah and Prophets affirm that God never abandons Israel, even when they sin. Leviticus 26:44 – "Yet for all that . . . I will not reject them or abhor them to destroy them utterly and break My covenant with them, for I am the LORD their God."

14. Hebrews 8:10–11 quotes Jeremiah 31:33–34, which states that the law is written on human hearts. (a) The author of Hebrews does not fully capture the original prophetic intent. Torah study remains central; prophecy means a profound, more universal understanding, not the absence of Torah. Multiple times, the Hebrew Bible discusses the spiritual aspect of the law (Deut. 6:4–5; 30:6; Jer. 32:40; Ezek. 11:19; 36:26). (b) Hebrews uses this verse to claim that the Messianic promise is already fulfilled in Jesus. This prophecy clearly has not yet come to pass. The world is not yet filled with the universal knowledge of God (Isaiah 11:9).

15. Hebrews 9:3–4 says, "3 Behind the second curtain was a second section called the Most Holy Place, 4 having the golden altar of incense and the ark of the covenant covered on all sides with gold, in which was a golden urn holding the manna, and Aaron's staff that budded, and the tablets of the covenant." (a) Aaron's rod is misplaced here, since it was not kept in the Ark of the Covenant/Testimony (1 Kgs. 8:9). (b) According to Exodus 30:6 (cf. Exod. 16:33–34; 26:33; 40:3, 26), the altar of incense was outside the Holy Place in front of the veil, not inside the Most Holy Place behind the veil.[4] (c) Likewise, the locations of the altar of incense and the pot of manna are incorrectly described. The jar of manna and Aaron's staff were placed beside or in front of the ark—not inside it (Bava Batra 14b).

16. Hebrews 9:11–12 describes Christ entering a "greater and more perfect tabernacle." (a) An opponent of the author would demand

4. Geisler and Howe, *When Critics Ask*, offers several hypothetical solutions to this problem, and those that follow. Readers must be the final judge.

evidence to support this assertion. The author is making an unverifiable theological claim rather than a factual description. (b) Hebrews' Jesus is a "high priest." However, he was not from the tribe of Levi or the family of Aaron which disqualified him under Torah law. (c) Hebrews claims Jesus entered a heavenly "tent" not made with hands. The Torah specifies earthly service in a physical sanctuary. See Exodus 25:8–9 – "Make Me a sanctuary, that I may dwell among them . . . exactly as I show you . . ." (d) There is no concept in the Torah of an invisible, heavenly sanctuary being entered by a human being's offering of blood. (e) Hebrews says that Jesus offered his own blood. Human blood sacrifice is strictly forbidden (Lev. 17:10–12). Only the blood of kosher animals—which was offered by Levitical priests in the Temple under God's instructions—is valid for sacrificial purposes. (f) The author of Hebrews claims that Jesus was a once-for-all atonement. However, the Torah requires ongoing, communal sacrifices by Levitical priests (Exod. 29:42; Lev. 16). (g) The author continues to claim the "eternal redemption" through the death of Jesus. In contradiction, the Torah states redemption comes through repentance and obedience, not a one-time act. The Torah commands ongoing sacrifices—daily (Tamid), weekly (Shabbat), and yearly (Yom Kippur) (Exod. 29:42; Lev. 16). (h) Hebrews 9:12 implies that Jesus' blood alone secures redemption. However, true atonement requires Teshuvah (repentance), *Vidui* (confession), charity, prayer, and, when applicable, animal offerings.

17. Hebrews 9:19 says, "For when Moses had declared every commandment of the law to all the people, he took the blood of calves and goats, with water and scarlet wool and hyssop, and sprinkled both the book itself and all the people." The author of Hebrews contradicts the Torah on several points. (a) Goats were not used at the Ratification of the Covenant. (b) No water was used. (c) No hyssop was used. (d) No scarlet wool was used. (e) There was no mention of Moses sprinkling the book. Exodus 24:5–6 explicitly states, "5 And he sent young men of the people of Israel, who offered burnt offerings and sacrificed peace offerings of oxen to the Lord. 6 And Moses took half of the blood and put it in basins, and half of the blood he threw against the altar," while Exodus 24:8 adds, "And Moses took the blood and threw it on the people and said, 'Behold the blood of the covenant that the Lord has made with you in accordance with

all these words'" (ESV). (f) There is no mention of goats or calves in that passage. Hebrews introduces animals not used in the original covenant ceremony. (g) Hyssop, scarlet wool, and water are used in the purification ritual of the red heifer (Num. 19), and the cleansing of a leper (Leviticus 14).

18. Hebrews 10:1 says, "The law is only a shadow of the good things that are coming—not the realities themselves. For this reason, it can never, by the same sacrifices repeated endlessly year after year, make perfect those who draw near to worship" (ESV). Therefore, the author of Hebrews suggests that the Law is only a "shadow of the good things to come" and not perfect in itself. (a) In contradiction, Psalm 19:7 says, "The law of the Lord is perfect, reviving the soul; the testimony of the Lord is sure, making wise the simple" (ESV). (b) This proclamation in Hebrews mischaracterizes and diminishes the significance of the Law (Torah) in Judaism and oversimplifies its role. (c) The offerings (*korbanot*) are divinely commanded means to attain purity, atonement, and closeness to God. (d) The Torah itself declares that its commandments are for all generations (e.g., Deut. 12:28). (e) The repetition is not a failure, but a recognition that human beings need ongoing purification and connection to God. Therefore, the sacrifices facilitate an ongoing relationship and a cycle of repentance. Perfection is a process, not a one-time event.

19. Hebrews 10:5 says, "Sacrifice and offering you did not desire, But a body you have prepared for me." (a) This verse is a mistranslation or reinterpretation that is based on the Greek or a Greek text. In fact, the psalmist David wrote: "Sacrifice and offering you did not desire; my ears you have opened." (Ps. 40:6, verse 7 in the Jewish numbering). The passage cited in Hebrews 10:5 cannot be found in the Hebrew Bible. (b) Hebrews 9:22 then contradicts Hebrews 10:5 by insisting that "without the shedding of blood there is no forgiveness." (c) The author of Hebrews uses this altered quote to claim that Jesus came into the world with a body that was prepared for death, which would render regular acts of sacrifice obsolete. (d) This statement is fallacious and demonstrates a complete misunderstanding of what the Torah says. Jesus' death was not necessary for people to be reconciled with God and receive forgiveness and atonement. Believers are challenged to find one verse in the Hebrew Bible where God explicitly prescribes the shedding of Jesus' blood and death

on the cross as the only means for humanity to be reconciled with God and receive forgiveness and atonement for their sins. If God is omnipotent, He is not limited in His ability to forgive. The Hebrew Bible does not state that the shedding of the blood of a supposedly sinless man is the only means for a person to be reconciled with God and receive forgiveness and atonement.

Nevertheless, Christian commentators and theologians persist in making the claim that the shedding of blood is necessary to receive forgiveness. However, Scripture repeatedly demonstrates that this is not the case. For example, the Bible tells us that money can be used for atonement: "You shall take the atonement money of the children of Israel, and shall appoint it for the service of the tabernacle of meeting, that it may be a memorial for the children of Israel before YHVH, to make atonement for yourselves" (Exod. 30:16, ESV). Here, money is sufficient, without blood. Fine flour could also be used to atone for sin: "If, however, he cannot afford two doves or two young pigeons, he is to bring as an offering for his sin a tenth of an ephah of fine flour for a sin offering" (Lev. 5:11, ESV). Flour is sufficient without blood.

Perhaps the most contemptible, despicable, and detestable member of the Jewish people in the entire Hebrew Bible is Manasseh, the king of Judah. The Hebrew Bible holds nothing back in describing his multiple abominations:

> Manasseh was twelve years old when he became king, and he
> reigned in Jerusalem fifty-five years. 2 He did evil in the eyes
> of the Lord, following the detestable practices of the nations
> the Lord had driven out before the Israelites. 3 He rebuilt the
> high places his father Hezekiah had demolished; he also erected
> altars to the Baals and made Asherah poles. He bowed down to
> all the starry hosts and worshiped them. 4 He built altars in the
> temple of the Lord, of which the Lord had said, "My Name will
> remain in Jerusalem forever." 5 In both courts of the temple of
> the Lord, he built altars to all the starry hosts. 6 He sacrificed
> his children in the fire in the Valley of Ben Hinnom, practiced
> divination and witchcraft, sought omens, and consulted mediums and spiritists. He did much evil in the eyes of the Lord,
> arousing his anger. 7 He took the image he had made and put
> it in God's temple, of which God had said to David and to his
> son Solomon, "In this temple and in Jerusalem, which I have
> chosen out of all the tribes of Israel, I will put my Name forever.
> (2 Chron. 33, ESV)

Consequently, God permitted the Assyrians to conquer Judah. "So the Lord brought against them the army commanders of the king of Assyria, who took Manasseh prisoner, put a hook in his nose, bound him with bronze shackles and took him to Babylon" (2 Chron. 33:11). What did the imprisoned king do? In the following verses, the Hebrew Bible reports what happened next:

> 12 In his distress he sought the favor of the Lord his God and humbled himself greatly before the God of his ancestors. 13 And when he prayed to him, the Lord was moved by his entreaty and listened to his plea; so he brought him back to Jerusalem and to his kingdom." (ESV)

God forgave Manasseh of his sins and unfaithfulness (v. 19). God absolved Manasseh after he humbled himself, repented, and prayed to the Lord. Remember, this man had sacrificed his children in a fire, erected altars to Baal, practiced divination and witchcraft, sought omens, consulted mediums and spiritists, and desecrated the Holy Temple. This chapter in the Hebrew Bible repudiates any thought that God requires blood to atone for sins.

Since God can forgive, there is no need for the "sacrifice" of which the author of Hebrews speaks. God is almighty and pardons all people for their sins. God is almighty— He can do what He likes. God is merciful—He forgives whom He wills. He is not an unmerciful God. Claiming God requires blood for atonement and pardon is to limit God's power.

(e) The author of Hebrews implies Jesus' body replaces the Temple offerings. However, human sacrifice is forbidden in the Torah. God desires sacrifices and sincere obedience. Psalm 40 rebukes empty ritual without devotion, not the sacrificial system itself. (f) The author of Hebrews claims this verse was spoken by Christ "when he came into the world," treating it as a prophecy of Jesus' incarnation. Psalm 40 is not messianic. It is a personal psalm of David, which expresses gratitude, devotion, and a desire to obey God's Torah. It contains no reference to a future Messiah or atonement through death.

Cockerill identifies two additional errors:

> Second, Hebrews has the plural, "whole burnt offerings," at the beginning of v. 6 instead of the singular "whole burnt offering" found in most manuscripts of Ps 40:6b.[10] Third, Hebrews reads "you were not pleased" instead of "you did not" "request" at the end of v. 6: "With whole burnt offerings and sin offerings you

were not pleased. Finally, in the last line of this quotation Hebrews reads, "to do, o God, your will" instead of "to do your will, o my God, I have resolved" (Ps 40:8).12 Hebrews has omitted "my," and put "o God" before instead of after "your will," and terminated the quotation before the words "I have resolved."[5]

20. Hebrews 10:10 says, "And by that will we have been sanctified through the offering of the body of Jesus Christ once for all." (ESV) (a) Hebrews says people are "sanctified through the offering of the body of Jesus." In the Torah, sanctification (Hebrew: *kedushah*) comes through keeping God's decrees/statutes and performing them. See Leviticus 20:7–8 – "Sanctify yourselves and be holy . . . keep My statutes and do them" (ESV) (b) Claiming that a person's body was "offered" for sanctification is essentially a form of human sacrifice. God never accepts a human being as a sin offering or sanctifying agent. (c) Hebrews 10:10 promotes the idea that one sacrifice—once and for all—sanctifies everyone forever. The Torah explicitly commands ongoing, repeated sacrifices for different kinds of sins and occasions. Moreover, a single offering, even if it was valid, cannot override God's command for perpetual observances. (d) The author completely contradicts the words of the prophets, who explicitly foretold that the animal sacrificial system *would return in the Messianic age*. Therefore, if Jesus was *the final sacrifice* "once and for all," why would the Bible command that animal sacrifices must be fully restored in the Messianic era? (Isa. 56:7; Jer. 33:17–18; Ezek. 43:22; 44:27–31; 45:4, 17–25; Zech. 6:12–13; 14:21)
21. Hebrews 10:11 says, "And every priest stands daily at his service, offering repeatedly the same sacrifices, which can never take away sins." (ESV) (a) Hebrews misrepresents the sacrificial system by stating that sacrifices can never take away sins. This verse directly contradicts the Torah itself, which repeatedly states that specific offerings atone for sin (Lev. 4:26; 5:10; Num. 15:28). Judaism recognizes that sacrifices alone are insufficient—they must be accompanied by teshuvah (repentance) and moral action. However, when appropriately performed, sacrifices do affect atonement for specific categories of sins (e.g., unintentional violations). (b) The author misunderstood the purpose of the sacrificial system. The daily (Tamid) offerings and others were not primarily about the removal of

5. Cockerill, *The Epistle to the Hebrews*, 435.

sin, but about maintaining the covenantal relationship with God, expressing gratitude, devotion, national responsibility, and teaching spiritual discipline and humility. (c) The author suggests that sin offerings occur daily, which contradicts the teachings of the Torah. Once again, the author completely contradicts the words of the prophets, who explicitly foretold that the animal sacrificial system would return in the Messianic age. See the verses cited above. (d) The Levitical priesthood was commanded by God (Exod. 28:1; Lev. 16:34).

22. Hebrews 10:18 says, "Where there is forgiveness of these, there is no longer any offering for sin" (ESV). (a) Hebrews contradicts the Torah's ongoing requirement for sacrifices. The Torah explicitly commands repeated sin offerings as part of an eternal covenant (Num. 28:3). The Torah does not teach that a single event or offering eliminates the need for further offerings. The claim "no more offerings for sin" directly rejects God's commandments. (b) Hebrews teaches that forgiveness has already been achieved through Jesus' death, making further offerings unnecessary. Forgiveness is not automatic or tied to someone else's death. Each person must actively turn back to God (Ezek. 18:21–22). (c) Hebrews implies that Jesus' death ended the need for the Torah's entire system of atonement. The Torah is described as an eternal covenant. See Exodus 31:16–17 – "It is a sign forever . . ." (cf. Deut. 29:28). (d) Once again, the author contradicts the words of the prophets, who explicitly foretold that the animal sacrificial system *would return in the Messianic age.* See the verses cited above. (e) The Torah also commands a sacrifice for unintentional sins: "You shall do the same on the seventh day of the month for anyone who has sinned through error or ignorance; so you shall make atonement for the temple" (Ezek. 45:20). (f) Moreover, why would the Messiah, who is called "the prince" on several occasions in the book of Ezekiel, *bring a sin sacrifice on behalf of himself* and the nation? "On that day the prince shall provide for himself and all the people of the land a young bull *for a sin offering*" (Ezek. 45:22, ESV). (g) In suggesting that animal sacrifices had been rendered obsolete by the death of Jesus, the author of Hebrews also overlooks the fact that Jewish practices continued for approximately forty years until the destruction of the Second Temple in 70 CE. (h) Moreover, if God no longer commanded animal sacrifices, why

did the disciples continue visiting the Second Temple after the alleged sacrifice and atoning death of Jesus? "The next day, Paul took the men and purified himself along with them. Then he went to the temple to give notice of the date when the days of purification would end and the offering would be made for each of them" (Acts 21:26; ESV).

23. Hebrews 11:11 says: "By faith Sarah herself received power to conceive, even when she was past the age, since she considered him faithful who had promised." (a) This claim is not true. Some commentators suggest that Sarah doubted God's word and did not believe she would conceive a child. Genesis 18:9–15 is explicit on this point:

> 9 They said to him, "Where is Sarah your wife?" And he said, "She is in the tent." 10 The Lord said, "I will surely return to you about this time next year, and Sarah your wife shall have a son." And Sarah was listening at the tent door behind him. 11 Now Abraham and Sarah were old, advanced in years. The way of women had ceased to be with Sarah. 12 So Sarah laughed to herself, saying, "After I am worn out, and my lord is old, shall I have pleasure?" 13 The Lord said to Abraham, "Why did Sarah laugh and say, 'Shall I indeed bear a child, now that I am old?' 14 Is anything too hard for the Lord? At the appointed time I will return to you, about this time next year, and Sarah shall have a son." 15 But Sarah denied it, saying, "I did not laugh," for she was afraid. He said, "No, but you did laugh." (ESV)

This laughter is viewed by commentators (e.g., Rashi) as a moment of doubt, rather than one of faith. (b) There is debate over whether Sarah is the subject of this verse. Some ancient manuscripts and Greek grammatical structures suggest that Abraham, rather than Sarah, is the subject. Some scholars and translations (e.g., NIV footnotes, earlier Greek texts) read it as: "By faith he [Abraham] received power to father children."

24. Hebrews 11:12 says, "Therefore from one man, and him as good as dead, were born descendants as many as the stars of heaven and as many as the innumerable grains of sand by the seashore" (ESV). (a) Hebrews implies that the fulfillment of God's promise to Abraham—descendants "as many as the stars"—came through faith

in Jesus, which ultimately led to the establishment of the church. Hebrews spiritualizes or universalizes the promise, later applying it to Christians (see Gal. 3:29). This is a theological repurposing that is not found in the Torah. In the Torah, the promise to Abraham is national: a multitude of physical descendants (the Jewish people). (b) However, Abraham was far from dead. He lived until the ripe old age of one hundred and seventy-five (Gen. 25:6), some seventy-five years after the birth of Isaac. In Genesis, Abraham is depicted as vital and active into old age. (c) The verse focuses solely on Abraham. Both Abraham and Sarah were involved in the miracle of Isaac's birth. Genesis emphasizes Sarah's barrenness and old age as much as Abraham's. Focusing only on Abraham obscures the full scope of the miracle, which involved both parents and misses Sarah's transformation from doubt to joy (Gen. 21:6).

25. Hebrews 11:17 says, "By faith Abraham, when he was tested, offered up Isaac, and he who had received the promises was in the act of offering up his only son" (ESV). (a) Hebrews uses this verse (and surrounding verses) to support the idea that the Akedah foreshadows Jesus' death. Isaac is seen as a type of Christ—"the only beloved son" given up in sacrifice by the father. This interpretation allegorizes the Akedah into a Christian salvation model, not a Jewish test of faith and covenant. Judaism sees the Akedah as a test of Abraham's trust in God (Gen. 22:1) and a rejection of pagan human sacrifice. (b) Hebrews likely uses "only son" (monogenēs in Greek) to emphasize typological parallels between Isaac and Jesus, which distorts the actual Torah narrative for theological purposes. (c) Hebrews misrepresents the Akedah as an "offering." In Genesis 22:12, Isaac was never actually offered. God stopped Abraham. The Torah is very clear that no actual offering occurred. Isaac remained unharmed, and Abraham sacrificed a ram in his place. (d) The Epistle to the Hebrews ignores God's explicit prohibition of human sacrifice. In reality, Hebrews' framing of the event leans toward a theology that accepts human death (i.e., Jesus) as a legitimate offering. (e) The author of Hebrews is wrong on this point. Isaac was not only Abraham's "only son." At the time of the Akedah (the offering of Isaac), Abraham had an older son, Ishmael, through Hagar.

26. Hebrews 12:2 says, "Looking to Jesus, the founder and perfecter of our faith, who for the joy that was set before him endured the

cross, despising the shame, and is seated at the right hand of the throne of God" (ESV). (a) This statement claims that faith begins and is completed through Jesus. Faith (*emunah*) in the Hebrew Bible is directed toward God, not any human intermediary. Faith is not "founded" by Jesus; it is established through the covenant with Abraham (Genesis 15:6), the giving of the Torah at Sinai (Exod. 19–20), and the words of the prophets (Isaiah, Jeremiah, etc.). (b) Verse 2 frames Jesus' execution as a noble act of faith and obedience. Judaism rejects the idea of redemptive human suffering or death as the foundation of faith. Human sacrifice is absolutely forbidden in the Torah (Lev. 18:21; Deut. 12:31). (c) the phrase ". . . and is seated at the right hand of the throne of God" implies that Jesus shares in God's authority and position—common in Christian theology. Claiming someone is seated beside God implies a dual authority, which borders on idolatry (*shittuf* — combining God with another being). (d) The author implies the idea of atonement through death. While suffering has meaning in Jewish tradition, it is never seen as the mechanism of atonement for others' sins. The idea that Jesus' death provides universal atonement contradicts the Torah's view that each person is responsible for their own sins (Ezek. 18:20).

27. Hebrews 13:12 says, "So Jesus also suffered outside the gate in order to sanctify the people through his own blood" (ESV). (a) This verse implies that Jesus' blood brings sanctification, which is central to Christian atonement theology. In Torah law, human blood is never used for atonement or sanctification. Moreover, the Torah forbids human sacrifice and never permits using a person's blood to cleanse or sanctify others (Lev. 17:1; Deut. 12:31). (b) the author of Hebrews misapplies the Yom Kippur ritual to Jesus. The Yom Kippur sin offering was an animal prescribed by God, slaughtered by the Levitical priest, and brought into the Temple. Jesus was not a priest, not of the tribe of Levi, not sacrificed in the Temple, and executed by Roman authorities, not as a *korban* (offering) under Toah law. (c) Hebrews claims Jesus' death sanctifies the people. In Judaism, sanctification (*kedushah*) is achieved through the observance of the *mitzvot* (commandments) and living a holy life, not by someone else's death. (Leviticus 19:2).

28. Hebrews 13:20–21 says, "20 Now may the God of peace who brought again from the dead our Lord Jesus, the great shepherd of

the sheep, by the blood of the eternal covenant, 21 equip you with everything good that you may do his will, working in us that which is pleasing in his sight, through Jesus Christ, to whom be glory forever and ever. Amen" (ESV). (a) Jesus' resurrection is not a Jewish proof of messiahship. The true Messiah will bring peace to the world (Isa. 2:4), rebuild the Temple (Ezek. 37:26–28), regather all exiles to Israel (Isa. 11:11–12), and cause universal knowledge of God (Isa. 11:9). Since none of these things happened, Jesus' resurrection (even if assumed true) does not fulfill Jewish messianic prophecy. (b) Hebrews implies a new, eternal covenant ratified by Jesus' blood (i.e., his death), which replaces or fulfills the Torah covenant. The Torah responds that the eternal covenant was already made at Sinai (Exod. 19:5; Deut. 29:28). A human death—especially an unlawful Roman execution—cannot form or validate a covenant under Jewish law. The Torah is already described as eternal (Ps. 119:89) and unchanging (Deut. 13:1 [12:32 in Christian Bibles]). (c): Jesus, as a mediator or instrument of God's Will, contradicts the Torah. God alone is the source of strength and holiness. Judaism does not require or accept a human intercessor or mediator between humanity and God (Deut. 30:14). The Torah teaches that every person can access God directly through prayer, repentance, and observance of the Torah. Elevating Jesus to this role is theologically incompatible with Jewish monotheism and violates the principle of direct relationship with God. It is nothing less than idolatry. (d) Giving glory to Jesus misplaces the Divine Glory. Glory (*kavod*) belongs to God alone in Judaism. The Hebrew Bible is unequivocal. Isaiah 42:8 – "I am the LORD, that is My name; and My glory I will not give to another" (ESV). Attributing eternal glory to a human being—especially one executed by a pagan empire—violates core Jewish theology.

What the Hebrew Bible Says About the Coming of the Messiah

In contrast to the Christian worldview, the Hebrew Bible is explicit about the Messianic age. It contains many "exhaustive" or verifiable prophecies that will be realized worldwide simultaneously, no matter where the Messiah appears:

1. The resurrection of the dead (Isa. 26:19). Imagine deceased children, husbands, wives, siblings, grandparents, and friends suddenly reappearing.
2. No more death (Isa. 25:8). Imagine people on their literal death bed, and seconds before death, they fully recover.
3. There will be no more hunger or illness (Isa. 25:8). Imagine millions of people facing massive starvation and death, and their needs are suddenly fulfilled.
4. There will be no more weapons of war (Ezek. 39:9). Imagine all weapons suddenly disappearing and being transformed into plowshares or other tools.
5. World peace will prevail (Isa. 2:4; Mic. 4:3). There will suddenly be no fighting anywhere.
6. The Messiah will rule at a time when all people can come to acknowledge and serve one God (Isa. 66:23).
7. Knowledge of God will fill the world as the waters cover the seas (Isa. 11:9; 40:5; Hab. 2:14; Zeph. 3:9–13).
8. In the Messianic era, *all* people will believe in God and proclaim His Unity (Zech. 14:9).

No one will need to be told when the Messianic age arrives. It will be a self-evident, cosmic, transformative, and transcendental worldwide event. This event will be all-encompassing and undeniable. Therefore, it is self-evident that the author of Hebrews was in error.

Lastly, the reader must inquire about *what* the Messiah *will do* rather than *who* the Messiah *is*. The author of the Epistle to the Hebrews and other "believers" in Jesus would argue that many unfulfilled miraculous and prophetic events will occur during the *parousia*, the "second coming." This topic requires further elaboration.

The Christian view of prophecy is "front-end loaded." In contrast, the Jewish view is "back-end loaded." The reality is that the author of Hebrews and his fellow Jewish Christians (i.e., believers) had been waiting approximately forty years after the death of Jesus for his return. Additionally, believers would have been waiting approximately fifty to eighty years after the death of Jesus when the Acts of the Apostles were being made public. In the eyes of doubters, the alleged *parousia* is merely a device for addressing the doubt and skepticism faced by people then and throughout the past 2,000 years. Moreover, it is no less than an example of confirmation bias and cognitive dissonance.

The Hebrew Bible Teaches that Blood Sacrifice is Not Required for the Forgiveness of Sins

If a "New Covenant" resulted from Jesus' blood and death on the cross, there would be no need for the Great Commission (Matt. 28:19–20). If Jesus was the Messiah, and the Messianic age started approximately two thousand years ago, there would be no need for Christian evangelicals, missionaries, preachers, and theologians to preach the gospel of Jesus to one's neighbor or brother. If Jesus' blood and death on the cross were the once and for all time atonement for humankind's iniquities and sins, then why is it necessary to teach about Jesus in an attempt to know him? Moreover, why would it be necessary to convert members of the Jewish, Islamic, Hindu, or other theistic faiths to Christianity? Jeremiah 31 is explicit in its teaching that God can forgive sins without the need for a sacrifice:

> 33 For this is the covenant that I will make with the house of Israel after those days, declares the Lord: I will put my law within them, and I will write it on their hearts. And I will be their God, and they shall be my people. 34 *And no longer shall each one teach his neighbor and each his brother, saying, 'Know the Lord,' for they shall all know me, from the least of them to the greatest, declares the Lord. For I will forgive their iniquity, and I will remember their sin no more.* (ESV)

Contrary to the assertions made by the author of Hebrews, the blood of Jesus and his death on the cross did not fulfill any of the future promises of the New Covenant as outlined in Jeremiah. Moreover, the Hebrew Bible refutes the idea that someone can die for your sins:

> Num. 35:33 You shall not pollute the land in which you live, for blood pollutes the land, and no atonement can be made for the land for the blood that is shed in it, except by the blood of the one who shed it.
>
> Deut. 24:16 Fathers shall not to be put to death because of their children, nor shall children be put to death because of their fathers. Each one shall be put to death for his own sin.
>
> Ps. 49:7 (49:8 in the Hebrew Bible) Truly no man can ransom another, or give to God the price of his life,

> Ezek. 18:20 The soul who sins shall die. The son shall not suffer for the iniquity of the father, nor the father suffer for the iniquity of the son. The righteousness of the righteous shall be upon himself, and the wickedness of the wicked shall be upon himself. (ESV)

The evidence presented above shows that the Epistle to the Hebrews not only contains numerous factual inaccuracies but also presents a flawed understanding of the historical context. It is also fundamentally mistaken regarding what the Hebrew Bible says about the coming of the Messiah and the requirement for blood sacrifices to take away people's sins. From a Jewish perspective employing the Bible, the two most objectionable claims contained in the Epistle relate to Jesus himself: he is God and he is the Messiah.

A First-Century Rabbi Addresses the Claims Made in the Epistle to the Hebrews that Jesus is God and that He is the Messiah

In the second century, Justin Martyr authored his *Dialogue with Trypho* (an imaginary Jewish interlocutor). This literary invention attempted to prove that Christianity is the new law for all people and to demonstrate from Scripture that Jesus is the Jewish Messiah. Employing this format, chapter six concludes with a hypothetical first-century Jewish opponent, Rabbi Troki, who engages in a theological debate with the author of the Epistle to the Hebrews. Paul said in Romans 1:16, "For I am not ashamed of the gospel, for it is the power of God for salvation to everyone who believes, to the Jew first and also to the Greek" (ESV). Our Rabbi is not ashamed of the Torah. (1) He is knowledgeable in Torah, (2) fluent in three languages, Aramaic, Greek, and Hebrew, (3) knows Greek translations of the Bible, and (4) familiar with Paul's writings. The Rabbis' letter is unabashedly polemical. He attempts to prove through Scripture that the arguments against Judaism in the author's Epistle are false. In particular, he endeavors to refute two specific claims referred to above: that Jesus is God (Heb. 1:8) and that he is the Messiah, or Christ (i.e., the title is used in Heb. 3:6; 9:28).[6] The Rabbi's speech is below. Imagine him addressing the author of the Epistle to the Hebrews in the cool of the evening, shortly before the destruction of the Temple in 70 CE.

6. The Greek word Χριστός (Christ) appears explicitly at least twelve times in Hebrews, often in connection with his roles as high priest, sacrificial offering, risen Lord, and eternal mediator.

Rabbi Troki's Reply to the Author of the Epistle to the Hebrews

I, Rabbi Troki, have received and carefully examined a copy of your sermon, "To the Hebrews." You claim to quote from our Holy Scripture. However, your writing reveals a lack of knowledge of our Holy Scripture, written in the Holy and Sacred Tongue of the Hebrew language. You pervert God's words. Let your soul be bound up in a bag with holes.

You are wrong on many levels. If Scripture is true, Jesus is not God and not divine. The nations of the world have many gods. Heaven forbids that God should ever become a man! Isaiah is clear: "I am the Lord; that is my name; my glory I give to no other, nor my praise to carved idols" (42:8, ESV). Jesus is not God's name. Admittedly, if God is omnipotent, God can do whatever God wants. However, the crucial issue is whether our omnipotent God would or would not become incarnate and take on visible human form. You either deliberately omit or are ignorant of numerous verses from Holy Scripture refuting your false claims.

How do you not know Exodus 3, which describes God's revelation to Moses at Horeb? Later, the event is repeated in Deuteronomy 4. How is it that you either omit or do not know verse 12? "Then the Lord spoke to you out of the midst of the fire. You heard the sound of words, *but saw no form; there was only a voice*" (ESV). Then, Deuteronomy continues:

> 15 Therefore watch yourselves very carefully. *Since you saw no form on the day* that the Lord spoke to you at Horeb out of the midst of the fire, 16 beware lest you act corruptly by making a carved image for yourselves, *in the form of any figure, the likeness of male or female*, 17 the likeness of any animal that is on the earth, the likeness of any winged bird that flies in the air, 18 the likeness of anything that creeps on the ground, the likeness of any fish that is in the water under the earth. 19 And beware lest you raise your eyes to heaven, and when you see the sun and the moon and the stars, all the host of heaven, you be drawn away and bow down to them and serve them, things that the Lord your God has allotted to all the peoples under the whole heaven . . . 23 Take care, lest you forget the covenant of the Lord your God, which he made with you, and make a carved image, the form of anything that the Lord your God has forbidden you. 24 For the Lord your God is a consuming fire, a jealous God. (Exod. 3:15–24, ESV)

The Torah is unequivocal. Nobody can worship God in any form.

Again, you display your abysmal ignorance or deliberate omission of the truth. In Exodus 33, the Torah describes Moses seeing the Glory of the Lord in the Tent of Meetings:

> 18 Moses said, "Please show me your glory." 19 And he said, "I will make all my goodness pass before you and will proclaim before you my name 'The Lord.' And I will be gracious to whom I will be gracious, and will show mercy on whom I will show mercy. 20 But," he said, "*you cannot see my face, for man shall not see me and live*." 21 And the Lord said, "Behold, there is a place by me where you shall stand on the rock, 22 and while my glory passes by I will put you in a cleft of the rock, and I will cover you with my hand until I have passed by. 23 Then I will take away my hand, and you shall see my back, but my face shall not be seen." (Exod. 33: 18–23)

Moses, the greatest of all prophets, was not permitted to see the face of God. Your Jesus is God incarnate in human flesh. How could thousands of people, including pagan Roman soldiers and political leaders, have been permitted to see the face of Jesus?

I have another question that I demand a straight answer to. Numbers 12 describes a crucial event:

> 5 And the Lord came down in a pillar of cloud and stood at the entrance of the tent and called Aaron and Miriam, and they both came forward. 6 And he said, "Hear my words: If there is a prophet among you, I the Lord make myself known to him in a vision; I speak with him in a dream. 7 Not so with my servant Moses. He is faithful in all my house. 8 With him I speak mouth to mouth, clearly, and not in riddles, *and he beholds the form of the Lord*. Why then were you not afraid to speak against my servant Moses?" (Num. 12:5–8, ESV)

God permits Moses only to see the "form of God." Therefore, even Moses could not behold the Lord Himself because no man can see the Lord and live (Exod. 33:18–24). Answer the following question: if Moses is only permitted to see the form or image of the Lord, and Jesus is God incarnate in human flesh, how can thousands of people, including pagan Roman soldiers and the political leadership, have been permitted to see the face of Jesus?

Have you read the Holy and Sacred Bible in the original Hebrew, the Holy and Sacred Tongue? Have you read about the creation of man? Genesis 1:26–27 and 2:7 speak in the language of man. It metaphorically describes God making Adam (man) in the "image" of God and forming him from the dust of the earth. These passages are open to divergent interpretations. Perhaps you are ignorant of the following explanation. The first human, Adam, was made in the image of God, which is the *image of God's name*. When read vertically in the Sacred and Holy tongue [Hebrew], the four-letter name of God (YHWH) forms the stick figure of a human being. The *yud* is the head, the first *hei* the arms, the *vav/waw* the trunk/vertebral column, and the final *hei* is the legs. Jesus was a human being, formed like all healthy humans, in the image of God's name.[7]

The Children of Israel are commanded not to worship anything *in the form of any figure, the likeness of male or female*. You believe Jesus is God. Heaven forbid! The burden of proof is on you to prove that Jesus appeared to Moses at Horeb. Moreover, the burden of proof is on you to prove that any of the numerous angelic appearances in the Hebrew Bible are Jesus or the spirit of Jesus (Gen. 18; 23:15; 32:22–32).

How can you, who are allegedly a learned man seriously maintain that Jesus is divine? Did the Children of Israel, living in Judea during the last hundred years or earlier, ever believe that a man can be God or that God can be a man? *The Messiah can only be a human being and not God*. Perhaps your learning is limited. Do you not know the teaching of the prophet Hosea? Hosea 11:9 declares: "I will not execute my burning anger; I will not again destroy Ephraim; *for I am God and not a man*, the Holy One in your midst, and I will not come in wrath"[8] (ESV).

Numbers 23:19 says, "*God is not man*, that he should lie, or a son of man, that he should change his mind" (ESV). Additionally, there is 1 Samuel 15:29, when God rejected Saul. The prophet Samuel declared, "And also the Glory of Israel will not lie or have regret, *for he is not a man*, that he should have regret" (ESV). God did not create man to worship a man. Listen carefully to what I am saying. *Nowhere* in the Holy and Sacred Bible does God explicitly state that "the Messiah" would be a God or even Godlike. However, you erroneously believe and proclaim that Jesus is the divine son of God. Heaven forbid and may God have mercy on your soul.

7. Numerous explanations of Genesis 1:26 exist in Rabbinic literature. They encompass intellectual, moral, spiritual, and relational aspects of humanity. (1) God's Presence in the Soul i.e., the Divine spark, (2) Humans as Reflectors of God's Glory, (3) Capacity for Holiness and Spirituality, (4) Rationality and Free Will, (5) Moral Freedom and the Ability to Choose Good, (6) Human Dignity and Respect, and (7) Moral and Ethical Characteristics.

8. See also Job 9:32; 33:12; Mal. 3:6; Ps. 146:3.

It seems that you do not know your Bible, for Hosea 3:4–5 categorically refutes any possibility that Jesus could be either the Messiah or God. It clearly says, "4 For the children of Israel shall dwell many days without king or prince, without sacrifice or pillar, without ephod or household gods. 5 Afterward, the children of Israel shall return and *seek the Lord their God, and David, their king*, and they shall come in fear to the Lord and to his goodness in the latter days" (ESV). First, notice that the Messiah is referred to as David, their king. Your Jesus was not from the line of David since he had no human father, nor was he ever a king. Second, the verse says that at a future time, the children of Israel will return to (a) the Lord their God and (b) their king. The king is mentioned separately from the Lord our God. Consequently, this verse provides unequivocal proof that the future Messiah (king) will not be God in the flesh but a human Davidic king at the end of days.

You are obviously unfamiliar with Jeremiah 30:8–9. It reinforces Hosea's message. "8 And it shall come to pass in that day, declares the Lord of hosts, that I will break his yoke from off your neck, and I will burst your bonds, and foreigners shall no more make a servant of him. 9 *But they shall serve the Lord their God and David their king*, whom I will raise up for them" (ESV). Here, the king is also mentioned separately from the Lord their God. Hence, the two are not the same.

Ezekiel 37:24–28 provides additional support for my argument. "24 My servant David shall be king over them, and they shall all have one shepherd. They shall walk in my rules and be careful to obey my statutes. 25 They shall dwell in the land that I gave to my servant Jacob, where your fathers lived. They and their children and their children's children shall dwell there forever, *and David my servant shall be their prince forever*" (ESV). Again, David is the king and is mentioned separately from the Lord their God (i.e., my rules, statutes, and land I gave them). The two are utterly distinct.

Excuse me for my lengthy response. Allow me to quote the instructions given by Moses our teacher in Deuteronomy 4:

> 15 You saw no form of any kind the day the Lord spoke to you at Horeb out of the fire. Therefore oversee yourselves, 16 so that you do not become corrupt and make for yourselves an idol, *an image of any shape, whether formed like a man or a woman*, 17 or like any animal on earth or any bird that flies in the air, 18 or like any creature that moves along the ground or any fish in the waters below. 19 And when you look up to the sky and see the

> sun, the moon and the stars—all the heavenly array—do not be enticed into bowing down to them and worshiping things the Lord your God has apportioned to all the nations under heaven. (Deut. 4:15–19, ESV)

Have you not read what the book of Deuteronomy says, nine chapters later?[9]

> 32 See that you do all I command you; do not add to it or take away from it. 1 If a prophet, or one who foretells by dreams, appears among you and announces to you a sign or wonder, 2 and if the sign or wonder spoken of takes place, and the prophet says, "Let us follow other gods" (gods you have not known) "and let us worship them,"3 you must not listen to the words of that prophet or dreamer. The Lord your God is testing you to find out whether you love him with all your heart and with all your soul. 4 It is the Lord your God you must follow, and him you must revere. Keep his commands and obey him; serve him and hold fast to him. (Deut. 9:32–34, ESV)

You either do not know what you are saying, or you are lying. You place a stumbling block before the blind (Lev. 19:14). Multiple biblical verses explicitly state that God is unique and there is only one God (Deut. 4:35, 39; 6:4; 32:39; 1 Kgs. 8:60; 2 Kgs. 19:15; 1 Chron. 17:20; Neh. 9:6; Ps. 86:10; Isa. 43:10–11; 44:6, 8; 45:21; 46:9; Zech. 14:9). How can Jesus be God if God the Father is God?

The Gospels (which we will assume, for the sake of argument, were written before Hebrews was composed) also refutes the idea that Jesus was God. They contain descriptions of Jesus that counter the idea that he possessed divine attributes.

1. While Jesus was with his disciples, he grew weary (John 4:6) (hence he was not omnipotent).
2. While Jesus was with his disciples, he was distressed (Mark 14:33–34) (hence he was not omnipotent).
3. While Jesus was on Earth, he died and was buried (Mark 15:37, 46) (hence he was not immortal).
4. While Jesus was with his disciples, he had limited knowledge: he was unaware of who had touched him (Mark 5:30), and he did

9. Deuteronomy 12:32–13:4 (Deuteronomy 12:32 in Hebrew texts, this verse (12:32) is numbered 13:1 in the AV).

not know the date of the Last Day (Mark 13:32) (hence he was not omniscient).

5. Jesus prayed to God his Father to take this cup from him (Mark 14:36) (hence, he was not omnipotent).
6. Jesus had power given to him (Matt. 28:18; John 5:19) (hence, he was not omnipotent).

Clearly, your knowledge of the Torah is deficient and lacking.

Second, the absolute minimum requirement for qualifying as "the Messiah" is being from the male bloodline (in Hebrew, *zera*) of King David. I have heard different stories about the birth of Jesus. I have no idea which of these stories is true. You provide no evidence that Jesus can be the Messiah. I have heard an account about Paul, the person who is known as the Apostle. Paul claims in Romans 1:3 that Jesus could trace his blood lineage to David. Paul's statement about the birth of Jesus is informative. Are you aware of what Paul wrote? He states in Galatians 4:4:

> But when the fullness of time had come, God sent forth his Son, *born of woman*, born under the law (ESV)

If you really believed that Jesus was born from a virgin (i.e., had no biological father), then you must have known that he could not have qualified as the Messiah. Are you ignorant of the Torah? In the Holy and Sacred Bible, God's word is explicit. The father must be a direct descendant of the male bloodline. Numbers 1:18 says, "and on the first day of the second month, they assembled the whole congregation together, *who registered themselves by clans, by fathers' houses*, according to the number of names from twenty years old and upward, head by head" (ESV).

If Jesus were the Messiah, as you believe, we would all be living during the Messianic age, which the Holy Bible explicitly describes. Since you and virtually all members of the Jewish people recognize this reality, then you must realize that Jesus could not be the Messiah. When did we ever see any of the following prophecies fulfilled?

1. The redemption of Israel.
2. The rebuilding of the Third Temple.
3. All Jews returning (i.e., the in-gathering) to the Land of Israel (Isa.43:5–6).

4. The world turns to the Jewish people for spiritual leadership and guidance (Zech. 8:23).
5. The knowledge of God filling the world as the waters cover the seas (Isa. 11:9; 40:5; Zeph. 3:9–13).
6. Everyone believes in God and proclaims His Unity (Zech. 14:9)
7. The Jewish people experience eternal joy and gladness (Isa. 51:11).

You suggest that the Messianic age will be fulfilled when Jesus returns, the so-called *parousia* or Second Coming. Your letter contains several references to this event:

1. The End of the Ages (9:26)
2. Expectation of the Parousia (9:28)
3. The Approaching Parousia (10:25)
4. The Imminent Parousia (10:37)
5. The Expectation of the Parousia (13:14)

However, your writings are deceptive and false. Your *parousia* is a theological construction designed to cover up the failure of your Jesus' prophesied *imminent* return. It has been approximately forty years since your God-man's death. Your problem is self-evident. Most witnesses of your Jesus have died. They leave behind a generation without access to firsthand accounts of the person you call the God-man. Your fellow believers face mockery, ridicule, sarcasm, and mounting pressure of doubt. You are writing to keep their hopes alive. "A fool takes no pleasure in understanding, but only in expressing his opinion" (Prov. 18:2, ESV).

The day is getting late, so I will finish here. There are numerous errors and falsehoods in your sermon. While they are not as many as the grains of sand along the seashore or the stars in the evening sky, they are numerous, nonetheless. You who have eyes and do not see. You who have ears and do not hear. You place stumbling blocks before the blind (Lev. 19:14). Repent and return to the Lord. Only then can the true God, the Creator of all, have mercy on your soul.

How Christians Might Reply to Rabbi Troki and Why Their Arguments Fail

Our imaginary first-century Jewish Rabbi appears to have scored a resounding victory against the author of the Epistle to the Hebrews. However, there are several objections that Christians could marshal against some of the Rabbi's arguments. Let us briefly examine them:

(a) Do the Doctrines of the Trinity and the Incarnation Invalidate the Rabbi's Objections?

First, many Christians would take umbrage at the Rabbi's argument that since God cannot grow weary, be distressed, or die, Jesus cannot be God. In a similar vein, the Rabbi argues that since Jesus (unlike the Father) did not know the date of the Last Day, Jesus must be less than God. In response, Christians appeal to the doctrines of the Trinity and the Incarnation. Jesus, they say, was God the Son (not the Father). In addition, Jesus assumed a human nature when he came and lived among us. Hence, it is hardly surprising that he exhibits human limitations, such as weariness, sadness, bodily death, and ignorance.

In response, any attempt to read the doctrine of the Trinity into the New Testament is anachronistic. The formula "in the name of the Father, Son, and Holy Spirit" appears once in the entire New Testament (Matt. 28:19), where it is mysteriously presented without any explanation. We are not told what the relation between the Father, Son, and Holy Spirit is. Indeed, there is nothing to suggest that these three individuals are the same being or that they are all equal and co-eternal.

The Christian bishop Theophilus of Antioch began to refer to God, his Word (Logos), and his Wisdom (Sophia) as a τριάς or Triad around 180 CE. About thirty years later, in 210 CE, the Latin theologian Tertullian coined the term *Trinitas* (or Trinity) to refer to the Father, Son, and Holy Spirit. However, readers should note that early Christian notions of the Trinity were heretical, judged by the standards of the Nicene Creed, to which the vast majority of contemporary Christians subscribe: Tertullian, for instance, did not believe that the Son and Holy Spirit existed from all eternity, and unlike later Christians who viewed the Father, Son, and Holy Spirit as omniscient, Tertullian believed the Son to be ignorant of the date of the Last Day. Writing in the mid-third century, the Christian theologian Origen declared the three Divine Persons to be co-eternal but not equal: only the Father is considered the one true God, while the Son is referred to as "God" in a derivative sense, being eternal with the Father. The fully developed concept of a Trinity of three co-equal, co-eternal Divine Persons, who were nonetheless One Being, was not formulated until the fourth century, at the ecumenical Councils of Nicaea (325 CE) and Constantinople (381 CE). At any rate, what is certain is that the notion that God is a "Compound Unity" of three persons did not exist in the first century.

Likewise, the concept of the Hypostatic Union—i.e., the notion that Jesus possessed two natures, divine and human— evolved (continuing or gradual revelation). No Scriptural verses from the Hebrew Bible justify the claim that God can become a man. Only in John's Gospel (c. 90–100 CE) are we explicitly told that God's Word, or *Logos*, became flesh and lived among us (John 1:1–2, 14), but this *Logos*, which is called *theos* (God), is carefully distinguished from *ho theos* ("*the* God"). What is more, in the same Gospel, Jesus refers to the Father as "the one true God" (John 17:3) and as "my God and your God" (John 20:17), who is "greater than I" (John 14:28). Clearly, he did not equate himself with God the Father.

Some can argue that the Christian doctrine of the incarnation that Jesus is God made man, is implicit in the writings of the second-century bishop and theologian Irenaeus (c. 180 CE). It was first articulated by Tertullian (c. 210 CE), who referred to "One Person—Jesus, God and Man" and taught that the Son of God assumed a human soul and a human body.[10] However, it was not until the fifth century that the Christian Church, at the ecumenical Council of Chalcedon (451 CE), provided the definitive formulation of the Hypostatic Union, declaring that Christ is "one person in two natures," fully divine and fully human, without confusion, change, division, or separation. This view became the orthodox Christian understanding of Christ's nature. Entire books, encyclopedia entries, and journal articles have been written on this subject by people on both sides of the religious aisle. The point here is that the doctrine has to be read back into Scripture by those who already embrace it.

(B) Does "born of a woman" Rule Out the Virgin Birth?

Second, many Christian Bible commentators and theologians would vigorously contest our imaginary Rabbi's claim that the phrase "born of a

10. Tertullian, *Adversus Praxeam*, chapter 27.

woman" is at odds with the doctrine of the virgin birth, arguing that it refers to the humanity of Jesus, which began at a definite point in time, unlike Jesus' divine nature, which existed from all eternity. Readers need to understand that according to mainline Christianity, Jesus was simultaneously 100 percent God and 100 percent man, with no sin in him whatsoever. This view is the doctrine of the *Two Natures of Christ* (or the Hypostatic Union), discussed above. However, what mainline Christian theology overlooks is that Jesus' direct lineage through the male line to David cannot be established. Consequently, Jesus cannot be considered the Messiah. The concept of a virgin birth is thus irrelevant.

It is unknown whether the author of Hebrews had any prior information about whether Jesus was born from a virgin or had a biological father who could trace his ancestry directly back to David. If he had prior knowledge, when, where, and from whom did he receive it? These questions are unanswerable.

Finally, detractors point out that the author of Hebrews does not provide any details about the conception and birth of Jesus, the identities of Mary and Joseph, the visit of the magi, or Jesus' early life, baptism, and temptation in the wilderness.[11]

(c) Can the Parousia Explain Why Key Messianic Prophecies Have Not Been Fulfilled?

Third, in response to our imaginary Rabbi's argument that Jesus cannot be the Messiah since the redemption of Israel, the rebuilding of the Third Temple, and the return of the world's Jews to Israel have not yet materialized. Christian apologists, Bible commentators, and theologians argue that the messianic age will be fulfilled when Jesus returns (Acts 1:11). Skeptics and detractors counter that the second coming (*parousia*) is a theological construction that deals with the failure of Jesus' prophesied *imminent* return. The Gospels and Acts were composed approximately forty to seventy years or even later after Jesus' death, and many witnesses had died by then. That reality left a generation without access to firsthand accounts of Jesus' tradition. Moreover, Hebrews, which was presumably composed before the destruction of the Second Temple in the year 70,

11. Modern commentators and theologians will counter that many details in the New Testament are not multiply attested: Matthew's guard at the tomb, Luke's travelers on the way to Emmaus, and John's account of Jesus being pierced on his side by a Roman soldier while on the cross.

addressed the challenges faced by the survivors of the first and second generations of believers. They encountered mockery, ridicule, sarcasm, and the mounting pressure of doubt. Jesus had been dead for almost forty years. The Gospels (Matt. 10:6–7, 23; 16:28; 24:23; Mark 9:1; 14:61–62; Luke 21:28, 32) and Hebrews (9:28; 10:25; 37) clearly express Christian anticipation of Jesus' *imminent* return to the current generation. The concept of *parousia* addresses the challenges faced by skeptics of that generation and reflects believers' adaptation and reinterpretation of prophecies related to Jesus' imminent return. In psychology and sociology, this kind of adaptation is referred to as *confirmation bias* by denial, reinterpretation, and making excuses.

Many Jewish community members in the author's time expected a Messiah who would be a political and military leader who would liberate Israel from Roman rule and restore the kingdom of Israel. Jesus, whom the Romans crucified, did not fit this expectation. How did the author of Hebrews and Jewish Christians come to view him as the Messiah? They did so by redefining the Messiah's role.

CONCLUSION

In conclusion, the Epistle to the Hebrews is a combination of sermon and polemical text (from a Jewish perspective) written by a devout and sincere believer in Jesus, who is attempting to convince Jewish people and fellow believers in Jesus that Christianity is superior to Judaism. On the contrary, all it "proves" is that the author considered his opinions correct and valid. The central message of this chapter is that the statements made in the Epistle to the Hebrews are unable to establish the reliability of the author's claims and that the Epistle's arguments are far from compelling and convincing. This chapter also engages with and systematically challenges the claims of the Epistle's anonymous author. It presents the reader *with* a *cumulative argument* against the author of the Epistle. Its impact solidifies the Epistle's *unsustainability*. Ultimately, it is up to the reader to judge the success or failure of this argument.

7

Worldview and Horizons: Christianity and Islam

Horizon may be defined as one's "preunderstanding." It is how historians view things as a result of their knowledge, experience, beliefs, education, cultural conditioning, preferences, presuppositions and worldview. Horizons are like sunglasses through which a historian looks. Everything she sees is colored by that horizon. Take baseball, for example. In a baseball game, if there was a close play at second base, do you think the runner was safe or out? It depends on whether your son is the guy stealing second or the shortstop tagging him. When we read books about Jesus, we find ourselves in agreement or disagreement with certain authors usually based on whether the Jesus they reconstruct is like the one we prefer.[1]

When it comes to historical investigations, our biases can significantly shape our conclusions. These biases—called "horizons"—are influenced by many factors: our race, gender, nationality, political beliefs, religious convictions, upbringing, and the communities we belong to. These personal "horizons" act like tinted sunglasses, affecting the way we interpret the world and the data we encounter. This is why different historians can look at the same evidence and draw entirely different

1. Licona, *The Resurrection of Jesus*, 38.

conclusions. And it's not just Christians who have biases, myself included—everyone does.[2]

INTRODUCTION

Ruth Flanagan makes a pertinent observation, "The term 'worldviews' is employed across disciplinary boundaries, yet with no agreed definition it may actually obscure rather than clarify meaning . . . Within each discipline, differing definitions and employment of the term have evolved which, even within the same discipline, can be contradictory."[3] The concept of worldview is a topic of discussion in philosophy, psychology, sociology, economics, anthropology, and religion/theology. The term worldview was coined in Immanuel Kant's (1724–1804) work, *Critique of Judgment* (1790).[4]

Kant writes:

> If the human mind is nonetheless to *be able even to think* the given infinite without contradiction, it must have within itself a power that is supersensible, whose idea of a noumenon cannot be intuited but can yet be regarded as the substrate underlying what is mere appearance, namely, our intuition of the world" [*Weltanschauung*]. For only by means of this power and its idea do we, in a pure intellectual estimation of the magnitude, comprehend the infinite in the world of sense *entirely under* a concept, even though a mathematical estimation of the magnitude by *means of numerical concepts* we can never think it in its entirety.[5]

David Naugle elaborates: "That last phrase—"our intuition of the world"—is an English translation of Kant's coined German term *Weltanschauung*."[6] The term "Weltanschauung" is a compound of *Welt* ('world') and *Anschauung* ('perception' or 'view'). It was later popularized by Georg Wilhelm Friedrich Hegel (1770–1831).

2. Licona (@drmikelicona), "Michael Licona on Instagram: When It Comes to Historical Investigations."

3. Flanagan, "Worldviews," 331–32.

4. Naugle, *Worldview: The History of a Concept*, 58.

5. Kant, *Critique of Judgment*, 111–12, emphasis on Kant's worldview.

6. Naugle, *Worldview: The History of a Concept*, 13.

CHRISTIAN THEISM AND WORLDVIEW VERSUS ISLAM

Christian fundamentalists (who are predominantly Evangelical Protestants) share numerous beliefs. The following doctrinal position and statement of faith is from a representative of a theologically conservative institution: Biola University.

> There is one God, eternally existing and manifesting Himself to us in three Persons: Father, Son and Holy Spirit.
>
> . . . He was put to death by crucifixion under Pontius Pilate. God raised from the dead the body that had been nailed to the cross. The Lord Jesus after His crucifixion showed Himself to be alive to His disciples, appearing unto them by the space of 40 days. After this, the Lord Jesus ascended into heaven, and the Father caused Him to sit at His right hand in the heavenly places, far above all rule and authority and power and dominion, and every name that is named, not only in this world, but also in that which is to come, and put all things in subjection under His feet, and gave Him to be Head over all things to the Church.
>
> The Lord Jesus, before His incarnation, existed in the form of God and of His own choice laid aside His divine glory and took upon Himself the form of a servant and was made in the likeness of men. In His pre-existent state, He was with God and was God. He is a divine person possessed of all the attributes of Deity, and should be worshiped as God by angels and man. . . .
>
> By His death on the cross, the Lord Jesus made a perfect atonement for sin, by which the wrath of God against sinners is appeased and a ground furnished upon which God can deal in mercy with sinners. He redeemed us from the curse of the law by becoming a curse in our place.[7]

Therefore, Biola University and other institutions adopt a "presuppositional" view (one must presuppose the truth of the Christian vision of theism).

Given this presuppositional worldview, Melchizedek's connection with the Epistle to the Hebrews is significant. Melchizedek makes eight appearances in the Epistle to the Hebrews (Heb. 5:6, 10; 6:20; 7:1, 10, 11, 15, and 17). The eight verses in Hebrews that discuss Melchizedek are intricately interconnected, building an elaborate theological argument concerning the supremacy of Jesus Christ and his priesthood.

7. "Theological Positions,"; cf. "Doctrinal Position"; "Moody Believes."

Hebrews 5:6 (First mention of Melchizedek): This verse quotes Psalm 110:4, stating that Jesus is a priest "according to the order of Melchizedek." The connection to Melchizedek is important because it contrasts the priesthood of Jesus with the Levitical priesthood. Unlike the Levitical priests who were part of a hereditary system, Melchizedek is a priest who was not part of that system, and Jesus' priesthood shares this unique characteristic.

Hebrews 5:10 (Jesus as high priest): This verse further develops the theme by emphasizing that Jesus was appointed by God as high priest "according to the order of Melchizedek." This insight is part of the argument that Jesus' priesthood is superior to the Levitical priesthood and that he is uniquely qualified due to his eternal nature, as seen in the mysterious figure of Melchizedek, who is both king and priest, without a known genealogy.

Hebrews 6:20 (Jesus as the forerunner): In this verse, the author explains that Jesus—having entered the "inner sanctuary" as a forerunner—has become a high priest "forever, in the order of Melchizedek." This verse emphasizes the eternal nature of Jesus' priesthood, contrasting it with the temporary nature of the Levitical priests. It ties Jesus' role as high priest to the mysterious and enduring nature of Melchizedek's priesthood, which was not bound by time or lineage.

Hebrews 7:1–3 (Melchizedek's enigmatic role): These verses recount the story of Melchizedek from Genesis 14, which describes him as both the king of Salem and the priest of the Most High God and sets the stage for understanding Christ's similar dual role as both King and Priest. He is presented as a figure without a recorded genealogy, beginning, or end, symbolizing a priesthood that is eternal and not tied to earthly lineage. This claim helps establish the idea that Melchizedek's priesthood is a type or shadow of the eternal and superior priesthood of Christ. Jesus' priesthood is described as superior because it is in the order of Melchizedek, which transcends the limitations of the Levitical priesthood.

Hebrews 7:10 (The significance of Melchizedek's priesthood about Levi): This verse references the interaction between Melchizedek and Abram from Genesis 14:18–20, where Melchizedek blesses Abram. The phrase "still in the loins of his father" refers to the idea that Levi—the ancestor of the Levitical priesthood—was in the genealogical line of Abram and was thus "present" when Abram met Melchizedek. Therefore, Melchizedek's priesthood predates the Levitical priesthood. This reality highlights the superiority of Melchizedek's priesthood over the Levitical priesthood, even before the Levitical priesthood was established. Jesus—being of the Melchizedekian order—transcends the Levitical system, highlighting his eternal priesthood. Therefore, verse 10 points to the eternal nature of Melchizedek's priesthood and by extension Jesus' priesthood, which is superior to the Levitical line.

Hebrews 7:11 (The need for a new priesthood): This verse presents a rhetorical question that strengthens the argument for the superiority of Jesus' priesthood. The Levitical priesthood—while established under the Mosaic law—was never able to bring true perfection or complete reconciliation with God. The Levitical priesthood could not bring "perfection," meaning that the system was incomplete and could not fulfill God's ultimate purpose. Something being outside the Levitical system, greater and more eternal was required. This reality establishes the necessity for a new and greater priesthood, one that originates from the order of Melchizedek and is fulfilled by Jesus.

Hebrews 7:15 (The emergence of a better priesthood): Here, the comparison between Jesus and Melchizedek is even more explicit, in that it reinforces the belief that Jesus' priesthood is superior because it is not based on human lineage or the rituals of the Law but is established by God's eternal will. This verse emphasizes that Jesus, as a priest "like Melchizedek," further clarifies the uniqueness and superiority of his priesthood. The comparison between Jesus and Melchizedek shows that Jesus' priesthood fulfills the true and eternal purpose of the priesthood. It is not bound by genealogy, sacrifice, or ritual but is permanent and effective, offering a better way to salvation.

Hebrews 7:17 (Jesus as a priest forever): This verse cites Psalm 110:4 again, emphasizing that Jesus' priesthood is eternal. The declaration that Jesus is a priest "forever" connects directly to Melchizedek's mysterious and timeless role. The fact that this priesthood is "forever" highlights the key distinction between Jesus' priesthood and the Levitical priesthood. The latter was temporary and required constant renewal through successive generations.

These eight verses combined highlight the superiority of Jesus' priesthood, which is "in the order of Melchizedek." Melchizedek is a type of Christ's eternal priesthood. The Melchizedekian priesthood is characterized by its timeless and eternal nature. It is not bound by time, and it offers a more profound and more permanent reconciliation with God than the Levitical priesthood, which was rooted in a temporal, human system. Through the figure of Melchizedek, the author of Hebrews establishes that Jesus' priesthood is superior because it is eternal, not dependent on lineage, and because it provides a perfect, final means of salvation. Melchizedek himself is a type (or shadow) of Christ's priesthood. The author of Hebrews presents Melchizedek as a mysterious figure whose characteristics—being both a king and priest—point to Jesus. This typology is fulfilled in Christ, who perfectly and eternally fulfills the dual roles of priest and king (cf. Heb. 7:15–17). Therefore, Jesus is the Messiah.

However, the reader must examine these eight verses in the context of the Epistle to the Hebrews. The author is explicit about Jesus. He is more than a high priest after the order of Melchizedek. From a Christian worldview, the reader must accept the following assertions made about Jesus in Hebrews:

> He is God's Son [1:2], he was appointed heir of all things [1:2], he is the one through whom he (Jesus) made the universe [1:2], he is the radiance of God's glory and the exact representation of his (i.e., God's) being [1:3] he sustains all things by his powerful word [1:3], he sat down at the right hand of the Majesty in heaven [1:3], he is superior to the angels [1:4], all angels will worship him [1:6], God promises him, "Your throne, O God (referring to Jesus) will last for ever and ever" [1:8], his years will never end [1:12], he suffered death, so that by the Grace of God he might taste death for everyone [2:9], he has been found worthy of greater honor than Moses [3:3], he is the Son of God [4:14], he is the source of eternal salvation to all who obey him [5:9], he is without a biological mother and father [7:3], he lives forever [7:23], he is able to save completely [7:25], he always lives to intercede for the people [7:25]; he is holy, blameless, pure, set apart from sinners, exalted above all the heavens [7:26], he sat down at the right hand of the throne of the Majesty in heaven [8:1], he serves in the sanctuary, the true tabernacle set up by the Lord [8:2], he is the mediator of a covenant which is superior to the old one [8:7], he obtained eternal redemption for us once and for all by his own blood [9:12], he offered himself unblemished to God, cleansing our consciences from acts that lead to death [9:14], he is the mediator of a new contract [9:15], he died as a ransom [9:15], he was sacrificed once to take away the sins of many people [9:28], he is the author and perfecter of our faith [12:2], he endured the cross, scorning its shame [12:2], he is the mediator of a new covenant [12:24], he suffered to make the people holy through his own blood [13:12], and he was brought back from the dead [13:20].

ISLAMIC THEISM AND WORLDVIEW

Islam is the second-largest religion in the world, with approximately two billion adherents. Its worldview is at odds with Christian theism. Sixteen highlighted examples of this religious worldview were identified by a literature review, as well as ChatGPT, Gemini, and Grammarly are enumerated below:

1. *View of God (Tawhid vs. Trinity)*

- Islam: Believes in the absolute oneness of God (Allah)—a central tenet called *Tawhid*. God has no partners or associates.
- Christianity: Beliefs in the doctrine of the Trinity—God is one but exists in three persons: the Father, the Son (Jesus Christ), and the Holy Spirit.

2. *Jesus Christ (Isa in Islam)*

- Islam: Jesus (Isa) is considered a prophet, not the Son of God in a literal sense. He is highly revered but not divine.
- Christianity: Jesus is the Son of God, the second person of the Trinity, and the Savior of humanity whose death and resurrection offer salvation.

3. *The Nature of Jesus' Death*

- Islam: Believes Jesus was not crucified; instead, someone else was made to appear like him, and Jesus was taken up into heaven by God.
- Christianity: Believes that Jesus was crucified, died, and was resurrected to atone for the sins of humanity.

4. *The Holy Spirit*

- Islam: The Holy Spirit is understood as the angel Jibril (Gabriel), a messenger of God.
- Christianity: The Holy Spirit is the third person of the Trinity, fully divine, and he works to guide, empower, and comfort believers.

5. *The Bible vs. The Qur'an*

- Islam: The Qur'an is considered the final and unalterable word of God, revealed directly to the Prophet Muhammad. The previous

Scriptures (the Torah, Psalms, and Gospels) are viewed as having been corrupted over time.

- Christianity: The Bible, comprising of the Old and New Testaments, is regarded as the divinely inspired Word of God, with the New Testament primarily focusing on the life and teachings of Jesus Christ.

6. *Salvation*

- Islam: Salvation is achieved through faith in one God (Allah), righteous deeds, and submission to Allah's will. Salvation is achieved through good deeds, prayer, charity, and following the Five Pillars of Islam.
- Christianity: Salvation is through faith in Jesus Christ as Lord and Savior, who atoned for sin through his death and resurrection. Grace, not works, is central to Christian salvation.

7. *Original Sin*

- Islam: It does not teach the doctrine of original sin. God forgave Adam and Eve's disobedience, and all humans are born sinless.
- Christianity: Beliefs in original sin—all humans inherit a sinful nature due to the fall of Adam and Eve, which requires redemption through Jesus Christ.

8. *Prophethood*

- Islam: Muhammad is considered the last of the prophets, the Seal of the Prophets. There is no prophet after him.
- Christianity: Believes in the finality of Jesus Christ as the ultimate revelation of God. Prophets existed in the Old Testament, but there is no belief in a new prophet after Jesus.

9. *The Concept of Sin*

- Islam: Sin is viewed as an act opposing Allah's will. It can be forgiven through sincere repentance and good deeds.
- Christianity: Sin is an offense against God, and only the death and resurrection of Jesus can provide forgiveness of sin through faith.

10. *Heaven and Hell*

- Islam: Heaven (*Jannah*) and Hell (*Jahannam*) are real places of eternal reward or punishment based on one's faith and deeds.
- Christianity: Believes in eternal life in Heaven and eternal suffering in Hell, but salvation is primarily centered on faith in Jesus Christ. Hell is often seen as an eternal separation from God.

11. *The Day of Judgment*

- Islam: The Day of Judgment is a fundamental belief representing the day when all humans will be resurrected and judged by God based on their deeds and faith.
- Christianity: The Day of Judgment is also a central belief as is the day when all individuals are judged, based on their relationship with Christ and whether they accepted him as their Savior and obeyed His command to "Love one another as I have loved you."

12. *The Afterlife*

- Islam: The afterlife is a key belief. Those who follow Allah's guidance will be rewarded with eternal bliss in *Jannah*, while those who reject it face eternal punishment in *Jahannam*.
- Christianity: Beliefs in an afterlife where believers in Christ are rewarded with eternal life in Heaven, and non-believers face eternal separation from God.

13. *The Nature of Scripture*

- Islam: The Qur'an is the literal, eternal word of God, revealed in Arabic, unchanged and preserved since its revelation.
- Christianity: The Bible is divinely inspired but also composed by human authors over centuries. It is not considered the literally dictated word of God in the same way the Qur'an is in Islam (however, this is disputed by "conservative" Christian denominations.)

14. *Revelation*

- Islam: The Qur'an is the final and most complete revelation from God, superseding previous scriptures such as the Torah and the Gospels.

- Christianity: Believes the Bible is God's revelation to humanity, with the New Testament focusing on the life, teachings, and resurrection of Jesus.

15. *The Concept of Messiah*

- Islam: Jesus is a prophet and the Messiah, but not divine. He is expected to return to defeat the Antichrist (*Dajjal*) and establish justice.
- Christianity: Jesus is the Messiah, the Son of God, whose death and resurrection are central to salvation and the establishment of God's kingdom.

16. *Intercession of Jesus*

- Islam: Does not accept the intercession of Jesus. Only Allah can forgive sins, and individuals must seek forgiveness directly from Him.
- Christianity: Jesus can intercede on behalf of believers, praying to God on their behalf.

These sixteen points outline key theological and Scriptural differences between Islam and Christianity. The reader should note that Christians do not agree on every point. They continually debate the concepts of God, salvation, and sacred texts, some of which directly contradict the material in the Epistle to the Hebrews.

The Epistle to the Hebrews in the New Testament presents Melchizedek in a highly significant light. Several concepts in the Epistle that are related to Melchizedek are highly problematic in Islam.

- *Theological Monotheism*: Islam's strict monotheism rejects the idea of any being, even Melchizedek, having eternal or divine characteristics. The claim that Melchizedek is "without father or mother" would contradict the Islamic understanding of God's singularity (*Tawhid*) and the human nature shared by all prophets, saints, and righteous people. The Qur'an teaches that all humans, including prophets, are born with earthly genealogies.
- *Rejection of Jesus' Priesthood*: In Christianity, Melchizedek's priesthood is viewed as eternal and as a foreshadowing of Christ's priesthood, which is considered eternally valid and universal. Islam, however, rejects the idea that anyone other than Allah could hold such an eternal, divine position. The Christian concept of priesthood in Islam is fundamentally different because God is the only

true priest, and there is no intermediary between humans and God in the Islamic faith. In Islam, every believer has direct access to God, and the concept of a priesthood is unnecessary.

- *The Role of Jesus*: Hebrews teaches that Jesus is the ultimate high priest, in the order of Melchizedek, and that his sacrifice has fulfilled the need for any further priestly mediation. Islam rejects Jesus' divinity, viewing him as a prophet and not the literal Son of God or a mediator of salvation. Therefore, the idea of Melchizedek's priesthood prefiguring that of Christ is incompatible with Islamic theology, which does not accept Jesus as a divine figure or a mediator in the way Christianity does.
- *Jesus' Sacrifice*: In Hebrews, Melchizedek's priesthood is linked to the sacrifice of Jesus on the cross as the ultimate atonement for sin. Islam rejects the crucifixion and atonement theology found in Hebrews, as well as the idea that any human, including Jesus, could offer a divine sacrifice for sin. The Qur'an teaches that salvation is through submission to God, and no human sacrifice is needed.[8]

The expression and concept of the "Son of God" is misunderstood. Joseph Cumming elaborates that "words used in the sacred Scriptures can have different senses (*wujūh*), according to the context of the verses and the occasions of their revelation (*asbāb nuzūlih*ā)."[9] He identified and described four different symbolic senses:

- First: In one sense, all human beings are children of God. Acts 17:28–29 says: "We are all the offspring of God." Similarly, Luke 3:38 says that Adam, peace be upon him, was "the son of God," and all who are children of Adam (*banī Ādam*) are thus children of God (*abnā' Allāh*).
- Second: There is a special sense in which the Gospel says that all who believe in *al-Sayyid al-Mas*ī become children of God. This sense appears in the Gospel text that we are considering in this book. It says about *al-Sayyid al-Masī*: "To all who received him, to those who believed in his name, he gave the right to become children of God, who were born not of blood, nor of the will of the flesh, nor of the will of a man, but of God." (John 1:12–13)

8. See (Sura Al-Baqarah 2:112; Sura Ali 'Imran 3:85; Sura Al-Hajj 22:37; Sura Al-An'am 6:164; Sura Al-Baqarah 2:48)

9. Cumming, "What is the Meaning of the Expression."

- Third: The Gospel uses the expression "son of God" in a special sense to refer to the King of Israel whom the children of Israel (*banī Isrā'īl*) awaited, according to the prophecies in the Tōrah.
- Fourth: There is one more important symbolic sense in which the Gospel text we are considering in this book uses the term "Son." This sense is very close to the meaning of the term "Word of God" (*kalām Allāh*). As we noted above, in the Arabic language, the word of a speaker can be called "the daughter of his lips." In our article in this book on *kalām Allāh*, we observed that both the Qur'an and the Gospel assert that God's *kalām* is eternal (*azalī*) and uncreated, subsisting in God's essence (*qā'im bi-dhāt Allāh*) and that God created all things through His *kalām*. We also observed that both the Qur'an and the Gospel assert that *al-Sayyid al-Masī* can be called *kalimat Allāh*.[10]

Approximately two billion people of the Islamic faith reject many aspects of the Christian worldview. Islam opposes many of the Epistle to the Hebrews' teachings regarding Melchizedek as related to Jesus because they contradict core Islamic beliefs, which creates an unbridgeable gulf between the two faiths. It seems that the non-negotiable abyss cannot be closed. Islamic beliefs and the Islamic understanding of Scripture continue to elude many Christians. This text provides helpful information to explain why Muslims cannot accept Jesus as a high priest in the order of Melchizedek or as the savior of the world. Understanding the gulf between Christians and Muslims requires an understanding of the Islamic worldview.

10. Cumming, "What is the Meaning of the Expression."

8

Skeptics and Detractors

> Dogmatism and skepticism are both, in a sense, absolute philosophies; one is certain of knowing, the other of not knowing. What philosophy should dissipate is certainty, whether of knowledge or ignorance. (Betrand Russell)[1]

INTRODUCTION

In contrast to Christian and Islamic theism, numerous alternative philosophical worldviews exist: agnosticism, skepticism, atheism, naturalism, nihilism, secular humanism, modernism, and postmodernism. Moreover, there are also alternative religious worldviews: Judaism, Buddhism, Taoism, Confucianism, Pantheism, and Hinduism. On many grounds, skeptics and others question the reliability of Hebrews. The author is anonymous. The Epistle to the Hebrews is an exhortatory letter to encourage and assure believers in their faith.

Craig Koester writes, "Hebrews is one of the earliest extant Christian sermons."[2] Grindheim says, "The Letter to the Hebrews is an artistically crafted sermon."[3] Koester elaborates that "Although it has been traditionally called an "epistle," the idea that Hebrews is a sermon or speech has gained broad support, and many recognize that the work draws on

1. Russell, "Philosophy for Laymen," 38–49.
2. Koester, "Hebrews, Rhetoric, and the Future of Humanity," 103.
3. Grindheim, *The Letter to the Hebrews*, 13.

the devices of classical rhetoric."[4] Craik Oester comments, "It was not intended to be objective. Hebrews was written about thirty to seventy years after Jesus' death, at a time when many of the early Christian witnesses were dying off or already dead' Therefore, Hebrews was composed for a generation who did not know any eyewitnesses or have access to first-hand accounts of the Jesus tradition and for those at risk of losing their faith. Its author wants to prove that Jesus is the Messiah, the Son of God, the high priest, sinless, and the one who made a one-time sacrifice for all humanity."[5] At this point, skeptics and others pose a fundamental question: does it make sense to accept the Epistle's account of Melchizedek and his relationship to Jesus? They reiterate that an anonymous author wrote the Epistle to the Hebrews, which contains numerous unverifiable claims based on theological reasoning.

Skeptics and others challenge the claims in the Epistle of the Hebrews. Given that its author is anonymous, how are they to "evaluate the *rationality* of the author's belief?" No matter how sincere a person is, believing something to be true does not necessarily make that belief accurate. If the reader does not know the author's identity or where and when he composed Hebrews, how can they successfully interpret what it means?[6] Moreover, many of the Epistle's claims are subjective opinions (employing eisegeses) of a committed, passionate, and evangelizing believer are. They are unverifiable, unfalsifiable, and contradict both the Hebrew Bible and the Qur'an.

Questions Relating to Genesis 14

1. When, where, and by whom was Genesis 14: 18–20 composed?
2. Is Genesis 14:18–20 history, legend, or midrash?
3. Were verses 18–20 an interpolation?
4. Who was Melchizedek?
5. Is Melchizedek the name of a person, an epithet, or a title?
6. Where was Melchizedek ruling?
7. Who gave and who received the tithe?

4. Koester, "Hebrews, Rhetoric, and the Future of Humanity," 103.
5. Oester, "Book of Hebrews."
6. See Neusner, "Sanders' "Paul and the Jewish People,"" 416.

8. Why did Abram or Melchizedek give a tithe?
9. Who or what is El Elyon [God Most High]?
10. Who gave and who received a blessing? Why?

Questions Relating to Psalm 110

1. When, where, and by whom was Psalm 110 composed?
2. Is Psalm 110 a coronation, a royal psalm, a messianic text, or all three?
3. Who is YHWH talking to?
4. What does the Hebrew word *leʿolam* mean?
5. What does the Hebrew phrase "in the order of Melchizedek" mean?
6. How can Jesus be the person the psalm is talking about if verses five and six have not been fulfilled?

Unresolvable Questions Relating to the Epistle to the Hebrews

1. When, where, and by whom was the Epistle to the Hebrews composed? Crucially, nothing is known about the author's character, education, profession, whether he was Jewish or a pagan, or if he wrote other, now lost works.
2. Did the author "embellish" the text in order to facilitate his missionary agenda and propagate his faith?
3. What biblical authority did Church councils have in making the Epistle to the Hebrews classified as canonical and, therefore, as equal or superior to the Hebrew Bible (Scripture) despite Deuteronomy 4:2; 12:32; and Proverbs 30:6?
4. What genre does Hebrews belong to?
5. Is Hebrews' theology a form of midrash?
6. How does the author know Jesus was appointed heir of all things and that he is the one through whom God created the worlds? [Heb. 1:2]
7. How does the author of Hebrews know Jesus reflects God's glory and is the exact imprint of His very being? [Heb. 1:3]

8. How does the author of Hebrews know Jesus is superior to the angels? [Heb. 1:4]
9. How can Jesus atone for people's sins if this action violates the Hebrew Bible and the Qur'an?
10. What proof is there that Jesus is superior to Moses? [Heb. 3:3]
11. How do Psalm 2:7 and Psalm 110:4 show that Jesus is a high priest? [Heb. 5:5–6]
12. How was Jesus made perfect? [Heb. 5:9] What does it mean to be made perfect?
13. How can Jesus be the source of eternal salvation [which violates the Torah and the Qur'an]? [Heb. 5:8–9]
14. How can Jesus be a one-time sacrifice if the Hebrew Bible instructs us that "the Messiah"—named "the Prince"—*will bring a sin sacrifice on behalf of himself and the nation*?

> Ezek. 45:22 On that day the prince shall *provide for himself* and all the people of the land a young bull for *a sin offering*. (ESV)

9

Conclusion

HEBREWS

The author of Hebrews is unashamed of his beliefs. There is a vital link between Jesus' resurrection and his high priesthood, as described by the author of Hebrews, who declares in no uncertain words:

1. Jesus [the Son] *made purification for sins* (Heb. 1:3).
2. Jesus was crowned with glory and honor because of the suffering of death *so that by the grace of God, he might taste death for everyone* (Heb. 2:9).
3. [How did this happen?] Jesus [the Son] "*learned obedience through what he suffered*" and *was "made perfect*" (Heb. 5:9).
4. [Consequence] Jesus *became the source of eternal salvation to all who obey him*. (Heb. 5:9)
5. [How does Jesus save his followers?] Jesus [the Son] is able to save to the uttermost those who draw near to God through him since *he always lives to make intercession for them* (Heb. 7:25).
6. [Moreover] Jesus [the Son] has no need, like those high priests, to offer sacrifices daily, first for his own sins and *then for those of the people* (Heb. 7:27).
7. [Why not?] Since he did this once and for all *when he offered up himself* (Heb. 7:27)

8. [How did he accomplish this?] Now may the God of peace who brought again from the dead our Lord Jesus, the great shepherd of the sheep, by *the blood of the eternal covenant*, equip you with everything good that you may do his will, working in us that which is pleasing in his sight, through Jesus Christ, to whom be glory forever and ever (Heb. 13:20–21).

CONCLUSION

Melchizedek is an enigmatic figure. The author of Hebrews utilizes typology to explain the exalted position he occupies as high priest. Achieving this objective requires utilizing Genesis 14:18–20, Psalm 110:1–4, and select passages in the Hebrew Bible. By comparing the acclaimed priesthood of Jesus to that of Melchizedek, the author argues that he is both the Christ and the son of God. However, in Christian theology, Jesus is more than a priest or a high priest. He is the Messiah, the Son of God, and the paschal lamb whose death and blood are the unique means of humanity's salvation. This position is sincerely advocated by Christian apologists, Bible commentators, and theologians, who also appeal to Paul's assertion in 1 Corinthians 15 that Jesus' death and resurrection are foretold in Scripture.

The mainline Christian worldview is multifaceted. Crucially (but not exclusively): (1) The Bible, consisting of all the books of the Old (Hebrew Bible) and New Testaments, is the Word of God, a supernaturally given revelation from God Himself. (2) There is one God, eternally existing and manifesting Himself to us in three Persons: Father, Son, and Holy Spirit. (3) Jesus is Lord and Christ (Messiah). (4) Jesus is our high priest. (5) By his death on the cross, the Lord Jesus made a perfect atonement for sin. (6) He rose from death and ascended to heaven. (7) Jesus sits at the right hand of the throne of the Majesty in heaven and serves in the sanctuary (i.e., the true tabernacle set up by the Lord. (8) There, he serves as a mediator and a new covenant.

Skeptics and detractors (adherents of Judaism and Islam, and others) categorically reject the claim made by the anonymous author of Hebrews, Paul, in 1 Corinthians 15:1–4, and by modern-day Christian theologians that Jesus' death, burial, and resurrection fulfilled biblical prophecies. The collective arguments in rebuttal to the creed found in 1 Corinthians 15:1–4 include the following points:

1. Scripture does *not* explicitly say that Christ (the Messiah) had to die for our sins or be buried and rise again on the third day.
2. Jesus did *not* fulfill numerous prophecies that the Messiah was expected to accomplish during his lifetime.
3. Jesus did *not* fulfill the conditions for being the paschal lamb listed in the Hebrew Bible.
4. Jesus' blood on the cross was *not* a requirement for atonement. Consequently, *no* sins were atoned for by Jesus' crucifixion and death. Moreover, Leviticus 17:11 has *nothing* to do with Jesus and the atonement of sins.

Moreover, Jewish and Muslim detractors argue that both the Hebrew Bible and the Qur'an are clear and unequivocal in refuting the many claims made in the Epistle to the Hebrews and 1 Corinthians 15. According to the Hebrew Bible and Qur'an, the Messiah is not God, not part of a Trinity, not God incarnate in human flesh, not a man without a biological mother and father, not superior to angels, not the Creator of the heavens and the earth, not superior to Moses, not a great high priest, not a priest in the order of Melchizedek, not a mediator of a better covenant, not sinless (and hence exempt from offering a sacrifice for sin), not a one-time sacrifice (vicarious atonement) for humanity's sins, and not someone prophesied to die, be raised by God on the third day, ascend into heaven and return thousands of years later (the *parousia*).

Further investigation into the Melchizedek thread, as referenced in Genesis 14, Psalm 110, and the Epistle to the Hebrews, is essential. To fully grasp the significance of this figure, we must extend our analysis beyond these three core biblical texts. An in-depth study must engage with a broader array of materials, especially those found among the Dead Sea Scrolls, the Apocrypha, the Pseudepigrapha, the Talmud, midrash, haggadic, and rabbinic literature. These sources can provide invaluable insights and context crucial for a more comprehensive understanding of the Melchizedek thread.

Appendix

RABBINIC LITERATURE REVIEW ABOUT MELCHIZEDEK BY TOPIC

1. Melchizedek was born circumcised

   a. Abot de R. Nathan (2nd - 6th-century commentary)

   "Likewise, [Melchizedek] was born circumcised, as it says 'And Melchizedek, king of Salem" [interpreted as the king who was Salem, "complete" or "perfect," hence, circumcised].

   b. Bereshit Rabbah 26:3 (5th century)

   "Noah begot three sons, Shem, Ḥam, and Yefet"—but was Yefet not the eldest?, Initially, however, you should deal with the one who was righteous, born circumcised, the one whom the Holy One blessed be He associated His name with him, from whom Abraham was destined to descend, who served as High Priest, and in whose territory the Temple was built.**Malkitzedek was king of Salem, which is Jerusalem* (see Bereshit Rabbah 56:10). [The issue of circumcision in these sources concerns whether the new Christian church could lay claim to being a covenant people through their adoption of the Melchizedek priesthood.][1]

   c. Bereshit Rabbah 43:6 (5th century)

   "King of Salem [Shalem]"—Rabbi Yitzḥak the Babylonian says: He was born circumcised. **Melekh shalem, translated earlier*

1. "Bereshit Rabbah 26.2."

"king of Salem," can also mean "the perfect king," meaning that he was born in a perfected state, having had no need for circumcision.

2. Melchizedek is Shem:

    a. "Rabbi Joshua said: Abraham was the first to begin to give a tithe. He took all the tithe of the kings and all the tithe of the wealth of Lot, the son of his brother, and gave (it) to Shem, the Son of Noah, as it is said, 'And he gave him a tenth of all.'"[2]

    b. Bereshit Rabbah 43:6

"Melchizedek king of Salem took out bread and wine, and he was a priest of God, the Most High" (Genesis 14:18). "Melchizedek king of Salem . . ."—that is what is written: "Daughter of Tzor, the wealthiest of the people will seek your favor with gifts" (Ps. 45:13).

"Melchizedek king of Salem"—this place renders its inhabitants righteous, [and this is why he was called] Melchizedek, [and we find as well] "Adoni Tzedek [king of Jerusalem]" (Josh. 10:1). Jerusalem itself is called righteousness [*tzedek*], as it is stated: "Justice [*tzedek*] abided in it" (Isaiah 1:21).

"King of Salem [Shalem]"—Rabbi Yitzḥak the Babylonian says: He was born circumcised. [**Melekh shalem, translated earlier "king of Salem," can also mean "the perfect king," meaning that he was born in a perfected state, having had no need for circumcision.*][3]

3. Melchizedek acted as a priest and handed down Adam's robes to Abram (Numbers Rabbah 4:8):

GARMENTS OF SERVICE

This understanding finds textual support in two mediaeval compilations, *Bemidbar Rabbah* and *Midrash Tanhuma* (Buber). The similarity of these two retellings, both to each other and to the texts discussed above in the section on Garments of Protection, are many. To facilitate comparison between the texts I have presented them in parallel.

2. Friedlander, *Pirke de Rabbi Eliezer*, 195.
3. "Bereshit Rabbah 43:6."

Midrash Tanhuma (Buber) Toledot:12	Bemidbar Rabbah 4:8
A person must honour the Shabbat in their clothing, and it says *And call the Shabbat—'delight'* (Is. 58:13), and with what should Israel honour the Shabbat? With food and drink and clean clothes. For from the beginning God did just this as it says, *And GOD, God, make garments of skins for Adam and his wife and clothed them* (Gen. 3:21).[51] And what are the *garments of skin*? They are the clothes of the High Priest who was dressed by the Holy Blessed One for the honour of the world.	*Take the Levites [in place of the first-born]* (Num. 3:45)
Moreover the Rabbis taught that before the construction of the Sanctuary, private altars were permitted and the firstborn did the service.	Said our Rabbis, 'why did the Holy Blessed One command the redeeming of the firstborn of Israel by the Levites? For initially the firstborn did the service, until the tribe of Levi stood up [in the aftermath of the Golden Calf debacle and won the right of bringing the offerings for their clan].
Therefore the Holy Blessed One dressed the First Adam in the clothes of the High Priest since he was the firstborn of the world.	This began with the Creation of the world.[52] The First Adam was the firstborn of the world and when he brought a sacrifice - as it says, *[what could] please GOD more than oxen, than bull with horns and hooves* (Ps. 69:32)[53] – he would wear the clothes of the High Priest as it says *And GOD, God, make garments of skins for Adam and his wife and clothed them* (Gen. 3:21). They were garments of praise,[54] and the first born would do the service in them.
	And when Adam died, he passed them on to Seth. Seth passed them on to Methusaleh [his grandson]. When Methusaleh died he passed them on to Noah.

Noah came and passed them to Abraham.	And Noah stood and brought a sacrifice as it says, *[And Noah took] of every clean animal [he offered burnt offerings.]* (Gen. 8:20) Noah died and passed them to Shem—but was Shem a first-born, wasn't Yephet the firstborn as it says *the big brother, Japheth* (Gen. 10:21)?[55] Rather Noah foresaw the chain of descent of the ancestors [Abraham, Isaac & Jacob] came from [Shem]. Shem died and passed it to Abraham [his ninth generation descendant]—but was Abraham a firstborn? Rather because he was righteous he passed to him the birthright . . .
And Abraham passed them to Isaac. And Isaac passed them to Esau—who was the first born, and Esau saw his wives were worshipping strange gods, so he (Esau) hid[56][the garment] in his mother's house.[57] When Jacob stood and took the birth-right from Esau, Rebekhah said, 'since Jacob has taken the birthright from Esau, by rights he [Jacob] should wear these clothes, as it says *Rebekhah took the coveted clothes of Esau her oldest son* (Gen. 27:15). Jacob entered before his father and he smelled them, as it says *And he smelled his clothes and he blessed him* (Gen. 27:27).[4]	Abraham died and passed it to Isaac. Isaac stood and passed it to Jacob—but was Jacob a firstborn? Rather you will find that Jacob took it from Esau with cunning, he said to him '*First sell me your birthright*' (Gen. 26:31). You might think that Jacob had no reason for saying to Esau that he should sell him the birthright, rather Jacob wanted to bring sacrifices and could not because he wasn't a firstborn.

4. Melchizedek-Shem: The first reference occurs in the passage dedicated to the handling of the tradition of *intercalation* among the Patriarchs:

> The text says that "Noah handled on the tradition to Shem, and he was initiated in the principle of intercalation; he intercalated the years and he was called a priest, as it is said, "And Melchizedek king of Salem . . . was a priest of God Most High" (Gen. 14:18). Was Shem the Son of Noah a priest? But because he was

4. Gordon, "Garments of Skin."

the first-born, and because he ministered to his God by day and by night, therefore was he called a priest.[5]

5. Melchizedek called Jerusalem "Salem":

Genesis Rabbah 56:10

> Abraham called it [Jerusalem] Yireh, as it is stated: "Abraham called the name of that place The Lord will see [*yireh*]." Shem called it Shalem, as it is stated: "Malki Tzedek king of Shalem" (Gen. 14:18). The Holy One blessed be He said: 'If I call it *Yireh*, as Abraham called it, Shem, a righteous man, will have a complaint. If I call it Shalem, Abraham, a righteous man, will have a complaint. Instead, I shall call it Yerushalayim, as both of them called it, - *Yireh*, Shalem—Yerushalayim.'[6]

6. Melchizedek's school was one of three places where the Holy Spirit (*Ruach HaKodesh*) manifested himself:

Babylonian Talmud Makkot 23b

> The Gemara cites a somewhat similar statement. Rabbi Elazar says: In three places the Divine Spirit appeared before all to affirm that the action taken was appropriate: In the court of Shem, in the court of Samuel the Ramathite, and in the court of Solomon. The Gemara elaborates: This occurred in the court of Shem, as it is written in the context of the episode of Judah and Tamar: "And Judah acknowledged them and said: She is more righteous than I [*mimmenni*]" (Gen. 38:26). How did Judah know that Tamar's assertion that she was bearing his child was correct? Perhaps, just as he went to her and hired her as a prostitute, another person went to her and hired her as well, and he is not the father. Rather, a Divine Voice emerged and said: It is from Me [*mimmenni*] that these secrets emerged. God affirmed that her assertion was correct and that it was His divine plan that Judah would father a child from Tamar.[7]

7. Melchizedek brought out bread and wine:

Bereshit Rabbah 43:6

5. Friedlander, *Pirke de Rabbi Eliezer*, 53.
6. Bereshit Rabbah 56:10.
7. "Makkot 23B:3."

"Melchizedek king of Salem took out bread and wine, and he was a priest of God, the Most High" (Gen. 14:18).

"Melchizedek king of Salem. . ."—that is what is written: "Daughter of Tzor, the wealthiest of the people will seek your favor with gifts" (Ps. 45:13).

"Melchizedek king of Salem"—this place renders its inhabitants righteous, [and this is why he was called] Melchizedek, [and we find as well] "Adoni Tzedek [king of Jerusalem]" (Josh. 10:1). Jerusalem itself is called righteousness [*tzedek*], as it is stated: "*Justice [tzedek] abided in it*" (Isaiah 1:21).[8]

8. The Rabbis taught that Melchizedek acted as a priest:

Genesis Rabbah 43:7

Rabbi Judah said in Rabbi Nehorai's name that Melchizedek's blessing yielded prosperity for Abram, Isaac, and Jacob.

"And he was a priest of God, the Most High"—Rabbi Abba bar Kahana and Rabbi Levi, Rabbi Abba bar Kahana said: Any time wine is written in the Torah it connotes a [negative] impact, **As when Noah (Gen. 9:21) and Lot (Gen. 19:32–35) became drunk, both instances leading to humiliating consequences.* except for this one.[9]

9. Melchizedek blessed Abram:

Genesis Rabbah 43:7

Rabbi Judah said in Rabbi Nehorai's name that Melchizedek's blessing yielded prosperity for Abram, Isaac, and Jacob.

"He blessed him, and he said: Blessed is Abram to God, the Most High, Acquirer of heavens and earth"—from whom did He acquire them?[10]

10. The fear of Abram after meeting with Melchizedek:

"Fear not, Abram. Whom did he fear? Rabbi Berekiah said: He feared Shem (whose descendants, viz. Chedorlaomer and his sons, Abraham had slain), as it is written, 'The isles saw, and feared' (Isa 41:5): just as islands stand out in the sea, so were

8. "Bereshit Rabbah 43:6."
9. "Bereshit Rabbah 43:7."
10. "Bereshit Rabbah 43:8."

Abraham and Shem outstanding in the world. And feared: Each one feared the other. The former (Abraham) feared the latter, thinking, Perhaps he nurses resentment against me for slaying his sons. And the latter (Shem) feared the former, thinking, Perhaps he nurses resentment against me for begetting wicked offspring." This passage shows that not only was Melchizedek Shem, but the four kings of the Elamite opposition were sons of Shem.[11]

11. Melchizedek received tithes from Abram:

In *Pirke R. El.*, chapter 28, we find the following passage:

"Rabbi Joshua said: Abraham was the first to begin to give a tithe. He took all the tithe of the kings and all the tithe of the wealth of Lot, the son of his brother, and gave (it) to Shem, the Son of Noah, as it is said, 'And he gave him a tenth of all.'"[12]

12. Melchizedek instructed Abram in the Torah:

Genesis Rabbah 43:6

"[He] took out bread and wine, and he was a priest of God, the Most High"—Rabbi Shmuel bar Naḥman and the Rabbis, Rabbi Shmuel said: He revealed to him the laws of the High Priesthood. **Melchizedek brought bread and wine in order to show Abraham the priestly rites involving these items.* "Bread"—this alludes to the showbread; "and wine"—this alludes to the libations. The Rabbis say: He revealed Torah [precepts] to him, as it is stated: "Come, partake of my bread, and drink of the wine that I have mixed" (Prov 9:5). **The speaker in this verse is divine wisdom, the Torah. It refers to its teachings metaphorically as bread and wine.*[13]

13. Rabbi Hana bar Bizna citing Rabbi Simeon Hasida identified Melchizedek as one of the four craftsmen of whom Zechariah wrote in Zechariah 2:3:

Sukkah 52b [The William Davidson Talmud (Koren—Steinsaltz)]

11. Orlov, "Melchizedek Legend."
12. Friedlander, *Pirke de Rabbi Eliezer*, 195.
13. "Bereshit Rabbah 43:6."

> Apropos the end of days, the Gemara cites another verse and interprets it homiletically. It is stated: "The Lord then showed me four craftsmen" (Zech. 2:3). Who are these four craftsmen? Rav Ḥana bar Bizna said that Rabbi Shimon Ḥasida said: They are Messiah ben David, Messiah ben Yosef, Elijah, and the righteous High Priest, who will serve in the Messianic era.[14]

14. Tamar was descended from Melchizedek:

[Ephraim Miksha'ah the disciple of Rabbi Meir said in the latter's name that Tamar was descended from Melchizedek]

Genesis Rabbah 85:10

> "Moreover, behold, she conceived through harlotry"—it teaches that she would pat her belly and say: I am pregnant with kings; I am pregnant with redeemers. **The phrase "moreover, behold, she conceived through harlotry" is understood to imply that she was not embarrassed that she had conceived; on the contrary, she was proud, even though onlookers assumed that it had occurred through harlotry (Yefe To'ar).* "Take her out and she shall be burned"—Efrayim the cucumber seller [*makshaa*], **Cucumbers are kishuim; alternatively, makshaa refers to one who poses many questions [kushyot].* student of Rabbi Meir, said in the name of Rabbi Meir: Tamar was the daughter of Shem, as it is written: "The daughter of a man who is a priest, [if she shall profane herself by acting as a harlot . . . she shall be burned in fire]" (Leviticus 21:9); that is why [Judah said]: "Take her out, and she shall be burned." **Shem is identified by the Sages (see Nedarim 32b) as Malkitzedek, of whom the verse states that "he was a priest to God, the Most High" (Genesis 14:18). Consequently, if a daughter of Shem had committed adultery, she would have incurred the punishment of burning.*[15]

15. The priesthood was taken from the entire clan of Shem and became the exclusive privilege of Abraham's seed:

> Nedarim 32b
> Rabbi Zekharya said in the name of Rabbi Yishmael: The Holy One, Blessed be he intended to bring forth the priesthood from Shem, as it is written, and he [Melchizedek] was the priest of the

14. "Sukkah 52B:11."
15. "Bereshit Rabbah 85:10."

most high God. But because he gave precedence in his blessing to Abraham over God, he brought it forth from Abraham . . . Said Abraham to him, 'Is the blessing of a servant to be given precedence over that of his master?' Straightway it [the priesthood] was given to Abraham, as it is written, The Lord said unto my Lord . . . The Lord hath sworn, and will not repent, Thou art a priest for ever, after the order of Melchizedek, meaning, 'because of the words of Melchizedek,' hence it is written, And he was a priest of the most High God [implying that] he was a priest, but not his seed.[16]

Or

Nedarim 32b

R. Zechariah said on R. Ishmael's authority: The Holy One, blessed be He, intended to bring forth the priesthood from Shem, as it is written, 'And he [Melchizedek] was the priest of the highest God' (Gen. 14:18). But because he gave precedence in his blessing to Abraham over God, He brought it forth from Abraham; as it is written, 'And he blessed him and said, Blessed be Abram of the most high God, possessor of heaven and earth, and blessed be the most high God' (Gen. 14:19). Said Abraham to him, 'Is the blessing of a servant to be given precedence over that of his master? Straightaway it [the priesthood] was given to Abraham, as it is written (Ps. 110:1), 'The Lord said to my Lord, Sit thou at my right hand, until I make thine enemies thy footstool;' which is followed by, 'The Lord hath sworn, and will not repent, Thou art a priest for ever, after the order of Melchizedek' (Ps 110:4), meaning, 'because of the word of Melchizedek.' Hence it is written, And he was a priest of the most High God, [implying that] he was a priest, but not his seed.[17]

16. "Nedarim 32B:6."

17. Orlov, "Melchizedek Legend." He quotes, *The Babylonia Talmud, Seder Nedarim*. London: Soncino Press, 1936), 98–99.

Bibliography

Alexander, Thomas D. "A Literary Analysis of the Abraham Narrative in Genesis." PhD diss., University of Belfast, 1982.

Allison, Jane Elizabeth. "A Study of the Priestly Christology of the Epistle to the Hebrews." MA thesis, Durham University, 1991.

Al-Mehri, A. B., ed. *The Qur'ān: With Sūrah Introductions and Appendices: Saheeh International Translation*. Birmingham: Maktabah, 2010.

Alter, Michael J. *The Name Israel*. Eugene, OR: Resource Publications, 2023.

———. *Resurrection and Its Apologetics: Jesus' Death and Burial*. Vol. 1. Eugene, OR: Wipf and Stock, 2024.

Alter, Robert. *The Book of Psalms: A Translation with Commentary*. New York: Norton, 2009.

Amerding, Carl E. "Were David's Sons Really Priests?" In *Current Issues in Biblical and Patristic Interpretation: Studies in Honor of Merrill C. Tenney*, edited by Merrill C. Tenney and Gerald F. Hawthorne, 75–86. Grand Rapids: Eerdmans, 1975.

"Ancient Near East." Wikipedia, April 27, 2025. https://en.wikipedia.org/wiki/Ancient_Near_East.

Andersen, Francis I. "Genesis 14: An Enigma." Edited by David P. Wright, David Noel Freedman, and Avi Hurvitz, 497–508. Winona Lake, IN: Eisenbrauns, 1995.

Anderson, A. A. *The Book of Psalms. vol. 2, Psalms* 73–150. London: Oliphants, 1972.

Anderson, Cory. "An Examination of the Figure of Melchizedek in Hebrews 7:3," February 21, 2020. https://www.academia.edu/42036784/AN_EXAMINATION_OF_THE_FIGURE_OF_MELCHIZEDEK_IN_HEBREWS_7_3.

Anyabwile, Thabiti M. *The Gospel for Muslims: An Encouragement to Share Christ with Confidence*. Chicago: Moody, 2010.

Attridge, Harold W. *Hebrews: A Commentary on the Epistle to the Hebrews*. Philadelphia: Fortress, 1989.

Babcock, Bryan. "Who Is My Lord in Psalm 110?" *Crucible* 8, no. 2 (2017): 1–23.

Barker, Margaret. "Who Was Melchizedek and Who was God?" http://www.margaretbarker.com/Papers/SBLMelchizedek.pdf. Society of Biblical Literature Meeting, San Diego, CA, 2007.

Barr, James. *Biblical Words for Time*. London: SCM, 1969.

Bateman, Herbert W. "Jesus, God's Different Priest: (Hebrews 7:11), 10AD." http://www.hwbateman.com/data/articles/1f6cddof-2865-4832-96b6-37e049c400a4/hebrews-8.1_5f_2.pdf.

———. "Jesus, Our Eternal Intercessor" (Hebrews 7:25). February 17, 2016. Htpp://www.hwbateman.com/data/articles/1f6cddof-2865-4832-96b6-37e49c400a4/Hebrews-8.1_5f_2.pdf.

———. "Psalm 110, 1 and the New Testament." *Bibliotheca Sacra*, no. 194 (1992): 438–53.

Baylis, Charles Passant. "The Author of Hebrews' Use of Melchizedek from the Context of Genesis." ThD., Dallas Theological Seminary, 1989.

Bellarmine, Robert. *A Commentary on The Book of Psalms*. Translated by John O'Sullivan. Dublin: James Duffy, 1866.

"Bereshit Rabbah 26:2." Sefaria. https://www.sefaria.org/Bereshit_Rabbah.26.2?lang=bi.

"Bereshit Rabbah 43:6." Sefaria. https://www.sefaria.org/Bereshit_Rabbah.43.6?lang=bi.

"Bereshit Rabbah 43:7." Sefaria, n.d. https://www.sefaria.org/Bereshit_Rabbah.43.7?lang=bi&with=all&lang2=en.

"Bereshit Rabbah 43:8." Sefaria, n.d. https://www.sefaria.org/Bereshit_Rabbah.43.8?lang=bi.

"Bereshit Rabbah 56:10." Sefaria, n.d. https://www.sefaria.org/Bereshit_Rabbah.56.10?lang=bi.

"Bereshit Rabbah 85:10." Sefaria, n.d. https://www.sefaria.org/Bereshit_Rabbah.85.10?lang=bi&with=all&lang2=en.

Berlin, Adele, and Marc Zvi Brettler, eds. *The Jewish Study Bible*. 2nd ed. Oxford: Oxford University Press, 2014.

Besant, Annie. *Freethinker's Text Book, Part II Christianity*. London: Charles Watts, n.d.

Bird, Chad L. "Typological Interpretation within the Old Testament: Melchizedekian Typology." *Concordia Journal* 26 (2000): 36–52.

Birnbaum, Philip. *A Book of Jewish Concepts*. New York: Hebrew Publishing, 1975.

Bodinger, Martin. Martin Bodinger's "L'énigme de Melkisédeq" 1994 essay, translated., 2021. https://earlywritings.com/forum/viewtopic.php?t=7739.

Boyarin, Daniel. *The Jewish Gospels: The Story of the Jewish Christ*. New York: New Press, 2012.

Bratcher, Robert G., and William David Reyburn. *A Translator's Handbook on the Book of Psalms*. New York: United Bible Societies, 1991.

Brooks, Walter Edward. "The Perpetuity of Christ's Sacrifice in the Epistle to the Hebrews." *Journal of Biblical Literature* 89, no. 2 (1970): 205–14. https://doi.org/10.2307/3263051.

Brown, Michael, and Yisroel Blumenthal. "The Real Jewish Messiah: Dr. Brown's Notes for Debate with Yisroel Blumenthal." AskDrBrown, May 15, 2017. https://thelineoffire.org/article/the-real-jewish-messiahdr.-browns-notes-for-debate-with-yisroel-blumenthal.

Brown, Raymond. *The Message of Hebrews: Christ Above All*. Downers Grove, IL: Inter-Varsity, 1984.

Bruce, F. F. *The Epistle to the Hebrews*. Grand Rapids: Eerdmans, 1964.

Bryant, Jacob. *The Sentiments of Philo Judeus Concerning the AOrOS, or Word of God*. Cambridge, 1797.

Buchanan, George Wesley. *Hebrews (The Anchor Bible Commentary)*. Garden City, NY: Doubleday, 1972.

———. *To the Hebrews*. Garden City, NY: Doubleday, 1972.

Carson, D., and Douglas Moo. *An Introduction to the New Testament*. Grand Rapids: Zondervan, 2005.

Catechism of the Catholic Church. "Paragraph 3. Jesus Christ was Buried." In *Catechism of the Catholic Church*, Vatican City: Libreria Editrice Vaticana, 162–163. Distributed by United States Catholic Conference, 2000.

———. "Part One: The Profession of Faith." In *Catechism of the Catholic Church*, Vatican City: Libreria Editrice Vaticana, 13–18. Distributed by United States Catholic Conference, 2000.

———. "I Believe In Jesus Christ, His Only Son, Our Lord." In *Catechism of the Catholic Church*, Section Two: "The Profession of Christian Faith." Vatican City: Libreria Editrice Vaticana, 106–114. Distributed by United States Catholic Conference, 2000.

Chabad.org. "Aggadah - Jewish Knowledge Base" 2025. https://www.chabad.org/search/keyword_cdo/kid/10816/jewish/Aggadah.htm.

Chan, Alan Kam-Yau. *Melchizedek Passages in the Bible: A Case Study for Inner-Biblical and Inter-Biblical Interpretation*. Warsaw: De Gruyter Open, 2016.

Christian, Mark A. "Priestly Power That Empowers: Michel Foucault, Middle-Tier Levites, and the Sociology of 'Popular Religious Groups' in Israel." *The Journal of Hebrew Scriptures* 9 (2009): 1–81. https://doi.org/10.5508/jhs.2009.v9.a1.

Cockerill, Gareth Lee. "Building Bridges to Muslims or Syncretism: A Test Case." In *Contextualization and Syncretization: Navigating Cultural Currents*, edited by Gailyn Van Rheenen, 323–43. Pasadena, CA: Wiley Carey Library, 2006.

———. *The Epistle to the Hebrews*. Grand Rapids: Eerdmans, 2012.

———. "The Melchizedek Christology in Heb. 7:1–28." PhD diss., Union Theological Seminary in Virginia, 1976.

———. "Melchizedek or 'King of Righteousness?'" *Evangelical Quarterly: An International Review of Bible and Theology* 63, no. 4 (1991): 305–12. https://doi.org/10.1163/27725472-06304003.

Cohen, Yitchok. "Can You Elaborate More on Melkizedec Giving Tithes to Abraham and the Contradiction on Hebrews?" Quora, November 5, 2023. https://www.quora.com/Can-you-elaborate-more-on-Melkizedec-giving-Tithes-to-Abraham-and-the-contradiction-on-Hebrews

Combrink, H.J.B. "Some Thoughts on the Old Testament Citations in the Epistle to the Hebrews." *Neotestamentica* 5, no. 1 (1971): 22–36.

Cumming, Joseph. "What Is the Meaning of the Expression 'Son of God.'" Joseph Cumming, January 4, 2023. https://josephcumming.com/what-is-the-meaning-of-the-expression-son-of-god.

Dahood, Mitchell J. *Psalms III:* 101–150. Garden City, NY: Doubleday, 1970.

Dalgaard, Kasper. *A Priest for All Generations: An Investigation into the Use of the Melchizedek Figure from Genesis to the Cave of Treasures*. Kbh: Det Teologiske Fakultet, Københavns Universitet, 2013.

Davis, Barry C. "Is Psalm 110 A Messianic Psalm." *Bibliotheca Sacra* 157, no. 626 (2000): 160–73.

Day, John. "The Canaanite Inheritance of the Israelite Monarchy." In *King and Messiah in Israel and the Ancient Near East*, edited by John Day, 72–90. London: Bloomsbury, 1998.

Demarest, Bruce A. "Hebrews 7:3: A Crux Interpretum Historically Considered." *Evangelical Quarterly: An International Review of Bible and Theology* 49, no. 3 (1977): 141–62. https://doi.org/10.1163/27725472-04903003.

Denaux, Adelbert. "Jesus Christ, High Priest and Sacrifice According to the Epistle to the Hebrews." In *The Actuality of Sacrifice*, edited by Alberdina Houtman, Marcel Poorthuis, Joshua J. Schwartz, and Joseph Turner, 107–22. Leiden: Brill, 2014.

Dick, Michael B. "The Neo-Assyrian Royal Lion Hunt and Yahweh's Answer to Job." *Journal of Biblical Literature* 125, no. 2 (2006): 243–70. https://doi.org/10.2307/27638360.

"Doctrinal Position: Liberty University." About Liberty, December 16, 2022. https://www.liberty.edu/about/doctrinal-statement/.

Donnelly, Stephen. "The Divine Rites and Rejection of the Priesthood: Melchizedek on the Margins of Early Jewish and Christian Interpretation." PhD diss., The Hebrew University of Jerusalem, 2014.

Dryer, Bryan R. "The Epistle to the Hebrews in Recent Research: Studies on the Author's Identity, His Use of The Old Testament, and Theology." *Journal of Greco-Roman Christianity and Judaism* 9 (2013): 104–31.

Edwards, James. *The Gospel According to Mark (PNTC)*. Grand Rapids: Eerdmans, 2002.

Eisenbaum, Pamela. "The Letter to the Hebrews." In *The Jewish Annotated New Testament*, edited by Amy-Jill Levine and Marc Zvi Brettler, 2nd ed., 460–88. Oxford: Oxford University Press, 2017.

———. "Ritual and Religion, Sacrifice and Supersession: Utopian Reading of Hebrews." In *Hebrews in Context*, edited by Gabriella Geraladini and Harold A. Attridge, 345–56. Leiden: Brill, 2016.

Elgavish, David. "The Encounter of Abram and Melchizedek King of Salem." In *The Encounter of Abram and Melchizedek King of Salem: A Covenant Establishing Ceremony*, 495–508. 2001.

Ellingworth, Paul. *Epistle to the Hebrews*. Chicago: Eerdmans, 1993.

———. "Just Like Melchizedek." *The Bible Translator* 28, no. 2 (1977): 236–30. https:doi.org/10.1177/020094377702800207.

Emadi, Matthew. "You Are Priest Forever: Psalm 110 and the Melchizedekian Priesthood of Christ." *SBJT* 23, no. 1 (2019): 57–84.

Emerton, J. A. "The Riddle of Genesis XIV." *Vetus Testamentum* 21, no. 4 (1971): 403–39. https://doi.org/10.2307/1517339.

Engnell, Ivan. *Studies in Divine Kingship in the Ancient Near East*. Oxford: Basil Blackwell, 1967.

Federow, Stuart. "Jeremiah 31:31." What Jews Believe, 2013. https://whatjewsbelieve.org/jeremiah-3131/.

Filvedt, Ole Jakob, and Martin Wessbrandt. "Exploring the High Priesthood of Jesus in Early Christian Sources." *Zeitschrift* für die *neutestamentliche Wissenschaft* 106, no. 1 (31, 2015): 96–114. https://doi.org/10.1515/znw-2015-0005.

Fishbeck, Nadine Braunda. "The High-Priestly Christology of the Letter to the Hebrews: A Fusion of Late Second Temple Theology and Early Christian Tradition." MA thesis, School of Theology of the University of the South, 2012.

Fisher, Loren R. "Abraham and His Priest-King." *Journal of Biblical Literature* 81, no. 3 (1962): 264–70. https://doi.org/10.2307/3264423.

Fitzmyer, Joseph A. "Melchizedek in the MT, LXX, and the NT." *Biblica* 81, no. 1 (2000): 63–69.

Flanagan, Ruth. "Worldviews: Overarching Concept, Discrete Body of Knowledge or Paradigmatic Tool?" *Journal of Religious Education* 68, no. 3 (2020): 331–44. https://doi.org/10.1007/s40839-020-00113-7.

Frangipane, Marcella. "Archaeological Evidence of the Political Economy in Pre-State and Early State Societies in the Near East. Mesopotamia and Anatolia, Some Remarks and Comparisons." *Frontiers in Economic History*, 2022, 91–110. https://doi.org/10.1007/978-3-031-08763-9_6.

Friedlander, Gerald, trans. *Pirkê de Rabbi Eliezer: According to the text of the ms. Belonging to Abraham Epstein of Vienna. transl. and annotated with introd. and indices.* New York: Hermon, 1965.

"G2962 - Kyrios - Strong's Greek Lexicon (KJV)." Blue Letter Bible, 2025. https://www.blueletterbible.org/lexicon/g2962/kjv/tr/0–1/.

Gammie, John G. "Loci of the Melchizedek Tradition of Genesis 14:18–20." *Journal of Biblical Literature* 90, no. 4 (1971): 385–96. https://doi.org/10.2307/3263610.

———. "Melchizedek: An Exegetical Study of Genesis 14 and the Psalter," 1962.

Geisler, Norman L., and Thomas A. Howe. *When Critics Ask: A Popular Handbook on Bible Difficulties.* Grand Rapids: Baker, 2004.

Germany, Stephen, and Peter Gemeinhardt. "Melchizedek: Hebrew Bible/Old Testament." In *Encyclopedia of the Bible and Its Reception*, edited by Breenan Breed and Constance F. Furey, 18:525–28. Berlin: Walter de Gruyter, 2020.

Gillingham, S. E., and John Day. "The Messiah in the Psalms: A Question of Reception History and the Psalter." In *King and Messiah in Israel and the Ancient Near East*, 209–37. Sheffield: Sheffield Academic, 1998.

Goldingay, John. "The Patriarchs in Scripture and History." In *Essays on the Patriarchal Narratives*, edited by A. R. Millard and D. J. Wiseman, 11–42. Leicester: IVP, 1980.

Gordon, Rabbi Jeremy. "Garments of Skin - an Unfinished Traditions' History of the Ultimate Midrash." October 11, 2019. http://rabbionanarrowbridge.blogspot.com/2019/10/garments-of-skin-unfinished-traditions.html.

Granerød, Gard. *Abraham and Melchizedek: Scribal Activity of Second Temple Times in Genesis 14 and Psalm 110.* Berlin: De Gruyter, 2010.

———. "Melchizedek in Hebrews 7." *Biblica* 90 (2009): 188–202.

Greear, J. D. *Breaking the Islam Code.* Eugene, OR: Harvest House, 2010.

Grindheim, Sigurd. *The Letter to the Hebrews.* Grand Rapids: Eerdmans, 2023.

Gruenwald, Ithamar. "Melchizedek." In *Encyclopedia Judaica*, edited by Fred Skolnik, 14:11. Detroit: Thomas-Gale, 2007.

Grypeou, Emmanouela, and Helen Spurling. *The Book of Genesis in Late Antiquity: Encounters Between Jewish and Christian Exegesis.* Leiden: Brill, 2013.

Gustavsson, Olivia Rizk. "The Melchizedek Mystery: The Life of Melchizedek After Melchizedek." Master's thesis, Univerisity of Gothenburg, 2020.

Guthrie, Donald. *The Tyndale New Testament Commentaries: The Letter to the Hebrews.* Leicester: Inter-Varsity, 1983.

Habermas, Gary R. *On the Resurrection.* Brentwood, TN: B & H Academic, 2024.

Hagner, Donald Alfred. *Encountering the Book of Hebrews: An Exposition.* Grand Rapids: Baker Academic, 2004.

Hahn, Scott. *Kinship by Covenant: A Canonical Approach to the Fulfillment of God's Saving Promises.* New Haven: Yale University Press, 2009.

Hambrick, Matthew R. "The Paradox of Melchizedek How the Author of Hebrews Utilized the Paradox to Harmonize Disharmony." PhD diss., Point Loma Nazarene University, 2007.

Hamilton, Victor Paul. *The Book of Genesis. Chapters 1–17.* Grand Rapids: Eerdmans, 1990.

Harrington, Daniel J. *What Are They Saying About the Letter to the Hebrews?* New York: Paulist, 2005.

Haywood, Robert. *Targums and the Transmission of Scripture into Judaism and Christianity*. Leiden: Brill, 2009.

"Hebrews 7:7." BibleRef.com, 2025. https://www.bibleref.com/Hebrews/7/Hebrews-7-7.html.

Hendel, Ronald. "Historical Context." In *The Book of Genesis: Composition, Reception, and Interpretation*, edited by Craig A. Evans, Joel N. Lohr, and David L. Petersen, 51–81. Leiden: Brill, 2012.

Henry, Matthew. *An Exposition of the Old and New Testament*. Philadelphia: Ed. Barrington & Geo. D. Haswell, 1828.

Heschel, Abraham Joshua. "Halakhah and Aggadah." My Jewish Learning, n.d. https://www.myjewishlearning.com/article/halakhah-and-aggadah/.

Horton, Fred L. *The Melchizedek Tradition: A Critical Examination of the Sources to the Fifth Century A.D. and in the Epistle to the Hebrews*. Cambridge: Cambridge University Press, 2005.

Hughes, Philip Edgcumbe. *A Commentary on the Epistle to the Hebrews*. Grand Rapids: Eerdmans, 1977.

Hydon, Paul Vernon. "The Priesthood of Jesus as Presented by the Epistle to the Hebrews." PhD diss., Boston university, 1941.

Ibn Ezra, Abraham ben Meir. *Ibn Ezra's Commentary on the Pentateuch: Genesis*. Translated by H. Norman Strickland and Arthur M. Silver. Vol. 1. New York: Mesorah, 1988.

Imran, Adil Nizamuddin. *Christ Jesus, the Son of Mary: A Muslim Perspective*. Lombard, IL: Book of Signs Foundation, 2009.

Instone-Brewer, David, Hermann L. Strack, and Paul Billerbeck. "Introduction to the English Translation." In *A Commentary on the New Testament from the Talmud & Midrash* 3, Vol. 3. Bellingham, xxi–xli. WA: Lexham, 2021.

Jobes, Karen H. *Letters to the Church: A Survey of Hebrews and the General Epistles*. Grand Rapids: Zondervan, 2011.

Johnson, Luke Timothy. *Hebrews: A Commentary*. Louisville: Westminster John Knox, 2006.

Josephus, Flavius. "The Jewish War." In *Josephus, Complete Works*, Book 6. Translated by William Whiston, 427–605. Grand Rapids: Kregel, 1960.

———. *Josephus, Complete Works*. Translated by William Whiston. Grand Rapids: Kregel, 1960.

Kampouris, Panagiotis L. "The Priesthood of Melchizedek in Biblical and Extra-Biblical Sources and Its Relevance to the Ancient Near Eastern Divine Kingship." In *Dialogue "Studies in Theology,"* 11:123–44. Patras, 2020.

Kang, Dae-I. "The Royal Components of Melchizedek in Hebrews 7." *Perichoresis* 10, no. 1 (2012): 95–124. https://doi.org/10.2478/v10297-012-0005-5.

Kant, Immanuel. *Critique of Judgment*. Translated by Werner S. Pluhar. Indianapolis: Hackett , 1987.

Karrer, Martin. "The Epistle to the Hebrews and the Septuagint." In *Septuagint Research: Issues and Challenges in the Study of the Greek Jewish Scriptures*, edited by Wolfgang Kraus and R. Glenn Wooden, 335–53. Atlanta: Society of Biblical Literature, 2006.

Kennedy, Gerald Thomas. "St. Paul's Conception of the Priesthood of Melchisedech: An Historico-Exegetical Investigation." PhD diss., The Catholic University of America, 1951.

Kilcrease, Jack D. *Self-Donation of God: A Contemporary Lutheran Approach to Christ and His Benefits*. Eugene, Or: Wipf & Stock, 2013.

Kim, Paulus Jinu. "Antitype of Jesus Christ Beyond the Type of Melchizedek on Hebrews." *Saint Paul's Review* 1, no. 1 (2021): 1–10. https://doi.org/10.56194/spr.v1i1.2.

The Kingdom of Zion. "History of Melchizedek." Academia.edu, March 7, 2023. https://www.academia.edu/41373027/History_of_MELCHIZEDEK_who_is_SHEM_and_would_eventually_become_the_MESSIAH_and_Savior_of_the_World.

Kistemaker, Simon J. *Exposition of the Epistle to the Hebrews*. Grand Rapids: Baker, 1985.

Kobelski, Paul J. *Melchizedek and Melchireša*. Washington, DC.: The Catholic Biblical Association of America, 1981. https://www.marquette.edu/maqom/KobelskiMel.pdf.

Koester, Craig R. "Hebrews, Rhetoric, and the Future of Humanity." *Reading the Epistle to the Hebrews*, (2002): 99–120. https://doi.org/10.2307/j.ctt1bhkpdr.10.

———. *The Anchor Yale Bible. 36, Hebrews: A New Translation with Introduction and Commentary*. New Haven, CT: Yale University Press, 2010.

Kravitz, Bentzion. "Jeremiah's New Covenant - Is There a Conspiracy to Hide the Truth?" Jews for Judaism, 31AD. https://jewsforjudaism.org/knowledge/weekly/jeremiah-s-new-covenant-is-there-a-conspiracy-to-hide-the-truth.

———. "Psalm 110 - A Jewish Perspective." Jews for Judaism, June 2005. https://jewsforjudaism.org/knowledge/articles/psalm-110-a-jewish-perspective.

Lake, John William. *Plato, Philo, and Paul: Or The Pagan Conception of a "Divine Logos" Shewn to have been the Basis of the Christian Dogma of the Deity of Christ*. London: T. Scott, 1874.

Lamarche, Janet. "The Meaning of Genesis 14: 11–24: A Syntactical and Redactional Analysis," Master's thesis, Concordia University, 2009.

Lane, William L. *Hebrews* 1–8. Waco, TX: Word, 1991.

Larsen, David J. "After the Order of Melchizedek – KTP Nederland District 29." April 16, 2016, https://ktpdistrict29.nl/gb/after-the-order-of-melchizedek/.

Leschert, Dale. "Hermeneutical Foundations of the Epistle to the Hebrews: A Study in the Validity of Its Interpretation of Some Core Citations from the Psalms." PhD diss., Fuller Theological Seminary,1991.

Levy, David M. "Who Is Melchizedek? Hebrews 7:1–10." Israel My Glory, 2006. https://israelmyglory.org/article/who-is-melchizedek-hebrews-71-10/#:~:text=Melchizedek%2C%20the%20king%2Dpriest%2C,believers%20everywhere%2C%20Jewish%20and%20Gentile.

Licona, Mike. *The Resurrection of Jesus: A New Historiographical Approach*. Downers Grove, IL: IVP Academic, 2011.

——— (@drmikelicona). "When it comes to historical investigations, our biases can significantly shape our conclusions. . ." Instagram, February 18, 2025. https://www.instagram.com/reel/DGgs1EURjnq/?hl=en.

"List of Rulers of Mesopotamia: Lists of Rulers: Heilbrunn Timeline of Art History: The Metropolitan Museum of Art." The Met's Heilbrunn Timeline of Art History, 2025. https://www.metmuseum.org/toah/hd/meru/hd_meru.htm.

Litwa, M. David. *How the Gospels Became History: Jesus and Mediterranean Myths*. New Haven: Yale University Press, 2020.

Loewen, Jacob A. "The Names of God in the Old Testament." *The Bible Translator* 35, no. 2 (1984): 201–7. https://doi.org/10.1177/026009438403500201.

Longenecker, Richard N. *The Melchizedek Argument of Hebrews: A Study in the Development and Circumstantial Expression of New Testament Thought*. Grand Rapids: Eerdmans, 1978.

MacArthur, John. *Hebrews*. Chicago: Moody, 1983.

MacDonald, Dennis R. *The Homeric Epics and the Gospel of Mark*. New Haven: Yale University Press, 2000.

Madsen, Ann Nicholls. "Melchizedek, the Man and the Tradition." MA thesis, Brigham Young University, 1975.

"Makkot 23B:3." Sefaria, n.d. https://www.sefaria.org/Makkot.23b.3?lang=bi.

Manson, William. *The Epistle to the Hebrews: An Historical and Theological Reconsideration*. London: Hodder and Stoughton, 1951.

Margalith, Othniel. "The Riddle of Genesis 14 and Melchizedek." *Zeitschrift für die Alttestamentliche Wissenschaft* 112, no. 4 (2000): 501–8. https://doi.org/10.1515/zatw.2000.112.4.501.

Mariottini, Claude. "Republicans v. Democrats = Old Testament v. New Testament." Dr. Claude Mariottini - Professor of Old Testament, August 7, 2006. https://claudemariottini.com/2006/08/07/republicans-v-democrats-old-testament-v-new-testament/.

Mason, Eric F. "Hebrews 7, 3 and the Relationship between Melchizedek and Jesus." *Biblical Research* 50 (2005): 41–62.

———. *"You Are a Priest Forever": Second Temple Jewish Messianism and the Priestly Christology of the Epistle to the Hebrews*. Leiden: Brill, 2008.

Mathews, Joshua G. *Melchizedek's Alternative Priestly Order: A Compositional Analysis of Genesis 14:18–20 and Its Echoes Throughout the Tanak*. Winona Lake: Eisenbrauns, 2013.

Maul, Stefan M. "Assyrian Religion." In *A Companion to Assyria*, 336–58. Heidelberg: Propylaeum, 2017.

Miller, Dave. "How Old Was Isaac When Abraham Was Told to Offer Him?" Apologetics Press, December 31, 2002. https://apologeticspress.org/how-old-was-isaac-when-abraham-was-told-to-offer-him-1272/.

Mitchell, Alan Christopher. *Sacra Pagina: Hebrews*. Collegeville, MN: Liturgical, 2007.

Mitchell, Margaret M. "Homer in the New Testament?" *The Journal of Religion* 83, no. 2 (2003): 244–60. https://doi.org/10.1086/491279.

Moffatt, James. *The Moffatt New Testament Commentary*. London: Hodder and Stoughton, 1928.

Moffitt, David McCheyne. "A New and Living Way: Atonement and the Logic of Resurrection in the Epistle to the Hebrews." PhD diss., Duke University, 2010.

"Moody Believes." Moody Believes | Moody Bible Institute, 2025. https://www.moodybible.org/beliefs/.

Moulton, H. K. "The Names and Attributes of God." *The Bible Translator* 13, no. 2 (1962): 71–80. https://doi.org/10.1177/000608446201300205.

Mundhenk, Norm. "Jesus Is Lord: The Tetragrammaton in Bible Translation." *The Bible Translator* 61, no. 2 (1962): 53–63.

Names of God Study Group. "How to Translate the Name." *The Bible Translator* 43, no. 4 (1992): 403–6.

Naugle, David K. *Worldview: The History of a Concept*. Grand Rapids: Eerdmans, 2005.

"Nedarim 32B:6." Sefaria, n.d. https://www.sefaria.org/Nedarim.32b.6?lang=bi&with=all&lang2=en.

NET Bible: New English Translation. Spokane, WA: Biblical Studies, 2006.

Neusner, Jacob, and E. P. Sanders. "Sanders' 'Paul and the Jewish People.'" *The Jewish Quarterly Review* 74, no. 4 (1984): 416–23. https://doi.org/10.2307/1454280.

Neyrey, Jerome H. "Without Beginning of Days or End of Life (Hebrews 7, 3) Topos for a True Deity." *Catholic Biblical Quarterly* 53, no. 3 (1991): 439–55.

O'Collins, Gerald, and Michael Keenan Jones. *Jesus Our Priest: A Christian Approach to the Priesthood of Christ*. Oxford: Oxford University Press, 2010.

Oepke, Albrecht. *Das Neue Gottesvolk in Schrifttum, Schauspiel, bildender Kunst und Weltgestaltung*. Bertelsmann: Gütersloh, 1950.

Oester, Craik. "Book of Hebrews: Guide with Key Information and Resources." BibleProject, n.d. https://bibleproject.com/guides/book-of-hebrews/.

Orlov, Andrei. "Melchizedek Legend of 2 (Slavonic) Enoch." 2000. https://www.marquette.edu/maqom/legend123.pdf.

Pahl, Steven. "Thematic Connections in Psalm 110 and Genesis 14 - An Intertextual Study." Thesis, Ambrose University College, 2013.

"Parallelomania." Wikipedia, March 18, 2024. https://en.wikipedia.org/wiki/Parallelomania.

Park, Sung Jin. "Melchizedek as a Covenantal Figure: The Biblical Theology of the Eschatological Royal Priesthood." Bible.org, April 4, 2011. https://bible.org/article/melchizedek-covenantal-figure-biblical-theology-eschatological-royal-priesthood.

Parsons, Mikeal C. "Son and High Priest: A Study in the Christology of Hebrews." *Evangelical Quarterly: An International Review of Bible and Theology* 60, no. 3 (1988): 195–216. https://doi.org/10.1163/27725472-06003002.

Paul, M. J. "The Order of Melchizedek (Ps 110:4 and Heb 7:3)." *Westminster Theological Journal* 49 (1987): 195–211.

Pedersen, Johs. *Israel – Its Life and Culture III–IV Johs. Pedersen*. Örebro/Schweden: A.-B. Littorin Rydén, 1947.

Peters, Melvin K.H. "Septuagint." In *ABD* 5, edited by David Noel Freedman, 5:1093–1104. NY: Doubleday, 1992.

Philo Judaeus. *The Works of Philo Judaeus: The Contemporary of Josephus*. Translated by Charles Duke Yonge. Vol. 1. London: Henry G. Bohn, 1854.

Power, Bruce A. "The Development of Priesthood in Ancient Israel." MA thesis, Universities of Winnipeg and Manitoba, 1986.

Punt, Jeremy. "Politics of Genealogies in the New Testament." *Neotestamentica* 47, no. 2 (2013): 373–98.

Purcell. "The King as Priest? Royal Imagery in Psalm 110 and Ancient Near Eastern Iconography." *Journal of Biblical Literature* 139, no. 2 (2020): 275–300. https://doi.org/10.15699/jbl.1392.2020.3.

Qasem, Mohammad. *A Closer Look at Christianity*. CreateSpace, 2014.

Rankin, Oliver Shaw. *Jewish Religious Polemic of Early and Later Centuries*. New York: Ktav, 1970.

Reiling, J. "Melchizedek." In *Dictionary of Deities and Demons in the Bible*, edited by Karl van der Toorn, Bob Becking, and Pieter W. van der Horst, 2nd ed., 560–63. Grand Rapids: Eerdmans, 1999.

Reiss, Moshe. "The Melchizedek Traditions." *Scandinavian Journal of the Old Testament* 26, no. 2 (2012): 259–65. https://doi.org/10.1080/09018328.2012.745279.

Remsburg, John E. *Christ: A Critical Review and Analysis of the Evidences of His Existence*. New York: The Truth Seeker, 1909.

Riggenbach, Eduard. *Der Brief an die Hebräer*. Leipzig: Deichert. 1922.

Roberts, David Francis. "Melchizedek; Melchisedec in the International Standard Bible Encyclopedia." International Standard Bible Encyclopedia Online, n.d. https://www.internationalstandardbible.com/M/melchizedek-melchisedec.html.

Rooke, Deborah W. "Jesus as Royal Priest: Reflections on the Interpretation of the Melchizedek Tradition in Heb 7." *Biblica* 81, no. 1 (2000): 81–94.

———. "Kingship and Priesthood: The Relationship Between the High Priesthood and the Monarchy." In *King and Messiah in Israel and the Ancient Near East*, edited by John Day, 187–208. Sheffield: Sheffield Academic, 1998.

Rosenberg, Roy A. "The God of Sedeq." *Hebrew Union College Annual* 36 (1965): 161–77.

Rosenfeld, Dovid. "Jeremiah 31 and the New Covenant." Aish.com, December 20, 2021. https://aish.com/jeremiah-31-and-the-new-covenant/.

Russell, Betrand. "Bertrand Russell: Philosophy for Laymen." Bertrand Russell | Philosophy for Laymen, 1946. https://users.drew.edu/~jlenz/br-lay-philosophy.html.

Ryle, Herbert Edward. *The Book of Genesis in the Revised Version*. Cambridge: The University Press, 1921.

Sailhamer, John H. *Genesis - Leviticus*. Edited by Tremper Longman and David E. Garland. Grand Rapids: Zondervan, 2009.

Sandmel, Samuel. "Parallelomania." *Journal of Biblical Literature* 81, no. 1 (1962): 1–13. https://doi.org/10.2307/3264821.

Sandnes, Karl Olav. "Imitatio Homeri? An Appraisal of Dennis R. MacDonald's 'Mimesis Criticism.'" *Journal of Biblical Literature* 124, no. 4 (2005): 715–32. https://doi.org/10.2307/30041066.

Sarna, Nahum M. *Understanding Genesis*. New York: Jewish Theological Seminary Press, 2015.

Schenck, Ken. "Echoes of Philo in the Sermon of Hebrews." Kenneth Schenck, January 1, 2019. https://www.academia.edu/41196885/Echoes_of_Philo_in_the_Sermon_of_Hebrews.

Scherman, Nosson, ed. *The Tanach: The Stone Edition*. Brooklyn, NY: Mesorah, 1996.

Scholer, John M. *Proleptic Priests: Priesthood in the Epistle to the Hebrews*. Sheffield: JSOT, 1991.

Schrock, David S. "5 Ways We See Jesus Serve as a Priest." Crossway, July 2022. https://www.crossway.org/articles/5-ways-we-see-jesus-serve-as-a-priest/.

Segal, Benjamin J. *A New Psalm: The Psalms as Literature*. Jerusalem: Gefen, 2015.

Shulman, Moshe. "Melchizedek as a Type of Moshiach." http://roshpinaproject.com, March 21, 2010. http://roshpinaproject.com/2010/03/19/melchizedek-as-a-type-of-moshiach/.

Sigal, Gerald. "Is Jeremiah's 'New Covenant' (Jeremiah 31:31–34) a Prophecy Fulfilled by the New Testament?" Jews for Judaism, n.d. https://jewsforjudaism.

org/knowledge/articles/is-jeremiahs-qnew-covenantq-jeremiah-3131-34-a-prophecy-fulfilled-by-the-new-testament.

———. *The Jew and the Christian Missionary: A Jewish Response to Missionary Christianity*. New York: Ktav, 1981.

Singer, Tovia. *Let's Get Biblical*. Monsey, NY: Outreach Judaism, 1998.

Skolnik, Fred, ed. "Aggadah or Haggadah." In *Encyclopaedia Judaica*, 21:454–59. Detroit: Thomson-Gale, 2007.

Small, Brian C. *The Characterization of Jesus in the Book of Hebrews*. Boston: Brill, 2014.

Speiser, E. A. *Genesis (The Anchor Bible)*. New York: Doubleday, 1965.

Spicq, Ceslaus. "The Epistle to the Hebrews." *Ultimate Reality and Meaning* 1, no. 3 (1978): 181–92. https://doi.org/10.3138/uram.1.3.181.

———. *L'Epitre aux Hébreux*. Paris: J. Gabalda et Cie, 1952.

Staley, Cale A. "The MELKISEDEQ Memoirs: The Social Memory of Melkisedeq Through the Second Temple Period." MA thesis, The University of Iowa, 2015.

Steyn, Gert Jacobus. "A Quest for the Assumed LXX Vorlage of the Explicit Quotations in Hebrews." PhD diss., Stellenbosch University, 2009.

Strack, Hermann Leberecht, and Paul Billerbeck. *A Commentary on the New Testament from the Talmud & Midrash*. Edited by Jacob N. Cerone. Translated by Joseph Longarino. Bellingham, WA: Lexham, 2022.

———. *Kommentar zum Neuen Testament aus Talmud und Midrasch*. Munchen: Beck, 1922.

"Sukkah 52B:11." Sefaria, n.d. https://www.sefaria.org/Sukkah.52b.11?lang=bi&with=all&lang2=en.

"Supersessionism." Theopedia.com, n.d. https://www.theopedia.com/supersessionism.

Tabor, James D. *Paul and Jesus: How the Apostle Transformed Christianity*. New York: Simon & Schuster, 2013.

Taggar-Cohen, Ada. "Covenant Priesthood Cross-Cultural Legal and Religious Aspects of Biblical and Hittite Priesthood." In *Levites and Priests in Biblical History and Tradition*, edited by Mark Leuchter, 11–24. Atlanta: SBL, 2011.

———. "Hittite Priesthood – State Administration in the Service of the Gods: Its Implications for the Interpretations of Biblical Priesthood." *BN*, no. 156 (2013): 155–75.

"Template: Rulers of the Ancient Near East." Wikipedia, March 5, 2025. https://en.wikipedia.org/wiki/Template:Rulers_of_the_ancient_Near_East.

Tertullian, Quintus Septimius Florens. *Tertullian Against Praxeas (Adversus Praxeam)*. Translated by Alexander Souter. London: Society for Promoting Christian Knowledge, 1920.

"Theological Positions." Biola University, 2025. https://www.biola.edu/about/theological-positions.

Thompson, James W. *Hebrews*. Grand Rapids: Baker Academic, 2008.

Thurston, Robert W. "Philo and the Epistle to the Hebrews." *Evangelical Quarterly: An International Review of Bible and Theology* 58, no. 2 (1986): 133–44. https://doi.org/10.1163/27725472-05802005.

Toy, Crawford Howell. *Quotations in the New Testament*. New York: Charles Scribner's Sons, 1884.

Troll, Christian W. *Muslims Ask, Christians Answer*. Hyde Park, NY: New City Press, 2003.

United Bible Societies. "How to Translate the Name." *The Bible Translator* 43, no. 4 (1992): 403–6. https://doi.org/10.1177/026009439204300402.

Vaillancourt, Ian J. "The Canonical Melchizedek." In *Reading Scripture, Learning Wisdom*, edited by Michael A.G. Haykin and Barry H. Howson, 3–21. Peterborough, Ontario: Joshua, 2021.

Van de Mieroop, Marc. *A History of the Ancient Near East, ca. 3000–323 BC*. 3rd ed. Hoboken: Wiley, 2015.

Van Gorder, A. Christian. *No God But God: A Path to Muslim-Christian Dialogue on God's Nature*. Maryknoll, NY: Orbis , 2003.

Vanhoye, Albert. *Structure and Message of the Epistle to the Hebrews*. Roma: Editrice Pontificio Istituto Biblico, 1989.

Vos, J. Cornelis de. "Abraham's Family in the Epistle to the Hebrews." In *Abraham's Family: A Network of Meaning in Judaism, Christianity, and Islam*, edited by Lukas Bormann, 299–315. Tübingen: Mohr Siebeck, 2018.

Wenham, Gordon J. *Genesis 1–15*. Nashville: Thomas Nelson, 2003.

Williams, Jay G. "Exegesis-Eisegesis: Is There a Difference?" *Theology Today* 30, no. 3 (1973): 218–27. https://doi.org/10.1177/004057367303000302.

Williamson, Ronald. *Philo and the Epistle to the Hebrews*. Leiden: Brill, 1970.

Zaia, Shana. "Kings, Priests, and Power in the Neo-Assyrian Period." *Journal of Ancient Near Eastern Religions* 19, no. 1–2 (2019): 152–69. https://doi.org/10.1163/15692124-12341308.

Zimmerli, Walther. "Abraham Und Melchisedek." In *Das Ferne Und Nahe Wort*, edited by Fritz Maass, 255–64. Berlin: De Gruyer, 1967.

Author Names Index

General Names Index

Subject Index

www.ingramcontent.com/pod-product-compliance
Lightning Source LLC
LaVergne TN
LVHW020539100826
845148LV00010B/1526